Twayne's United States Authors Series

EDITOR OF THIS VOLUME

Mason I. Lowance, Jr.

University of Massachusetts, Amherst

American Diary Literature
1620-1799

TUSAS 342

AMERICAN DIARY LITERATURE

1620-1799

By STEVEN E. KAGLE

TWAYNE PUBLISHERS
A DIVISION OF G. K. HALL & CO., BOSTON

For

Jill, Jonathan, and Matthew

Library of Congress Cataloging in Publication Data
Kagle, Steven E
American diary literature.
(Twayne's United States authors series; TUSAS 342)
Bibliography: p. 194-200
Includes index.
1. American diaries. I. Title.
PS409.K3   818'.03   79-14396
ISBN 0-8057-7280-4

Contents

About the Author
Preface
Acknowledgments
Chronology

1. The Diary   15
   The Diary as Art;
   The Diary Tradition in America

2. The Spiritual Journal   29
   Puritan Diaries;
   Michael Wigglesworth;
   David Brainerd;
   Quaker Diaries;
   John Woolman;
   Methodist Diaries;
   Francis Asbury;
   Lorenzo Dow

3. Travel Diaries   58
   Sarah Kemble Knight;
   Dr. Alexander Hamilton;
   Philip Vickers Fithian;
   Dr. John Morgan;
   Gouverneur Morris

4. Diaries of Romance and Courtship   82
   John Smith and William Black;
   Sally Wister;
   Anne Home Livingston

5. War Diaries   98
   Military Diaries;
   Dr. Lewis Beebe;
   Dr. Albigence Waldo;
   Charles Herbert;
   Dr. James Thacher;
   Josiah Atkins;

Civilian Diaries;
Margaret Morris;
James Allen;
Samuel Rowland Fisher

6. Life Diaries   142
   John Winthrop;
   Samuel Sewall;
   William Byrd;
   Multi-generation Diaries;
   Cotton Mather;
   John Adams

7. Afterword   183
   Notes and References   186
   Selected Bibliography   194
   Index   201

About the Author

Steven E. Kagle is Professor of English at Illinois State University where he teaches colonial and nineteenth century American literature, creative writing, and science fiction literature. He received an A.B. degree in English from Cornell University and holds M.A. and Ph.D degrees from the University of Michigan.

Professor Kagle is the editor of three books: *The Diary of Josiah Atkins* (New York Times and Arno Press, 1975), *Plymouth* (by Carol Gesner, published by *Exploration*, 1976), and *America: Exploration and Travel* (Popular Press of Bowling Green University, 1979). In addition, he is the author of various articles concerning diary literature, including "Diary of John Adams and the Motive of Achievement" (*Hartford Studies in Literature*, 1971), "Diary as Art: A New Assessment" (*Genre*, 1973), and "Societal Quest" (*Extrapolation*, 1971). He has also been the recipient of a grant from the National Endowment for the Humanities for work on the *Diaries of the American Revolution*. Professor Kagle is currently working on a book on nineteenth century American diaries, as well as a novel.

Preface

When I began this study of American diary literature, I thought I knew the best American diaries. A handful had received special prominence in literary histories and anthologies, and it seemed likely that these would satisfy my purpose. However, after considering the general neglect of the form, I soon decided there was little justification for such a judgment. Unlike most literary genres, diaries had received little systematic consideration, and therefore the occasional praise of individual American diarists offered little assurance that others were not as good or better. Consequently I concluded that it was my obligation to investigate this possibility.

I began my investigation with Matthews's invaluable bibliography, *American Diaries*. After initial checks to satisfy myself that I could rely on his judgments, I was able to rule out not only those diaries which were so brief or fragmentary as to be of little value, but also those listed as dull or poorly written. By excluding those diaries originally written in languages other than English and those by authors who, especially after the mid-eighteenth century, could not in any sense be classified as Americans, I had reduced the list still further. But even in the period before 1800 there still remained almost a thousand diaries. After locating and evaluating almost all of these, I searched for those diaries missing from Matthews's list, including those published after its completion or still in manuscript. From this list I finally selected the diaries considered in this book.

Selection of the best American diaries has only been a step toward my goal and not the goal itself. Unlike Arthur Ponsonby, whose volumes describe a large number of English, Scottish, and Irish diaries, I have not sought to present a complete catalogue of the more readable American diaries, because I believe that before such a list can be useful to a wide audience there must first be the categories and methodology for their study. On the other hand, I have not, as Fothergill has done in *Private Chronicles, A Study of English Diaries*, attempted an extended analysis of a few diaries, because there has been no work surveying the literature. The result is a work which, hopefully, takes the basic steps in both directions to the extent that the field can be opened up both to the serious scholar and to the casual reader.

When necessary, I have returned to the original manuscripts to check the accuracy of printed material or to examine the whole of a work published only in part. For the scholar there are few pleasures equal to the opportunity to read an original manuscript and through it to identify with the author in the process of composition, but manuscripts are not practical for most reading. Fortunately, in the centuries since the diaries here were written, most of the better works have been published; however, I have found some valuable works unpublished or published in an unsatisfactory form. In one case, *The Diary of Josiah Atkins*, I edited the work from manuscript to make a complete and accurate edition available to the public. I have found others which deserve such treatment. Many other diaries are available in books or journals which are so rare as to make them practically inaccessible. I hope that the growth of interest in diary literature will result in their republication.

To the extent that the value of individual American diaries and the importance of their tradition as part of our literary heritage can be recognized, my effort will be justified.

STEVEN E. KAGLE

Illinois State University
Normal, Illinois

Acknowledgments

I am indebted to the following institutions and their staffs for their permission and assistance in using their libraries and other facilities: the American Antiquarian Society, the American Philosophical Society, the Boston Public Library, Columbia University, Haverford College (especially the staff of the Quaker Collection), Illinois State University, the Massachusetts Historical Society, the Newberry Library, the New Haven Colony Historical Society, the New Jersey Historical Society, the Pennsylvania Historical Society, the University of Illinois, the University of Wisconsin at Madison, and Yale University.

I would also like to acknowledge the assistance of Ms. A. Attora, Ms. D. Austin, and Ms. A. Carr in preparing this material.

I am grateful to the following institutions for permission to quote from copyrighted diaries: Abingdon Press for *Journal and Letters of Francis Asbury*, I and II [1958]; Dietz Press, Marion Tinling and Louis B. Wright for *The Secret Diary of William Byrd of Westover 1709-1712* [1941] and *Another Secret Diary of William Byrd of Westover 1739-1741* [1942]; Dover Publications for *William Byrd's Histories of the Dividing Line between Virginia and North Carolina* [1967]; Farrar, Straus & Giroux for *Diary of Samuel Sewall* [1973]; Frederick Ungar Publishing Company for *Diary of Cotton Mather* [1957]; Harvard University Press for *The Earliest Diary of John Adams* [1966], & *The Diary of John Adams* [1961]; Houghton Mifflin Company for *A Diary of the French Revolution* [1939]; the New York Times and Arno Press for *A Relic of the Revolution* [1968], *Nancy Shippen, Her Journal Book, Journal of a Physician against Canada* [1968], *Military Journal of the American Revolution, Sally Wister's Journal* [1969], and *The Diary of Josiah Atkins* [1975]; Oxford University Press for *William Byrd of Virginia, The London Diary* [1958] and *The Journal and Major Essays of John Woolman* [1971]; Peter

Smith for *The Journal of Madam Knight* [1935] and *Diary of Michael Wigglesworth* [1970]; Scholarly Press for *Memoirs of the Rev. David Brainerd* [1970]; University of North Carolina Press of Virginia for *The Diary of Cotton Mather for the Year 1712* [1964] and *Journal and Letters of Philip Vickers Fithian 1773-1774* [1968].

Finally, I would like to thank both Illinois State University and the National Endowment for the Humanities for research grants which enabled me to complete this work.

Chronology

1620 The first entry of *Mourt's Relation*, the composite diary of William Bradford and Edward Winslow of the Plymouth settlement, begins as the Pilgrims first sight land on November ninth.

1630 On ship as part of the "Great Migration," John Winthrop begins his *Journal*, or *History of New England*.

1659 Michael Wigglesworth begins his spiritual journal.

1673 Samuel Sewall begins his diary which continues until 1729.

1697 On January 14 Samuel Sewall records his public confession of error for his actions as a judge in the Salem witchcraft trials.

1704 Sarah Kemble Knight's diary of her travels to New Haven and New York.

1720 The birth of John Woolman.

1728 The death of Cotton Mather. His diary begun by 1681 was kept until 1724.

1743 David Brainerd begins his mission to the Indians.

1744 In order to improve his health, Dr. Alexander Hamilton takes a journey from Maryland to New Hampshire and records his experiences in a diary, *The Itinerarium*.

1748 John Smith marries Hannah Logan on August 28.

1753 First known entry of the diary of John Adams, second President of the United States. The diary continues until 1804.

1764 Dr. John Morgan meets Voltaire and records the interview in his travel diary.

1771 Francis Asbury, later to be the first Methodist bishop in America, begins his diary and sets sail for his ministry in the colonies.

1773 Philip Vickers Fithian becomes a tutor on the Virginia plantation of the Carter family.

1777 While Washington's army winters at Valley Forge, Dr. Albigence Waldo keeps a diary of the suffering in camp and Sally Wister writes of her flirtations with officers lodged in private homes nearby.

1778 Charles Herbert and his companions celebrate the fourth of July in Old Mill Prison in England.

1781 Josiah Atkins dies in a military hospital while less than a hundred miles away his regiment is aiding in the Battle of Yorktown.

1789 The fall of the Bastille—one of the events of the French Revolution described in the diary of Governeur Morris, then serving as American Ambassador to France.

1799 Death of George Washington and the last entries of his diary.

CHAPTER 1

The Diary

ALMOST everyone knows what a diary is until it becomes necessary to define one. It is especially difficult to find a definition which will clearly distinguish between the diary and other forms of autobiography. Most people will agree that the core of such a definition is *a record of events or thoughts written as dated periodic entries*, but such a basic definition is not always adequate. Part of the problem arises from the fact that the appearance of a work does not always indicate the process of composition. The existence of dated sections in an autobiographical account does not prove that the sections were written shortly after the events occurred or even that the events were recorded sequentially. Some writers add to entries throughout a day; others wait a week before recording a series of entries from memory. How long a lapse is permitted between an event and its record before a work ceases to be a diary and becomes an autobiography? The allowable extent of revision is another problem. How extensively can a work be altered and still retain its generic identity? Still another part of this problem involves the question of artistic intent. Does prior artistic intent or autobiographical conception prevent a work from being a true diary, or is such an intent or conception an essential part of a work of diary literature?

I offer no absolute standards, but I would suggest that the genre of an autobiographical work depends primarily on the extent to which the entries preserve the passage of time from entry to entry. A diary should preserve the gradual acquisition of knowledge and shifting of values that occur in life. The imposition on diary materials of a perspective or position formulated at a later point in time alters the identity of that portion of the material. Although I recognize the extent of revision to be a concern, I consider even extensive stylistic revision to be a less serious concern than more modest changes in temporal perspective.

Another group of problems involves possible limitations on the size and scope of the work: Are there limits to the brevity of a diary or its individual entries? To what extent can a diarist restrict the number of subjects he or she treats? Must the work focus on personal experience and, if so, can its focus be restricted to internal or external experience? Some restriction must be made. A daily, dated weather record satisfies the core definition as do certain historical records and official journals, but they are not true diaries. Most of the diaries discussed in this book are focused on a limited period and range of experiences, such as travel, war, or courtship; however, these works are not necessarily restricted to their primary subject. The writer who limits the scope of his work limits its ability to change through time. Such prior control is as destructive to the diary form as subsequent content revision. Just as an individual may for a period focus his life on a certain situation or action, so a diary may be focused; but a diary, like a human life, may resist such controls.

The question of emphasis on internal or external experience leads to a consideration of the distinction between diaries and journals. In common usage the two terms have been interchangeable, and many diarists and critics have used them in this way. There are, however, two distinct patterns which can be observed in the titles of the works themselves. The term journal is more frequently used for two distinct classes of works: "those kept as part of a job,"[1] especially those works kept as official records, and those focusing on internal rather than external concerns, ideas rather than events. This study uses the latter pattern as a basis for choosing between the two words, because the practice provides a useful critical tool for stressing the difference between these classes of experience as factors that promote and direct diary production. Since works focusing on external concerns predominate, the term diary may be used to identify the general form.

Of course, few diaries are strictly limited to internal or external concerns, spiritual or material realities; most have a dominant direction, and almost all have a single sustaining source. Many people keep diary-type records, and a large number of these are maintained for considerable periods; yet, few of these records deserve to be considered as diary literature in the highest sense of that term. What they lack is not only stylistic merit, but also an identifiable life of their own. The life of a diary is often born of a tension, a disequilibrium in the life of its author, which needs to be resolved or held in check. A journey, a new role, a spiritual crisis – these are some of the sources of tension that can bring about and sustain a diary. In some cases the tension represents a conflict between a pair of activities, motives, or goals. These conflicting elements may be represented in the diary as individual themes struggling for the diarist's attention. Whatever the tension and however great its disruptive effect on the diarist's life, it is a sustaining force for the diary. In a large number of cases the resolution of the tension, like the climax of a novel, signals the conclusion of the work.

A good novelist creates characters with distinct identities; a good diarist creates a distinct identity for his diary. A diary is both a work and a fictional person to whom that work is directed. In some cases that "person" is made omniscient and talked to as a god who already knows the nature of the communication; in other cases the knowledge and power of the diary personality is limited to the information previously communicated. It may be friendly, indifferent, or even hostile. Whatever its nature or adopted persona, the diary personality is separate from that of the author and capable of individual response. The work presents the reader with only one half of the dialogue that takes place between work and author, but the other half can frequently be intuited. As this dialogue broadens, new sources of tension may be introduced and new themes developed extending the life of the work.

The life and activity represented by such a dialogue extend the numerous uses of a diary. A diary may be useful as a piece of literature for its aesthetic value or for eventual incorporation into another literary form; it may be useful as a psychological document to offer insight into the development of the diarist's mind and behavior; it may be useful as a historical document preserving the events and characters of the past. One could continue in this way, listing scholarly disciplines and finding, for most, uses of value to either or both the diarist and students of the discipline.

Each type of diary tends to emphasize a different use. For example, spiritual journals tend to be used for such goals as the confession of sin or the search for evidence of divine intent. Travel diaries tend to analyze characteristics of a new area, the personal effects of dislocation, and so on. Some diarists use their record to preserve their actions for the future, others to direct their current activity. An understanding of the uses of a diary helps the reader to determine which parts of the work are of the greatest significance. As with any work of literature, the reader of a diary can impose his or her value system on it, but the good reader or critic will view significance as determined by the intrinsic nature of the work itself. In considering a diary we should guard ourselves against external criteria whether they be imposed by a scholarly discipline or personal interests. The test of significance should be the extent to which the part under examination develops or directs one of the themes that comprise the identity of the work.

A fundamental task for the reader of diary literature is mentally to divide the work into primary and secondary material, primary material being that which serves to advance one or more of the crucial themes, secondary material being that which provides a background of information against which the major themes are developed. A diary may be compared to a play in which the playwright has failed to separate the text from the stage directions. This task is left up to the reader. Certainly more is expected of the reader of a diary than that of many other forms of literature, but with some practice the process can be easily mastered.

As with any attempt at critical reading, the analysis of diary material also presents the danger of overinterpretation. For example, the patterns suggested by psychoanalytic theory are often compelling when dealing with the uncensored confidences of a diary, but the confidential and often casual nature of the diary keeping process may prompt responses not characteristic of the writer. One must be careful before labeling a statement of affection for one's mother as evidence of an Oedipal complex or a moment of despair as proof of a death wish. A diarist is less likely than other writers to be concerned about presenting a consistent attitude and more willing to record atypical feelings of the moment. A reader should seek persistent patterns as a basis for interpretation.

This tendency of the diarist to express the feelings of the moment, portraying an event "as he feels it was and not as more considered judgment might have more truly shown it to be," has been used as evidence of the inferiority of the diary form.[2] However, errors introduced by forgetting and rationalization increase with time, and the misconceptions and misinformation recorded in a diary may provide vital truths about the author's attitudes or beliefs at a given time. For example, in 1772, only a few years before he would become one of the leading figures in the American Revolution, John Adams wrote in his diary: "I was born Octr. 19, 1735. Thirty Seven Years, more than half the Life of a Man are run out.—What an Atom, an Animalcule I am!—The Remainder of my Days I shall rather decline, in Sense, Spirit, and Activity. My Season for acquiring Knowledge is past."[3] Although grossly erroneous in its assessment of both its author's past and future accomplishments, this statement gives the reader a unique insight into the writer's personality and so should be valued rather than dismissed.

Diary truth has other advantages over the retrospective truth of autobiography. If the diarist is often "a prisoner of the present,"[4] he is not, as the autobiographer, a prisoner of a single present. As Gordon Allport noted, "Diaries do not show the anachronistic fallacy of attributing to earlier years thoughts, feelings, and interpretations appropriate only to the moment of writing."[5] There may, of course, be self-deception in a diary. Yet the diary reader can often see through such deceptions, which then can add new dimension to the author's self-portrait. In any work, whether it be a diary or a novel, the veracity of a first-person narration is likely to be suspect. Even if the narrative is self-deprecating rather than prideful, a self-evaluation is rarely accepted as accurate unless subject to validation from another source or objective evidence. When the reader is able to see through a diarist's systematic self-deception, he is able to find a new security in his assessment of truth.

Important insights can often be found in contradictory "truths" which the author relates over a period of time, often resulting from a shift in the diarist's point of view. Such contradictions aid the reader in tracing the writer's developing character. Omissions, whether forced by the impossibility of recording the whole of a life or chosen by personal or artistic decision, can be equally important in evaluating a diary. Significant events often interrupt a diary record either by taking time usually allotted for composition or by providing an alternative outlet for the tension that motivated diary production. Such lapses may be an important source of evidence about a diarist's relation to his work.

It is important to remember that, more than almost any other form of literature, the writing process is part of the art work. In most literature the impression of the passage of time is created on the permanent page; in the diary the pages are separated by the real time of their creation. This situation contributes to the uniqueness of the diary as art.

I The Diary as Art

Although many literary critics have themselves kept diaries, the diary has largely been ignored as a subject for serious critical attention. This situation is unfortunate, because many diarists and writers in genres more commonly accepted as "literature" treat the same subjects and share a concern for the means by which these subjects can be expressed. However, such common interests have not sufficiently united them.[6] Only infrequently have critics assessed the expressive powers of the better diarists. Even less common has been any serious consideration of the genre.

Those critical of the artistic potential of the diary form maintain that diarists lack the artistic intent necessary for effective communication. They reason that since the diarist does not anticipate an audience, he is not motivated to expend his effort on organization or style. To support this view, those critical of the diary point to a number of diaries which are so fragmentary that they are inadequate for any reader other than the diarist himself.

Another reason given to justify the neglect of diary literature is that the very nature of the diarist's subject matter prevents creative achievement, that, by concerning himself with real rather than fictional events, the diarist has deprived himself of both creative choice and control. Those who support this argument maintain that only in a work not limited by real events is a writer sufficiently free to select and control events to produce a work of value.

The most frequently cited objection is based on the diary's periodic production. It is argued that by writing entries shortly after each individual event the diarist may fail to recognize both the true significance of the event and its relationship to future events, and that, as a result, diaries lack the necessary consistency and unity we expect of literature.

The objection based on the claim that diarists lack artistic and communicative intent may be refuted by dispelling the notion that such intent is essential to artistic success. The success of writers of other genres who created great art in private is an effective argument; however, it is not essential to a defense of the diary genre, because there is ample evidence that many diarists have written with the clear expectation of a future audience. Some, like Fanny Kemble, wrote their works as unsent letters addressed to a single reader; others, like John Winthrop, appear to have directed their diaries to a wider audience. Stylistic features of such diaries provide evidence that their writers' intentions went far beyond the mere presentation of factual information. Winthrop entitled his diary *The History of New England* and wrote in the third person as part of an attempt to give the impression of objectivity to his interpretation of events in the Massachusetts Bay Colony. Emerson's decisions to title his first journal "The Wide World" and to begin it with a flowery invocation to witches, fairies, and the spirits of the four elements are the kind of literary games that an author plays with an audience.[7] Diarists have shown their sense of audience by specifically addressing the reader, and some diarists have allowed their works to be openly read and criticized as a means of refining their art.

There is some measure of truth to the argument that a diarist's creative choice is hindered by the limitation of his subject matter to real and usually common events. However, even writers of fiction rarely choose unique events. The good diarist, as any good writer, makes the events of his record appear distinctive through his treatment of them. Indeed, as Kafka recognized in reading Goethe's diaries, the great diarist's stylistic skill can take a common event and "set fire to it."[8]

Although the individual mind and style of the talented diarist are adequate to allow creative choice, the adherence to real events may cause a writer to follow an inferior standard of truth. One writer may record a situation strictly according to the objective facts, while another records those facts ordered and colored by his own sensibility. Both are telling the truth, but the truth of the former is the truth of journalistic record, while the truth of the latter is the truth of literary art.

By valuing this creative subjective truth over objective fact, a diarist can surmount the problems arising from the necessity of treating real events. Of course, there is no reason to expect that because one diarist can surmount the obstacle of reality that all diarists can do so. Diarists are unequally gifted in their powers of perception and expression, and many are content to report journalistically. Nevertheless, a sufficient number have shown themselves able to deal creatively with the facts of their lives.

The objection that dealing with reality deprives the diarist of control is another argument that must be acknowledged, but if one accepts the contention that freedom of the will exists, one must then also admit that the diarist can exercise some control over the events in his record by controlling his own actions. As Leon Edel noted in the case of Boswell, a writer who is present at an event which he is recording can, if talented, exercise a substantial measure of control. Boswell, by becoming "a kind of organizer and scene shifter . . . could create occasions, incidents, encounters for the life he was ultimately to write . . . [and] by quiet manipulation place his subject in a better position for the biographical camera, improve on the accidents of life."[9]

In order to create a work of literary art a diarist must be creative in the way he lives his life as well as in the way he writes about it. A good diarist need not lead a life of great historical significance, but he must lead his life. If he merely reacts to events as they happen, he will be neither a great diarist nor a great man. As Gide wrote in his journal, "Rather than recounting his life as he has lived it, he [the artist] must live his life as he will recount it. In other words, the portrait of him formed by his life must identify itself with the ideal portrait he desires."[10]

The difficulties posed by periodic production form the greatest obstacle to the creation of an aesthetically successful diary. Ideally, periodic production need not cause any problem. There are numerous fictional diaries which, considered as examples of the more traditional genres, are accepted as works of art. However, in actual practice difficulties do arise which impede a diarist's artistic success.

Life rarely lives up to the standards of unity and completeness one usually expects from literature, and diaries show the results of this situation. However, some disunity or incompleteness may be acceptable and even desirable in art. Byron said in and of his diary, "God knows what contradictions it may contain. If I am sincere with myself . . . every page should confute, refute, and utterly abjure its predecessor."[11] This statement is not very different from the following which Whitman made in and of his poetry: "Let contradictions prevail! let one thing contradict another! and let one line of my poems contradict another!"[12]

Nevertheless, it must be admitted that even the best diaries have structural deficiencies, gaps which should be filled and extraneous material best omitted. If one examines works fashioned from diaries, one can see both the extent and the types of changes which need to be made. Even Thoreau's well-written journal required reshaping and reordering as well as selection to transform it into *Walden*.[13]

Many passages in works derived from diaries are both more vivid and more honest in their original forms. As Thoreau observed:

A journal is a record of experiences and growth, not a preserve of things well done or said. I am occasionally reminded of a statement which I have made in conversation and immediately forgotten, which would read much better than what I put in my journal. It is a ripe dry fruit of long-past experience which falls from me easily, without giving pain or pleasure. The charm of the journal must consist in a certain greenness through freshness and not in maturity. Here I cannot afford to be remembering what I said or did, my scruf cast off, but what I am and aspire to become.[14]

Critics have often mistaken this greenness for a fault and used works developed from diaries as proof of the inherent inadequacy of the parent genre. Such proof is faulty. The greatness of the derivative work need not devalue the original.

Unfortunately for the reputation of the diary form, revised diaries are usually considered to be changed in genre. Bradford's revised diary is often called history; Woolman's, au-

tobiography; Boswell's, biography; Parkman's, travel literature; and Thoreau's, essay. Some of such changes in generic
designation are justified; however, all too often the changes
which confer artistic respectability consist of little more than a
change of title and the removal of the dates separating entries.
Such changes do not really alter the generic identity of the
work.

The crucial factor in determining whether or not the derivative work is still a diary is the author's perspective. The most
characteristic features of the diary are the vividness and the
shift in point of view caused by periodic production. A diarist
approaches each succeeding entry changed by his new experiences and inspired by the immediacy of the impressions
he is about to record. The extent to which a derivative work
retains these characteristics should be a major factor in assign-
ing its genre. In many cases we will find that the derivative
work is still a diary.

A recognition of the value of revised diaries should not lead
us to ignore unaltered ones. These two types of diary may in
some ways be compared to a meadow and a garden; the ordered beauty of the latter should not be used as an indictment
against the natural beauty of the former. To appreciate diaries
we must formulate a criticism which takes into consideration
the process of diary keeping not as a source of flaws, but as a
source of features peculiar to the genre. For example, it may
be appropriate to read the dates and other intrusive notations
as though they were stage directions in a script. Through such
creative approaches to diary material we will become better
able to recognize its artistic value and to apply the standard
techniques of literary criticism. Diaries may then yield us
more of the rewards that other art forms have provided.

II   *The Diary Tradition in America*

Most critics have assumed that individual diarists wrote in a
vacuum, unaware of the work of other diarists and uncon-
cerned about the characteristics and development of the form.
This, however, is not universally the case. Many diarists have
shared their work, inspiring others not only to take up the
habit of diary keeping but also to respect the intrinsic value of

the genre. Bronson Alcott adopted his habit of diary keeping
from his mother, whose diary he had found "when a boy, hidden away in an old oaken chest." And he in turn passed it on to
his wife, his daughters, and his other "children," the pupils in
his school.[15] The value which Alcott placed in this legacy can
be seen in the following entry in which he describes spending
an evening with his students "reading, conversing, and recit-
ing their *Journals*. In these they are quite interested. I shall
trust much to this habit of recording their thoughts, feelings,
acts, and the events of the time in permanent form."[16] The
diaries of John Adams and Cotton Mather discussed at length
later in this volume are examples of a habit of diary keeping
passed from father to son for at least three generations.

Of course, the fact that many, if not most, of the better
diarists exchanged diaries with their associates does not prove
that they viewed the diary as literature. What makes these exchanges significant is that in many of them the diarists recorded in their own works their critical reactions to their reading and the advice which they themselves received. Obviously such critical discussions have not attracted the attention
accorded to the formal criticism associated with genres more
commonly accepted as literature; however, they have been
sufficient to give many diarists a conviction about the artistic
requirements and possibilities of their genre.

I shall attempt only to sketch the artistic and personal relationships which give life to this tradition, for not only are they
numerous and complex, but many that probably existed have
gone unrecorded. Nevertheless even a brief treatment of the
tradition should be sufficient to prove that it is far more extensive and important than most might expect. In pre-Civil War
America almost every major writer kept a diary. The list includes Taylor, Wigglesworth, Franklin, Brown, Irving,
Cooper, Bryant, Hawthorne, Emerson, Alcott, Fuller,
Thoreau, Melville, Dana, Longfellow, and Whitman. Most of
these writers kept extensive records and many encouraged
others in the practice. For example, Hawthorne once advised a
friend, "Think nothing too trifling to write down, so be it in
the smallest degree characteristic. You will be surprised to
find on perusing your journal what an importance and graphic
power these particulars assume."[17] The exchange of such

"graphic" writing resulted in a cross-fertilization of ideas and techniques which has greatly aided diarists in the development of their art.

Members of the Transcendentalist Club often exchanged diaries. For example, Bronson Alcott wrote in his *Journals*, "Miss Fuller called and sat an hour with me today. . . . I suffered her to take my 'Diary' from January to July to read. I have done this before, finding her one of the most intelligent of my contemporaries, having more insight into character than most."[18] Emerson too read and advised Alcott on his *Journals* and was sufficiently affected by what he read to record the following passage: "I cannot deny myself the pleasure of copying a passage from Mr. Alcott's Mss. Journal."[19] And of Thoreau's *Journal* Emerson wrote:

In reading Henry Thoreau's journal, I am very sensible of the vigour of his constitution. That oaken strength which I noted whenever he walked or worked, or surveyed wood lots, the same unhesitating hand with which a field-labourer accosts a piece of work, which I should shun as a waste of strength, Henry shows in his literary task. He has muscle and ventures on and performs feats which I am forced to decline.[20]

Of course, this reading and sharing of diaries is not the exclusive practice of Americans. Boswell exchanged his *Journals* with Johnson and several other acquaintances, relying on their advice in developing his skill as a diarist. Byron was given manuscript diaries to read and allowed his own to be passed from one reader to another. Gide too was an avid reader of diaries. Indeed he was so taken with Stendhal's *Journal* that he found himself imitating it. Similar exchanges of diaries and commentary on diaries can be found in many other periods and regions. Taken together these exchanges show that diarists have recognized the artistic potential of their genre.

Yet despite the importance of the diary in other cultures, there is a special significance to its appearance in America. Whitman in "Democratic Vistas" wrote that the key to American development had been "personalism" or "the perfect uncontamination and solitariness of individuality." The Puritans, eschewing the use of an intermediary between man and God, turned to the diary as a companion in their spiritual isolation; the pioneer explorers and settlers found the diary appropriate to record the self-sufficient life demanded by the frontier; the Transcendentalists found the diary to be in keeping with their principle of radical self-reliance. Individualism in America was rarely as "rugged" as it seems in America's mythos, but even in civilized America social pressures can call for the appearance of stoicism and self-sufficiency. In such situations the diary has been available and sanctioned as the confidant for feelings of loneliness, weakness, and doubt.

American literature at its best frequently extolls the isolated individual—Natty Bumppo scouting the forest, Ahab standing on the quarterdeck, Nick Adams fishing in northern Michigan. In such settings there may be others near, but their support is less felt than the separation of the character from the mass of humanity. The writers themselves are isolated and date their assumption of creative power from the moment in isolation. Just as Jonathan Edwards noted that God had chosen to grant him grace during a moment in which he was walking alone in the fields, so both Poe and Whitman in their poetry traced the assumption of their creative powers to a moment of isolation.[21] Emily Dickinson called loneliness "The Maker of the Soul"; certainly it was the maker of many American diaries.

The parents of the American diary tradition are the spiritual journal and the diary of travel and exploration. Spiritual and physical discoveries were often joined as in the works of William Bradford and John Winthrop, and where the forms seem separate their themes may be symbolically linked; however, these forms may be considered separately. In America, the spiritual journal is the first of the two to be fully developed. The fervency of religious belief in seventeenth-century America made spiritual concerns the highest object of American civilization. Exploration was important to the development of America, but the first early coastal explorations were made by Europeans rather than Americans. At first the East offered ample room for settlement; later the French and Indian Wars and the Quebec Act closed off westward expansion. Only after the Revolution and the Louisiana Purchase opened vast western tracts to American exploration did the diary of physical exploration become fully developed in America.

The eighteenth century had seen the development in America of the travel diary, the diary of romance and courtship, and the military diary. Then in the nineteenth century the opening of the frontier not only completed the development of the exploration diary, it also provided a symbolic equivalent in the spiritual journals of the Transcendentalists and their wide range of concerns about both nature and the spirit.

The development of the diary tradition includes a growth in the artistic self-consciousness of its authors. This development is not exclusive to the diary form. In other colonial American literature from sermons to poems there was an early tendency to favor content over style. Writers of seventeenth-century New England had stressed plain style as appropriate for the accurate representation of spiritual truth; writers of the eighteenth century, influenced by the Enlightenment, sought a writing style that would be orderly and free from ornament to match their belief in a logically ordered universe. There is an artistic beauty in the diaries of these periods, but it is the beauty of clear and simple forms. Just as the conflicts and themes in such works are sharply focused, so the language is direct and the imagery is drawn from common experience. There is conscious art in such diaries, but it is an art in keeping with the world of their authors.

CHAPTER 2

The Spiritual Journal

ITS early development and influence on subsequent diary types give the spiritual journal a prominent place in American diary literature. It served very special functions for the Puritans, Quakers, and Methodists, but was not limited to followers of these denominations. In colonial America the world of the spirit was at least as real and important as the physical world, and the motivation to consider concerns of the spirit was equally great. However, there were many obstacles to the open discussion of such concerns. Convictions of sin, doubts about salvation, and moral dilemmas were often too personal to be confided to an earthly auditor. Other obstacles such as the isolation of missionaries, circuit riders, and settlers on the frontier hindered systematic discussion of the world of the spirit. Prayer was valued, but it lacked a record for future consideration. The spiritual journal allowed its author to find a pattern which could reveal the truth of the past and plan the direction of the future.

I *Puritan Diaries*

The American Puritans of the seventeenth and early eighteenth centuries were among the most prolific diarists of all time. In some other societies aristocratic subgroups were also profoundly concerned with the keeping of diaries, but the Puritans' emphasis on literacy allowed most members of their society to involve themselves in the practice if they so chose. Unfortunately, numbers do not always assure quality, and only a few of the best American diaries come from this group; however, directly through the diary tradition or indirectly through their influence on American culture, the Puritans have had an important effect on many, if not most, of the important American diaries.

The major but not exclusive reason for the popularity of diary keeping by the American Puritans was an appreciation of its confessional, revelatory, and directive functions. By keeping a spiritual journal a Puritan could privately consider the conviction of sinfulness which his society viewed as a necessary step toward salvation, record natural and human events in which he could find God's principles, and plan actions or reason judgments to allow the better adherence to God's commandments.

Another important motive for many Puritan diarists was a journal's potential as a weapon against despair. For Calvinists like the Puritans, salvation was dependent on the arbitrary will of God to choose whom he would for salvation or damnation. The Puritan creed taught that the process by which sinful man became regenerate was rarely sudden or strikingly evident; rather, it was usually a long and difficult process the evidence of which would be difficult to perceive. Many Puritans hoped that by keeping a rigorously exact diary they would be able to find a pattern which would give them confidence in their own election.

Such spiritual motives are at the root of most Puritan diaries, but many of these are still not appropriately classified as spiritual journals. The diaries of John Winthrop, Samuel Sewall, and Cotton Mather will be examined later because, while containing to varying degrees the elements of the spiritual journal, they are continued over a long period and contain material and themes which suggest a less limited designation. Of course, even the works of Wigglesworth and Brainerd, discussed in this chapter as spiritual journals, have elements which suggest a broader classification. There is no clear dividing line between diary groups that will remove the necessity for human judgment in such determinations. The generic identity of a work which approaches or spans the boundaries of traditional definition is often determined by critical perceptions. The motives which inspire a diary are rarely pure and so make this process especially difficult.

II   *Michael Wigglesworth (1631-1705)*

Although chosen here as an example of the Puritan spiritual journal, Michael Wigglesworth's diary is no more a typical Puritan diary than Wigglesworth was a typical Puritan. He was a teacher and a minister in a land of farmers and tradesmen, a scholar in a society few of whose members possessed more than a grade-school education, and, later in his career, a popular poet in a culture which generally considered literature a wasteful pursuit. Rather, he represents the typical Puritan as a caricature represents its subject, as an exaggeration of its subject's most characteristic features. While few Puritans were ministers, Puritan society was marked by its piety, and the Puritan emphasis on the preeminence of the individual's relationship with God gave every person responsibilities once reserved for the clergy. While few Puritans were scholars, Puritan society was unusual in its day for its emphasis on education, and the Puritan expectation that every individual have the ability to relate to the Bible resulted in a literacy rate extreme for the period. And, while the Puritans devalued literature as pure art, their culture was to value increasingly the importance of the skillful use of language. The religious writings of the American Puritans gained great respect on both sides of the Atlantic, and the sermon which was the focal point for the Puritan service was a highly developed "literary" form.

Wigglesworth's interior life as revealed in his journal was also an exaggeration of the feelings and standards of the average Puritan. Wigglesworth went beyond the Puritan obligation to remind himself of his own sinfulness and expressed a self-loathing of almost unbelievable severity. Other Puritans made such assertions in their diaries, but these were usually tempered in such a way as to allow the reader to feel them as a symbolic debasing of the human soul before the magnificence of God; Wigglesworth's statements were expressed as absolutes with which few Puritans would have felt comfortable and suggested a special guilt that set him apart from other sinners.

We often think of the Puritans as religious extremists, but

their faith denied them the serene assurance of an extreme position. Carried only a degree further than the view accepted by their religious community, many of their virtues became vices and their orthodox beliefs, dangerous heresies. The Puritans believed that God commanded men to perform good works; yet the belief that good works could bring about salvation was the heresy of Arminianism. On the other hand, if the reliance on faith led to a devaluing of moral action, the Puritan risked the heresy of Antinomianism. A similar dilemma involved the Puritan view of human reason. The Puritans exalted reason as a weapon against scholasticism, but found it dangerous when it threatened to contradict scripture.

The Puritan walked an endless tightrope between such pairs of pitfalls. For most Puritans the fear of falling could be endured because for them the tightrope seemed strung near the ground; a deviation from orthodoxy threatened only temporary discomfort and an easy repentant climb back. But to Wigglesworth the tightrope seemed to stretch over the abyss where a single misstep could prove fatal to his soul. This perception produced an extraordinary paradox in Wigglesworth's journal—the coexistence of his conviction of extreme vileness and his equally extreme sense of pride.

The journal is full of Wigglesworth's self-deprecations. He cried, "Behold, I am vile,"[1] and consigned himself to "ly lowest in Hel" (p. 54). Several times he called himself "the chief of sinners" (p. 41) and prayed, "Deliver me above all things from that evil man myself" (p. 36). Yet in the same breath that he called himself a "wretched worm" (p. 55) or declared, "I . . . am daily captivated by my iniquitys" (p. 40), he berated himself for pride and vanity. How was it that pride and self-loathing could coexist in one soul? The answer to such a question requires both an understanding of the Puritan view of the process of grace and Wigglesworth's motives in keeping a journal.

For the Puritan the conviction of sin was an essential prerequisite for salvation. This consciousness of guilt brought forth the very contradictory hope to achieve sainthood. At the same time, the satisfaction which might come from good thoughts and behavior might lead to pride, the deadliest of sins. This yoking of opposites made any comforting resolution

almost impossible. On the very first page of his journal
Wigglesworth risked pride as he strove for purity:

Peevishness vain thoughts and especially pride still prevails in me. I
cannot think one good thought, I cannot do any thing for god but
presently pride gets hould of me: but I feel a need of christ's blood to
wash me from the sins of my best dutys and from all that deadness of
heart, and want of spirit for god this day. I find my heart prone to take
secret pleasure in thinking how much I do for others' good; but Lord
how little of it is done for the.   (p. 3)

Even when God assisted him toward good, the result was
often vanity. The only way to achieve peace seemed to be the
self-condemnation that brought a conviction of sin.

Only when his heart had been broken could Wigglesworth
find the love of God; however, as we see in the following account of a day of public humiliation, God would not always
abet the breaking of his heart and / or the submission of his
spirit:

I desir'd to bless god (so far as I know my owne heart). that as he had
giv'n me christ to be bread of life to me, so now he puts an opportunity into my hand to sue for supply of my great spiritual wants. but I
could not with all I could do get a melting broken heart this day; but I
had a hard heart besides all other plagues to spread before the lord:
Lord look down in mercy and let not my soul sinking iniquitys be my
ruin. I know not what to do: harden not my heart from thy fear. . . .
(p. 55)

As this last line suggests, Wigglesworth recognized that the
heart is not always subject to human will. As with Pharaoh in
Exodus the Lord might harden a heart in opposition to his own
commandments.

While searching his soul for the secret sin which would justify God's actions, Wigglesworth found an answer:

I came home and set my self seriously to meditate, and call over the
sins of my whole life by a Catalogue. And the Lord was pleased to set
in, and in some measure break my heart for them. showing me my
desert to be kickt out of this world because I haue not had naturall
affections to my natural father, but requited him and all my gover-
nours evil for good: and to be shut out of the world to come, because I
haue rebell'd against and dishonour'd and disregarded my heavenly
father, been a viper in his bosom where he has nourished me.   (p. 57)

Even though it is desirable to resist the temptation to make psychoanalytic interpretations from diary material, some recognition of the Oedipal nature of these comments is unavoidable. Wigglesworth himself drew the parallel between his divine and earthly fathers and his inability to express the love and affection which was due them. The above passage is only one of several which Wigglesworth entered in his journal in the months following his father's death. In another he wrote:

God brought to my mind . . . my want of love and dutifulness to my parents which I beg'd pardon of.
And the very next morning news is brought me of my father's death whereupon I set my self to confess before the Lord my sins against him in want of naturall affections to, and sympathy with my afflicted parents, in my not prizing them and their life which god hath graciously continued so long. My great request is for pardon of all former sins, and present deliverance from a stupid frame of spirit unsensible of gods visitation and my owne loss in losing such a friend. my humble supplication is to the Lord to sanctify his hand to me and all of us whom it concerns and to become a father of the fatherless and husband to the widdow.   (p. 50)

But such prayers and plans were not sufficient to avoid a sense of guilt. Wigglesworth was even concerned that he might "be secretly glad that . . . [his] father was gone" (p. 50). This self-accusation cannot be dismissed as a product of Wigglesworth's after-the-fact creation of guilt. There was a long-standing conflict between father and son which may have been one of the factors which motivated Wigglesworth to begin to maintain his journal.

When in the summer of 1652 Wigglesworth returned to Harvard College to work on his master's degree and to assume the post of freshman tutor, he was twenty-one years old, an age by which most Americans of the period had enjoyed at least a few years of independence and adult responsibility. However, Wigglesworth had not, and would not for years, fully shed the protective cocoon of enforced adolescence. Several factors had delayed his maturity: he had at the age of ten been removed from school to work on his father's farm; he had, less than two years before the start of the journal, undergone the religious conversion which fitted him for full church membership and which caused him to abandon his plans for a career in medicine and train instead for the ministry; and he had been profoundly dominated by his father who, though physically lamed by a back injury, was personally forceful. The diary provides a good example of this relationship between father and son. When in April of 1653 Wigglesworth returned home for a visit, he quickly regressed from the honored scholar to the incompetent child:

> I think I never had my folly so uncased, as since my coming home, both in my indiscretion in taking me so perplexed and chargeable a journey, in every point whereof much rash inconsiderateness and resolvedness upon it though to great disadvantage appears. And in sundry other respects makes my father an instrument of so discovering my weak and silly management of every business, that he makes my savour to stink in my owne nosethrils. this he did most eminently this week immediately after a proud fit of my owne. God abaseth the proud! My heart as 'tis asham'd of my self so it swells against my father, and cannot conceiv such things to proceed from loue, because that covers a multitude of infirmitys, but this rakes them open to the bottom. but whether he be to blame or no; surely I am, in causing such things and looking so much at man in the reproving them with discontent. (p. 14)

This excerpt is a key to the meaning of the journal, for it shows the interaction among the three most important "characters" in the work: Michael, the diarist; Edward, his earthly father; and God, his divine father. Michael's dilemma was to become successful, independent, and good, without feeling either the earthly superiority which would have placed him in competition with his father or the spiritual pride which would have made him appear presumptuous in the eyes of God.

When the *Diary* begins in February 1653,[2] the role relationship between father and son was undergoing a change which also was affecting the relationship between Wigglesworth and his God. As a student, Wigglesworth had been like a child, subject to the directions of his superiors, but by 1653 he had become the tutor, a spiritual father, responsible for the education and spiritual development of the students in his charge. The journal's first subject is Wigglesworth's ambiguous role:

> If the unloving carriages of my pupils can goe so to my heart as they doe; how then doe my vain thoughts, my detestable pride, my *un-*

*natural filthy lust that are so oft and even this day in some measure
stirring in me* how do these griev my lord Jesus that loves me infi-
nitely more than I do them? Do I take it heavily that my love is so
lightly made of? ah! lord Jesus how fearful is my despizing of thy
dying love. . . . ah! I cannot love thee, not fear to sin against thee,
although thou exercise me with such crosses, as again this day,
wherein I may read my owne ill carriages toward thee.   (p. 3)

In the role of father, Wigglesworth felt his own shortcomings
most acutely. He wished to become a loving father, but he felt
the need to berate himself for showing "too much doting affection" (p. 9); he wished to be a forceful father, but he found his
council unheeded. No result seemed to comfort him. When his
students succeeded, their success tempted him to prideful
satisfaction that he called "the daily fear of my soul" (p. 33);
when his students failed, he attributed their weaknesses to his
own and sought God's aid.

This pattern in which acts or thoughts whether good or bad
lead to an awareness of sin, leading in turn to a hope for divine
aid, is prevalent in the journal. Paragraphs or entries displaying this pattern usually begin with a confession of sinfulness
and end with a prayer for God's forgiveness and aid. When
occasionally in a unit of the diary Wigglesworth acknowledged a satisfactory state, event, or act, his achievement frequently brought forth thoughts of sin which then would have
to be resolved by prayer. To whatever extent Wigglesworth
was aware of this pattern, he acknowledged it as the design of
God, who determines all things according to his will.

This pattern of an individual's pursuit of a goal ordained by
a divine father and yet temporarily being frustrated by him is
common to the archetypal quest. In such a quest in literature
(including mythology and scripture), the hero pursuing the
quest requires a reconciliation with a heavenly father who for
a time appears to withhold his favor or forgiveness. Joseph
Campbell, who outlines this monomyth of the questing hero,
traces this pattern back to the primitive rite of passage, the
ritual required for a youth to become an adult member of his
society.[3] It is this transition period that Wigglesworth recorded in his journal.

As the rite of passage is at least symbolically sexual, sexual
maturity being an important component of socially perceived

manhood, it is not surprising that another of the sources of Wigglesworth's anxiety was sex. In one of the earliest entries he wrote, *"I find such unresistable torments of carnal lusts or provocation unto the ejection of seed that I find myself unable to read any thing to inform me about my distemper because of the prevailing or rising of my lusts"* (p. 4). These first pages of the journal frequently reveal Wigglesworth's concern about sexual fantasies. Even nocturnal emission was of grave concern to him especially when it was accompanied by lustful dreams. This concern with "filthy dreams" and "prevailing lusts" was a frequent topic in the early pages of the journal. Overt sexual references submerged for a time, reappearing later as part of a concern about general carnal lusts. This latter period went on until the beginning of 1654, when Wigglesworth started seriously to consider marriage.

Marriage, as Wigglesworth examined it, was not a choice made for love, but a practical arrangement by which he hoped to avoid the sins of desire and "dreams and self-pollution by night which my soul abhors and mourns for" (p. 79). Wigglesworth also expressed a concern that he had contracted a venereal disease, a fear which may reveal Wigglesworth's anxieties and lack of sexual knowledge, rather than evidence of actual sexual activity. Convinced by physicians that his disease was not a true venereal disease, he decided to marry for the preservation of purity and chastity. On May 18, 1655, he married his cousin Mary Reyner, and after some concern about his "intemperance in the use of marriage" (p. 88), his anxiety about sexual matters appears to have lessened.

As Wigglesworth's anxiety lessened, so did his diary production. The frequency and length of his entries were gradually reduced until they stopped in October of 1655.[4] They resumed again in February of 1656 when his first child, Mercy, was born, but after this point there were only a few sporadic entries and some documents included in the diary notebook. If the diary did, indeed, originate as a response to Wigglesworth's problems in assuming an independent role as a mature adult, it is certainly understandable that his diary-keeping habits and parenthood may have been related. Also relevant may have been another change which occurred in this period. In the summer of 1655 Wigglesworth considered and finally accepted a call to serve as pastor of the church at Malden,

Massachusetts. He even found himself able to handle the challenge of "double work" in carrying out the functions of both teacher and pastor (p. 90).

In this context we may see that, in the years covered by the journal, Wigglesworth's role in terms of personal authority, public position, and sexual behavior had radically changed; and, as those changes ended the inner conflict which prompted the journal, its production was no longer important. Wigglesworth had moved both in fact and self-image not merely from student and tutor to minister and teacher, but from child to father. These changes were not just the product of physical events such as the death of his father, his appointment to the ministry, and the birth of his first child, but also the effect of the diary as a ritualized working out of an inner conflict.

III   David Brainerd (1718-1747)

Many of the diaries written by missionaries are essentially concerned with the experience of the frontier; and so, despite their authors' religious occupations, their works are best included in a discussion of diaries of exploration and travel. Other diaries, including that of David Brainerd, are more appropriately considered as spiritual journals. One of the most crucial determinants in making such a categorization is the extent to which physical events are the primary concern of the writer.[5] Spritual journals can be centered about or explained in terms of physical events, but those events function to advance or symbolize a nonphysical development.

For most explorers and settlers the frontier is a physical entity, a wild and unknown terrain; for some it is also a cultural unknown, a society as strange and uncivilized as the land, but for a Puritan missionary such as Brainerd the true wilderness was internal, a feature of the human spirit. Like the settler and explorer, Brainerd sought to alter the wilderness, but as his conception of that wilderness included his own soul, he could not encounter the wild as a stranger. His attempts to tame his heart to the will of God were reflected in his actions, and his conversion of the Indians as recorded in the diary can be recognized as symbolic of his inner struggle.

In his *Memoirs of Brainerd*, a biography built around sec-

tions comprising most of Brainerd's journal, Jonathan Edwards
recognized that the principal value of the journal was as a record of its author's spiritual transformation. Edwards emphasized that a reader of the diary would not only see "the
external circumstances" of Brainerd's life, "but also what
passed in *his own heart* . . . ; the wonderful *change* he experienced in his mind and disposition; the manner in which that
change was brought to pass; how it continued; and what were
its consequences in his inward frames, affections, and secret
exercises."[6]

For the diary reader today, there is another parallel change
which is of equal importance to the religious one, and that is
the change from an intense concern for self to an almost totally
selfless interest in others, in this case the Indians of his ministry. This change is to some extent clouded by his identification
of the Indians' efforts to achieve salvation, by the success of
his personal ministry, and also by his need as a devout Calvinist to consider the achievement of good as beyond his
power and possible only to the extent that he acts as an agent
for God.

Brainerd's diary began long before he became a missionary,
but on his deathbed he decided to destroy his first two volumes and to insert a new preface in which he advised the
reader that his behavior in the first thirty pages of the remainder was similar to that in the destroyed portion except that it
"was more refined from some *imprudences* and *indecent
heats*" (p. 51). Some of this premissionary material is preserved in the autobiographical section. Here, after a summa-
tion of events of his earlier life and a few fitful entries,
Brainerd quoted passages in which he, in traditional Puritan
fashion, inquired into the state of his soul. His thoughts alternated between confessions of "great *sinfulness* and *vileness*"
and exaltations of the " 'ecstasy' which arose from his perception of divine love" (p. 49).

A typical entry from this early portion of Brainerd's journal
is the following of April 13, 1742:

I saw myself to be very mean and vile; and wondered at those who
showed me respect. Afterwards I was somewhat comforted in secret
retirement and assisted to wrestle with God, with some power,
spirituality, and sweetness. Blessed be the Lord, he is never unmind-
ful of me, but always sends me needed supplies; and from time to

time, when I am like one dead he raises me to life. Oh that I may
never distrust Infinite goodness!   (p. 57)

This frame of mind was still observable a year later as
Brainerd began his missionary work with the Indians on April
1, 1743:

I rode to Kaunaumeek, near twenty miles from Stockbridge, where
the Indians live with whom I am concerned, and there lodged on a
little heap of straw. I was greatly exercised with inward trials and
distresses all day; and in the evening, my heart was sunk, and I
seemed to haye no God to go to. Oh that God would help me!   (p. 95)

Although in his first year among the Indians he achieved some
success in his mission, Brainerd was still primarily self-con-
cerned and unable to relate to the Indians as individuals. In
this period his statements about being "greatly oppressed
with guilt and shame, from a sense of inward vileness and pol-
lution" were significantly similar to those Wigglesworth made
in the early portion of his journal. Even when Brainerd went
into the woods for secret prayer, he thought himself "the vilest
meanest creature upon earth," and he was so overcome by
emotion that he had physical symptoms: "when I rose from my
knees I felt extremely weak and overcome; I could scarcely
walk straight; my joints were loosed; the sweat ran down my
face and body; and nature seemed as if it would dissolve." To
this statement he added, "So far as I could judge, I was wholly
free from selfish ends in my fervent supplications for the poor
Indians" (p. 156). His denial, however, reinforced other evidence suggesting the opposite. Brainerd displayed a propriet-
ary attitude toward his congregation, not only in calling them
"my Indians," but also in describing their resistance to conversion more as one of the obstacles which *he* faced in his own
battle with the temptations of Satan than as a function of their
own personalities.

By the following year (1745), entries such as the following
show that Brainerd's attitude had begun to change:

Was obliged to leave those Indians at Crosweeksung.... When I
came to take leave of them and to speak particularly to each of them,
they all earnestly inquired when I would come again, and expressed
a great desire of being further instructed.... When I parted from

them, one told me, with many tears, "She wished God would change her heart"; another that "she wanted to find Christ"; and an old man, who had been one of their chiefs, wept bitterly with concern for his soul. I then promised them to return as speedily as my health and business elsewhere would permit, and felt not a little concern at parting, lest the good impressions then apparent upon numbers of them might decline and wear off. (p. 208)

Here the Indians had begun to be identified and treated as individuals, and this change accompanied a marked reduction in the extent of Brainerd's self-consciousness and melancholia.

A few days after the above entry Brainerd showed his new attitude more fully in a long sketch describing the conversion of the Indian who had served him as a translator. This event was highly significant for Brainerd, because it provided the first tangible evidence of success in the two years of his ministry. In terms of the development of the journal the sketch is important, because it is the first of a series that marks Brainerd's mature style. The form and tone of the sketch are typical of Puritan conversion narratives such as Edwards's "Personal Narrative" and is similar to Brainerd's own, which he included earlier in the work.

After announcing to his readers his hope that this biographical sketch would be a "satisfactory and agreeable" part of his own narrative in that this Indian had by functioning as an interpreter served as an extension of himself, he proceeded to describe the man's preconversion state: "Well fitted for his work . . . in regard to his desire that the Indians should conform to the manners and customs of the English," the interpreter had "little or no impression of religion upon his mind and in that respect was very *unfit* for his work. He indeed behaved *soberly* after I employed him; although before, he had been *a hard drinker* . . . still he seemed to have no concern about his own soul" (pp. 210-11). In this passage Brainerd showed that the future *saint* was still unregenerate; he had been good according to earthly standards but was deficient according to divine ones.

Brainerd then began to reveal the first signs of change on the part of his interpreter, who became interested in the discussion of "spiritual concerns" and addressed the other Indians with greater "fervancy." However, as is also common in such conversion accounts, these first signs of grace were followed by backsliding. The interpreter's spiritual state declined and he remained "careless and secure" until the climactic moment of actual election. Brainerd described the experience as follows:

> He fell into a weak and languishing state of body; and continued much disordered for several weeks together. At this season divine truth took hold of him, and made deep impressions upon his mind. He was brought under great concern for his soul; and his exercises were not now transient and unsteady, but constant and abiding. . . . After he had been some time under this exercise, while he was striving to obtain mercy, he says there seemed to be an *impassable mountain* before him. He was pressing towards heaven, as he thought; but "his way was hedged up with thorns, so that he could not stir an inch further." He looked this way, and that way, but could find no way at all. He thought if he could but make his way through these thorns and briers, and climb up the first *steep pitch* of the mountain, that then there might be hope for him; but no way or means could he find to accomplish this. Here he laboured for a time, but all in vain. He saw it was *impossible*, he says, for him ever to help himself through this unsupportable difficulty. "It signified just nothing at all for him to struggle and strive any more." Here, he says, he gave over striving, and felt that it was a gone case with him, as to his own power, and that all his attempts were, and for ever would be, vain and fruitless. Yet he was more calm and composed under this view of things, than he had been while striving to help himself. (pp. 211-12)

This conviction of personal helplessness in the attainment of salvation was for the Calvinist like Brainerd an essential step in the process of conversion, but Brainerd still distrusted the vivid metaphor of the mountain of thorns, because the despair expressed was not accompanied by a conviction of guilt, of personal responsibility for the situation. It was not until the interpreter added his new recognition that "*he had never done one good thing* . . . [although he] had done many things which folks call good" (p. 212), that Brainerd became satisfied that the conversion was valid.

Brainerd continued his account, tracing the changes in the interpreter's subsequent behavior until he could give the reader what he considered positive evidence of the permanence and hence genuineness of the change. The interpreter's resistance to spiritual temptation was so great that it could not be feigned: "It might justly be said he was become *another man*, if not a *new man*. His conversation and deportment were much altered; and even the careless world could not but wonder what had befallen him, to make so great a change in his temper, discourse and behavior" (p. 213).

Brainerd too had become a *new man*. His early despondency had been tempered by success; and, although he recorded that he had sweet thoughts of death prompted by a longing to be with God, he was "willing to stay awhile on earth" (p. 214) to continue the work of his ministry. This hopeful attitude was sustained by other successes which were recorded in the diary.

Another important conversion narrative which Brainerd noted was in part the result of that of the interpreter. An Indian who had seen the baptism of the interpreter and his wife was finally converted. This conversion was especially noteworthy for Brainerd, because the Indian had formerly been a "Conjurer and a murderer." Of these two crimes Brainerd considered conjuration to be far the more heinous because, as Brainerd maintained, in this case it was not just a series of "charms and juggling tricks" but the real or attempted use of magic. To understand Brainerd's reaction we must recognize that in this period the belief in the existence of magic was still strong. The suppression of the witchcraft trials in Salem was related more to a belief in their improper procedures and judgments rather than to a disbelief in the existence of witches. Also still prevalent was the suspicion that Indians were the initiates of the devil.

The conversion of this man was of especially great concern to Brainerd because this conjurer had used his reputation among the other Indians to hinder Brainerd's work:

" . . . and to him they gave heed," supposing him to be possessed of great power. When I have instructed them respecting the miracle wrought by Christ in healing the sick, and mentioned them as evidence of his divine mission, and the truths of his doctrine; they have quickly observed the wonders of that kind, which this man had performed by his magic charms. Hence they had a high opinion of him and his superstitious notions; which seemed to be a fatal obstruction to some of them in regard to their receiving the Gospel. I have often thought that it would be a great favour to the design of evangelizing these Indians, if God would take that wretch out of the world. (pp. 304-305)

But God found what Brainerd called "a more desirable method," taking away the man's powers of conjuration "so he does not now so much as know, how he used to charm and conjure" (p. 305). It was then that Brainerd's teaching began to take effect, and the conjurer's conviction of guilt finally led to hope. Then he too was "created anew." Brainerd's entry ended with the following anecdote:

There being an old Indian at the place where I preached, who threatened to bewitch me, and my religious people who accompanied me there; this man presently challenged him to do his worst; telling him that himself had been as great a conjuror as he; and that notwithstanding, as soon as he felt that word to his heart which these people loved, meaning the word of God, his power of conjuring immediately left him. "And so it would you," said he, "if you did but once feel it in your heart; and you have no power to hurt them, nor so much as to touch one of them." (p. 307)

Brainerd concluded the anecdote by comparing his follower to St. Paul as one who learned to support what he had once obstructed.

One of the most interesting of Brainerd's sketches is that of an Indian religious man whom he is unable to convert:

But of all the sights I ever saw among them, or indeed any where else, none appeared so frightful, or so near a kin to what is usually imagined of *infernal powers*, none ever excited such images of terror in my mind, as the appearance of one who was a devout and zealous Reformer, or rather, restorer of what he supposed was the ancient religion of the Indians. He made his appearance in his *pontifical garb*, which was a coat of *boar skins*, dressed with the hair on, and hanging down to his toes; a pair of bear skin stockings; and a great *wooden* face painted, the one half black, the other half tawny, about the colour of an Indian's skin, with an extravagant mouth, cut very much awry; the face fastened to a bear skin cap, which was drawn over his head. . . . As he came forward, he beat his tune with the rattle, and danced with all his might, but did not suffer any part of his body, not so much as his fingers, to be seen. No one would have imagined from his appearance or actions, that he could have been a human creature, if they had not had some intimation of it otherwise.

When he came near me, I could not but shrink away from him although it was then noon day, and I knew who it was; his appearance and gestures were so prodigiously frightful. He had a house consecrated to religious uses, with divers images cut upon the several parts of it. I went in, and found the ground beat almost as hard as a rock, with their frequent dancing upon it. (pp. 237-38)

Here we see the power of observation, which is one of the essential skills of a good diarist, used to advantage. We have not only a faithful and vivid representation of an Indian ceremony, but we have a recording of the emotional effect which the scene has on the diarist as physical reality is transformed through the consciousness of the diarist's personality.

Brainerd then went on to relate his conversations with the Indian zealot who led a good life but was not converted to Christianity:

He . . . had formerly been like the rest of the Indians, until about four or five years before that time. Then, he said, his heart was very much distressed, so that he could not live among the Indians, but got away into the woods, and lived alone for some months. At length, he says, God comforted his heart, and showed him what he should do; and since that time he had known God, and tried to serve him; and loved all men, be they who they would, so as he never did before. He treated me with uncommon courtesy, and seemed to hearty in it. I was told by the Indians, that he opposed their drinking strong liquor with all his power; and that, if at any time he could not dissuade them from it by all he could say, he would leave them, and go crying into the woods. It was manifest that he had a set of religious notions which he had examined *for himself*, and not taken *for granted*, upon bare tradition; and he relished or disrelished whatever was spoken of a religious nature, as it either agreed or disagreed with *his standard*. While I was discoursing; he would sometimes say, "Now that I like; so God has taught me"; &c and some of his sentiments seemed very just. (p. 238)

In this section the narrative takes a surprising turn. The pagan ceremonies which had seemed so frightening to Brainerd are revealed to have their roots in the same search for God, the same desire to return to the pure, primitive roots of religion which had motivated Brainerd's Puritan ancestors. The Indian even appears to have undergone a process similar to the Christian conversion which Brainerd had sought to

achieve through his mission. And it is to Brainerd's credit as a
diarist that while he did not repudiate his own principles he
did attempt to look beyond his initial reactions and to see the
Indian's integrity.

He concluded the section by writing of the zealot:

> He seemed to be sincere, honest, and conscientious in his own way,
> and according to his own religious notions; which was more than I
> ever saw in any other Pagan. I perceived that he was looked upon and
> derided among most of the Indians, as a *precise zealot*, who made a
> needless noise about religious matters; but I must say that there was
> something in his temper and disposition, which looked more like true
> religion, than anything I ever observed amongst other heathens.(pp.
> 238-39)

In these observations Brainerd revealed an interest in others
as individuals. As such they are evidence of Brainerd's development as man and diarist. When toward the end of the
journal he wrote of his inner calmness and composure, his
feelings were an appropriate result of the maturing process he
had recorded.

IV *Quaker Diaries*

The most characteristic feature of the Quaker[7] meeting is
that each congregant speaks as the spirit of God moves him
and reveals itself through him. This revealed truth or "inner
light" is not expected to be impersonal or abstract. Rather, as
the voice and language by which this truth is conveyed is human, so the members of the meeting expect that images and
examples will be drawn from the human condition and, in particular, from the human experience of the speaker. It is easy to
see how such a practice of public self-examination and revelation in the religious service could be extended to life in general and so find its expression in autobiography; autobiography not only extends the practice but also offers another opportunity for extending spiritual insights. By publishing an autobiography a Quaker could hope to make his life a witness for
God. Since a recording of the inspiration of the moment would
help to record accurately its essence, diaries prove a significant asset in writing such an autobiography.

George Fox, founder of the Society of Friends, kept a diary

and published it in revised form. His example provided a further impetus for both diary keeping and spiritual autobiography.[8] As a result, a large number of American Quakers kept diaries. However, Quaker diary keeping never reached the extent of the Puritan practice. One reason may be that in diary keeping personal needs are a more potent motivation than systematic theological objectives. The Quakers' relative freedom from the Puritans' uncertainty about salvation and their alternate opportunity for personal expression in the meeting would certainly affect their personal motivation for such a practice.

Commonly labeled in their titles as journals and frequently including a division into dated entries, these Quaker works are difficult to classify by genre. There is no clear line determining which may be appropriately considered diary literature. In choosing diaries for this work I have included only those originating in periodic production in which revision in the direction of autobiographical organization has left the entry framework and relationship of writer to document relatively intact, and in which the author has generally avoided extensive intrusions of commentary written for the revision to alter the reader's perception of those entries. I, therefore, have chosen to include only the journal of John Woolman as an example of this type of diary literature. There are other Quaker diaries which have survived without significant revision, but such revision is common in Quaker works of this period.

V *John Woolman (1720-1772)*

John Woolman's *Journal* in its published form is an amalgam of diary entries and sections of autobiography proper. Much of the diary material is preserved in or close to its original form, and some diary material may have been used in the composition of some sections not divided into entries. Significantly, the sense of a perspective shifting through time as we move from entry to entry, a feature characteristic of the diary form, is retained; and, most important to our consideration, the retention of surface fragmentation through division into periodic entries helps to unite form and content.

Instead of a continuous series of events relating to a single topic, Woolman's *Journal* develops three systematic concepts

48 AMERICAN DIARY LITERATURE

interweaving the events and opinions which support them like musical themes throughout the work. These concepts are: God's truth is composed of simple basic principles accessible through revelation; these principles operate in the world in a complex of events and appearances; and all God's truths and their appearances are interconnected by a chain of logic which can be followed by a combination of human reason and divine revelation. Broken into periodic entries, the work preserves the multiplicity and complexity of the events of the world as well as Woolman's lifelong attempts to discover God's plan. In Woolman's statement, "I have often felt a motion of love to leave some hints in writing of my experience of the goodness of God,"[9] his use of "hints" is more suited to the fragmented truth of the diarist rather than the systematic overview of the autobiographer.

A description of diary truth as fragmented should not be taken to suggest that Woolman's work is not unified. Instead of developing unity by the selection or emphasis of events according to thematic principles, a good diarist's awareness of essential themes emerges through the process of his record. Sections of autobiography proper included in Woolman's work serve as a preface to and commentary on the developments of the diary. All parts work together for the development of Woolman's themes. In one of the early autobiographical pages Woolman wrote of the difficulty of following the "openings of divine truth," and the corresponding difficulty of conveying the insights gained by that process:

As I lived under the cross and simply followed the openings of Truth, my mind from day to day was more enlightened; my former acquaintance was left to judge of me as they would, for I found it safest for me to live in private and keep those things sealed up in my own breast.

While I silently ponder on that change wrought in me, I find no language equal to it nor any means to convey to another a clear idea of it. I looked upon the works of God in this visible creation and an awfulness covered me; my heart was tender and often contrite, and a universal love to my fellow creatures increased in me. This will be understood by such who have trodden in the same path.   (pp. 28-29)

Given the exclusiveness of this divine language, Woolman could not directly convey its meanings, but he could offer its symbolic representation in events in life and visions. In an early diary form entry, Woolman recorded the following vision:

> ... As I opened my eyes I saw a light in my chamber at the apparent distance of five feet, about nine inches diameter, of a clear, easy brightness and near the center the most radiant. As I lay still without any surprise looking upon it, words were spoken to my inward ear which filled my whole inward man. They were not the effect of thought nor any conclusion in relation to the appearance, but as the language of the Holy One spoken in my mind. The words were, "Certain Evidence of Divine Truth," and were again repeated exactly in the same manner, whereupon the light disappeared.   (p. 58)

As the entry indicates both by its message and the means by which that message is transmitted, the certainty and simplicity of truth for Woolman rested on direct revelation and not on indirect means such as second-hand religious commentary or the analysis of human events.

Since a diary or an autobiography cannot directly convey the force of revelation, it must rely on secondary representation. As Woolman recognized that language lacks an exact correspondence to divine truth, so he found the same inadequacy in human events. The parallel between language and event is important here because, as Woolman recognized, some of the limitations of language can be overcome by providing numerous symbols and images which, while individually inadequate, can, taken together, circumscribe an area of meaning. In one entry truth is both a "tender seed" and the "presence of the Lord" which nourishes it (p. 63). In another the vehicle for that truth is the "Divine Fountain" and "the secret movings of the Heavenly Principle" in his own mind (p. 115). These images for Woolman were not contradictory, but rather were supplementary.

This use of language is not uncommon in literature. In "Song of Myself" Walt Whitman wrote, as an attempted answer to the questions, *"What is the grass?":*

> I guess it must be the flag of my disposition, out of hopeful green stuff woven.

> Or I guess it is the handkerchief of the Lord,
> A scented gift and remembrancer designedly dropt,

Bearing the owner's name someway in the corners, that we may see
    and remark, and say *Whose?* . . .

Or I guess it is a uniform hieroglyphic,
And it means, Sprouting alike in broad zones and narrow zones,
Growing among black folks as among white. . . .

Woolman like Whitman recognized that spiritual truth,
though simple in itself, is complicated by its multiple incarna-
tions. Multiple diary entries replicate the appearances of truth
in the world and allow the reader to induce God's goodness
from the events of Woolman's life. However, while Woolman's
work opens itself to the reader through inductive logic, Woolman's own logic was largely deductive. Beginning with the
principle that slavery was evil, Woolman deduced his culpa-
bility. Early in the work he explained, "When I ate, drank, and
lodged free-cost with people who lived in ease on the hard
labour of their slaves, I felt uneasy" (p. 38). Later this uneasiness about accepting the service of slaves is connected to
being obligated to those Friends who have given him free
food and lodging while traveling to speak for God. Recollect-
ing the scriptural warning that "a gift blindeth the eyes of the
wise and perverteth the words of the righteous," Woolman
gave money to the Negro servants as a means of keeping "clear
from the gain of oppression" (pp. 59-60). Only later did he logically construct an argument in which he clearly demonstrated
the chain of events which can make the nonslaveholding guest
guilty of slavery:

    In fifty pounds are four hundred half crowns. If a slave be valued at
fifty pounds and I with my horse put his owner to half a crown expense, and I with many others for a course of years repeat these expense four hundred times, then on a fair computation this slave may
be accounted a slave to the public under the direction of the man he
calls master.   (p. 141)

By a similar process Woolman refused to use sugar and thus to
add, however infinitesimally, to the demand which in turn
would raise the demand for slaves to produce it. Neither
would he take passage on a ship to the West Indies when he
concluded that his passage had been made cheaper because of

the extent of the sugar trade. In this manner the diary explores the connection between the basic divine principles and their complex effects.

As these themes appear and reappear in the diary connected with a multitude of different topics, they produce a document with the surface complexity and central unity which Woolman found in life. It is a world-view well suited to the diary form. It is perhaps also appropriate that, although Woolman revised the early portion of his work, he continued adding to it so that entries were included extending the work until it was interrupted by his death. Thus the diary never really concludes but rather extends, open to the world with which it deals.

VI *Methodist Diaries*

Following the lead of John Wesley,[10] the principal founder of their sect, and George Whitefield,[11] a leading revivalist whose preaching in America had a significant effect on the sect's development, many American Methodists took up diary keeping or continued the practice with increased vigor. Several of these were written with the hope that they might someday prove worthy of publication. Among the best of these diaries are those of Francis Asbury, the first American Bishop in America, and Lorenzo Dow, an itinerant preacher. The wide circulation of such diaries attests to the popularity and influence of the genre. Dow's diary, which he sold during his travels throughout America, went through many printings and had a diffuse but significant effect.

The characteristics of the Methodist sect had an effect on the character of the diaries that its American followers produced. The Arminian beliefs of Methodism allowed its members to look with far greater favor on the value of human good works and thus, in contrast to Puritan diaries, Methodist diaries place greater stress on physical acts and show less anxiety about an internal struggle for grace. Unlike the works of Quaker journalists they usually show little involvement with a search for direct divine revelation (Dow's diary is an important exception). As a result, they tend to focus outward to the world, giving a valuable picture of their world.

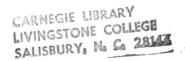

VII   *Francis Asbury (1745-1816)*

Asbury probably did not consider the possibility of publication when he began his diary, but later he began to write with this objective in mind. Toward this end he prefaced the diary with an autobiographical section to chronicle his life prior to his call to go to America, the point at which the first included diary entries begin. Later in the diary he reflected on this pre-diary period in the following lines: "Whilst I was a travelling preacher in England, I was much tempted, finding myself exceedingly ignorant of almost everything a minister of the Gospel ought to know. How I came to America, and the events which have happened since, my journal will show."[12] Even in context these two sentences lack an overt connection, but yoked together they imply that the journal will show what a minister should know and how, by learning that lesson in America, he overcame temptation.

The following excerpt reveals that the temptation to which Asbury referred was spiritual rather than physical: "Satan beset me with powerful suggestions, striving to persuade me that I should never conquer all my spiritual enemies, but be overcome at last. However, the Lord was near and filled my soul with peace. Blessed Lord, be ever with me, and suffer me not to yield to the tempter; no, not for a moment!" (I, p. 185). Asbury's anxiety arose whenever he became conscious of seeing great evil in the world and little fear of God in mankind. For a Calvinist such as Wigglesworth or Edwards these observations could be readily accepted as confirmation of their belief that few men were predestined by God for salvation. However, for a Methodist like Asbury, with his Arminian belief in the potential of all men, it signified the immensity of the work before him.

The earliest entries in the diary show Asbury preaching to the sailors on board his ship hoping, above all, to "be useful to souls"; but unfortunately he found only "deep ignorance and insensibility of the human heart" (I, p. 5). Nevertheless, Asbury persevered; bracing his back against the mizzenmast of the ship as it was buffeted by strong winds and rough seas, he preached to the unreceptive sailors, but even this exertion did not produce a visible effect:

I felt the power of truth on my own soul, but still, alas! saw no visible fruit: but my witness is in heaven, that I have not shunned to declare to them all the counsel of God. Many have been my trials in the course of this voyage; from the want of a proper bed, and proper provisions, from sickness, and from being surrounded with men and women ignorant of God, and very wicked. But all this is nothing. If I cannot bear this, what have I learned?   (I, p. 6)

What Asbury had learned from this experience and what he would learn in the many years covered in the diary was to work without the need for an earthly reward of any sort. Determined to "show the way" to other Methodists by leaving the cities and preaching in the country and along the frontier, Asbury gave up not only physical comforts, but also the easiest religious converts (I, p. 10). For most of his life Asbury traveled throughout the American colonies enduring hunger, fatigue, and illness, to preach to audiences which he found generally unreceptive. One comment he frequently made and which characterized his view of his own life as recorded in the diary was: "My soul is amongst lions" (I, p. 197). It is an image which converted danger to safety as Asbury knew that God preserves his Daniels."

As a work of art Asbury's diary suffers from a weak structure, but its style is strong and makes reading easy. Some of this fluency may be attributed to the fact that Asbury came to expect publication, began to revise his diary for that end, and actually published some parts of it during his lifetime. He was conscious of the value of a good diary and the problems involved in writing one. He also read diaries and used that experience to model his own work.

One might expect that a consciousness of possible publication and the reading of models would have a positive effect beyond that on fluency of style, but in Asbury's case the result may have been just the opposite. The following experience occuring midway in the diary reinforced a tendency already present in the work:

I was employed in reading Mr. Wesley's Journal; and I am now convinced of the great difficulty of journalizing. Mr. Wesley was, doubtless, a man of very general knowledge, learning, and reading, to which we may add a lively wit and humour; yet, I think I see too much credulity, long, flat narrations, and coarse letters taken from others, in his Journal: but when I come to his own thoughts, they are lively, sentimental, interesting, and instructing. The Journal of a minsiter of the Gospel should be theological: only it will be well to wink at many things we see and hear, since men's feelings grow more and more refined.   (II, pp. 42-43)

Asbury did try to be "refined" in subject and presentation. Yet there are many striking subjects in the diary.

Some of Asbury's best narrative passages are those in which he was retelling the experiences of others. These passages include Indian captivity narratives and even an account of an exorcism. Asbury could also on occasion refuse to "wink at" the problems he saw around him. In such emotional periods his diary became animated:

I confess my soul and body have been sorely tried. What blanks are in this country—and how much worse are rice plantations! If a man- of- war is "a floating hell," these are standing ones: wicked masters, overseers, and Negroes—cursing, drinking—no Sabbaths, no sermons. But hush! perhaps my journal will never see the light; and if it does, matters may mend before that time; and it is probable I shall be beyond their envy or good-will. O wretched priests, thus to lead the people on in blindness!   (II, p. 7)

Asbury's *Journal* has "seen the light" and his honest perceptions provide the substance that strengthens it.

VIII   *Lorenzo Dow (1777-1834)*

Although Lorenzo Dow considered himself a Methodist clergyman, the hierarchy of that church refused him ordination and repudiated many of his statements and works. One reason for these actions was that the Methodist church felt that his beliefs and practices tended toward the religious enthusiasm of the Quakers. Dow's own diary tends to support their judgment, for in its record of divinely directed dreams and conscious attention to direct and personal providential guidance, Lorenzo moved toward the Quaker position. Certainly the work seems more like Woolman's than like Asbury's.

The most obvious similarities relate to similar events and patterns. As in many spiritual narratives of the American colonies, the writers revealed a path to spiritual maturity that involved a serious illness which moved the spirit, a pulling away from youthful companions, early anxieties about speaking or otherwise involving oneself in religious gatherings, and finally a confirmation of faith. Equally significant aspects of the similarity of the two diarists are their emphasis on the importance of dreams and divine visions as a source of direction. Some of Dow's experiences were extensive and traumatic: in one section he recorded that after dreaming of being crucified and ascending into heaven, he went to pray in the forest where he heard voices calling from the tops of trees.

Similarity of event is less crucial in revealing a relationship than patterns of responses. Consider, for example, the autobiographical sections in which each author, recording the events of his youth, described the wanton killing of a bird. Woolman wrote of killing a robin:

... At first I was pleased by the exploit, but after a few minutes I was seized with horror, at having in a sportive way, killed an innocent creature while she was careful for her young. I beheld her lying dead, and thought these young ones, for which she was so careful must now perish for want of their dam to nourish them. After some painful consideration on the subject I took all the young birds and killed them, supposing that better than to leave them to pine away and die miserably. In this case I believed that the Scripture proverb was fulfilled, "The tender mercies of the wicked are cruel." ... For some hours [I] could think of little else but the cruelties I had committed. Thus he whose tender mercies are over all his works hath placed a principle in the human mind which excites to exercise goodness to every living creature. ... (pp. 24-25)

In his diary Dow wrote:

One day I was the means of killing a bird and upon seeing it gasp was struck with horror. And upon seeing the beast struggle in death it made my heart beat hard, as it would cause the thoughts of my death to come into my mind. Death appeared such a terror to me, I sometimes wished that I might be translated as Enoch and Elijah were; and at other times I wished that I had never been born.[13]

Despite the similarity between the initial events in these excerpts, their full meanings differ markedly. Woolman's episode became an example of the complex system of causality and moral responsibility which links physical events and divine principles; for Dow the experience was used to explain a personal emotional response in which the biblical allusions were devoid of spiritual guidance. The real similarity is in the heightened sensitivity and intense emotional response displayed by each writer. It prefigured the intensity with which each would pursue his religious convictions in the life he recorded in his diary.

As Woolman's work goes beyond the personal and the subjective to give a reasoned system, so Dow's diary goes beyond the limits of a purely spiritual account. Dow's diary gives an excellent portrait of the religious life and social customs of the common people of early America. Especially valuable are Dow's portraits of the camp meetings, the religious revivals of the frontier. Traveling with sparse provisions, riding mile after mile through all the difficulties of the wilderness, Dow managed to find surprisingly large groups to hear him. But large or small, in field, house, or tent, Dow related to the simple people and their needs. He might be interrupted by drunkards, threatened by rowdies, or pressured by members of rival religious persuasions; yet he managed to succeed. When "Satan's emissaries set up the Grog tents" near a camp meeting, Dow warned the people against them so their trade failed (p. 169). His power to influence was even miraculously extended so that the dumb spoke and backsliders flocked to his voice and aid with passionate enthusiasm.

Dow's own character followed the spontaneous promptings of faith rather than cool reason. As the journal shows, he often acted according to inner compulsion. In one entry he was "seized with an impulse to set off . . . so that . . . sleep departed." He tried to reject the impulse, but it returned "with double force" (p. 95). Mounting his horse, he rode nine miles, whereupon he unexpectedly met with an old man who, learning of Dow's calling, invited him home and gathered a congregation to hear him. In a parallel instance Dow was "awakened by a singular dream" warning that he had "disappointed the people through . . . neglect." Again he rose in the night, rode and learned that his impulse was providential, for his route was "nine miles beyond [his] . . . expectation" (p. 163). Had he not ridden when he did, he would have failed to reach on time the place appointed for his preaching.

The most striking of Dow's impulses is that which sent him,

while still a youth, across the ocean to Ireland to preach. Against all advice he went virtually without money to a strange country thousands of miles from home to speak on behalf of a sect that had few adherents. Yet by wit, luck, and, most importantly in Dow's mind, the providential support of God, he survived and enjoyed some measure of success. Seasickness made him doubt he would live to see Dublin, but the worst gale in many years did not stop him. A near wreck in a fog was averted when a mysterious sense of uneasiness roused the captain of Dow's ship at the crucial moment. In Ireland he just as narrowly, but surely, escaped difficulty and disaster. He recorded that when "sombody would frequently be robbed or murdered one day ... I would travel the same way the day before or after and yet was preserved and brought back in peace" (p. 121).

For his impulsiveness and fervency he gained the name "Crazy Dow"; but rather than struggling to repudiate it, he turned it to his advantage:

> Here too it was soon reported I was crazy, which brought many out to the different meetings: among whom was an old man, who came to hear for himself, and told the congregation that I was crazy, and advised them to hear me no more. I replied, people do not blame crazy ones for their behavior; and last night I preached from the word of the Lord; but when I come again I will preach from the word of the devil. This tried our weak brethren: however, the people came out by hundreds to hear the new doctrine. (p. 48)

The word of the devil that Dow delivered was from Luke 4:6-7 in which the devil tempts Christ in the wilderness. Such theatrical craziness contributed to Dow's success. It was "crazy" Dow the people came to hear, and it was the journal of "crazy" Dow they read. Sales of the journal were large, and Dow carried a supply of copies with him to support him on his travels and to earn funds for religious projects. But today we will find the craziness submerged in the romance of the past, and Dow's actions seem to blend into an appropriate picture of a little-examined side of American life in the early years of the Republic.

CHAPTER 3

Travel Diaries

JUST as exploring expeditions were directed to the West, so were many other travelers; settlers seeking new land, tourists seeking adventure, would-be trappers and merchants following the fur trade—these were only some of those who went west toward the frontier and the future. Of course, for most of the colonial period this westward movement was hindered by the Appalachian Mountains, first as a physical barrier and later as the demarkation of a British prohibition of colonial expansion. As a result, the earlier diaries do not extoll the symbolic significance of the West as do later works. But even when American diarists traveled in other directions, their works indicate a tendency toward identifying a direction of ideas and behaviors to parallel the physical directions. Sarah Kemble Knight, traveling to New York from her native Boston, conveyed a similar sense of moving away from civilization expressed by those diarists who were migrating toward the western frontier. Dr. Hamilton, traveling north for his health, suggested in his diary the same opposing directional associations with democratic egalitarianism and cultural elegance that Philip Vickers Fithian found when traveling in the opposite direction to become a tutor in Virginia. But whatever the direction of the journey or the value the diarist assigned to it, American diaries have tended to emphasize that the experience offers valuable knowledge to be carried home.

The assertion that travel leads to significant spiritual achievements is implicit in most diaries describing journeys. It is explicit in very few of those written in the seventeenth and eighteenth centuries, but the same observation may be made of other forms of American literature in this period. Only after the Revolution did works like Barlow's "Columbiad," extolling the spirit of discovery, become important in American writing. Other factors which might have accounted for this situation include the influence of the Romantic Movement. There were, of course, diarists like John Winthrop who extolled the divine mission of the American settlers, or like Sarah Kemble Knight who compared their journeys to the accomplishments of literary heroes; but in general such controlling images were not as directly or dramatically presented as those in many later works. They are, however, quite accessible to the reader who looks beyond overt raptures over the glories of the prairie.

I   Sarah Kemble Knight (1666-1727)

The introduction to the most recent edition of Sarah Kemble Knight's work begins, "Sarah Kemble Knight's Journal is the truest picture left to us of provincial New England."[1] But in an important sense Knight's portrait is not of New England at all. Of course, her narrative does give items of description of New England (and neighboring New York) from the conditions of its roads to the clothes of its inhabitants. However, most of her observations were sufficiently general that with minor alterations they could have been set in another part of America or even in England. This generality of setting presents little problem for us as readers, because setting is not the crucial element of the diary; character is. Moreover, it is not the character of particular individuals or a regional character that attracts our attention, but rather the character of the large section of humanity those individuals represent.

As we saw in considering spiritual journals, Knight's Puritan ancestors viewed human life as a serious business and mankind as divided between pious saints and blasphemous sinners. They allowed no middle ground between those destined for heaven and hell, and the smallest sin could be a sign of serious danger to the soul. But for Madame Knight the mass of humanity were neither holy men nor villains but simple fools. She did view folly as the result of sinful pride, covetousness, and so on, but considered most men as incapable of effecting truly evil ends. Therefore, the verbal whipping she applied as punishment was not the harsh lash of denunciation but the more subtle switch of satire.

In one of the earliest entries, she told of her attempts to obtain a guide being frustrated because all the men in the tavern were "tyed by the Lipps to a pewter engine" (p. 2). The tavern hostess offered to provide her son as a guide but asked an exorbitant fee. The resulting bargaining proceeded as follows:

I told her no, I would not be accessary to such extortion.

Then John shan't go, sais shee. No, indeed, shan't hee; And held forth at that rate a long time, that I began to fear I was got among the Quaking tribe, beleeving that not a Limbertong'd sister among them could out do Madm. Hostes. (p. 3)

When she did get escorted to the next tavern, Madame Knight found that the flaw of the hostess there was pride rather than covetousness. After rudely besieging Madame Knight with questions, the hostess ran "upstairs and putte on two or three Rings . . . and returning, set herself just before me, showing the way to Reding, that I might see her Ornaments, perhaps to gain the more respect. But," Madame Knight commented, "her Granam's new Rung sow, had it appeared, would affected me as much" (p. 7).

For many of her best accounts of human folly she repeated stories current in the neighborhoods through which she traveled. Typical is the following anecdote in which an Indian implicated in the theft of a hogshead was brought to the judge's house to be interviewed:

But his worship (it seems) was gone into the feild, with a Brother in office, to gather his Pompions [pumpkins]. Wither the malefactor is hurried, And Complaint made, and satisfaction in the name of Justice demanded. Their Worships cann't proceed in form without a Bench: whereupon they Order one to be Imediately erected, which, for want of fitter materials, they made with pompions—which being finished, down setts their Worships, and the Malefactor call'd, and . . . Interrogated after the following manner, . . . You sirrah, why did You steal this man's Hoggshead? Hoggshead? (replys the Indian,) me no stomany. No? says his worship; and pulling off his hatt, Patted his own head with his hand, sais, Tatapa—You, Tatapa—you; all one this. Hoggshead all one this. Hah! says Netop, now me stomany that. (pp. 35-36)

These stories are entertaining, but are not necessary as Knight produced an ample number of her own characters and incidents. In one entry she described the following scene:

Being at a merchants house, in comes a tall country fellow, wth his alfogeos full of Tobacco; for they seldom Loose their Cudd, but keep Chewing and Spitting as long as they'r eyes are open,—he advanc't to the midle of the Room, makes an Awkward Nodd, and spitting a Large deal of Aromatik Tincture, he gave a scrape with his shovel like shoo, leaving a small shovel full of dirt on the floor, made a full stop, Hugging his own pretty Body with his hands under his arms, Stood staring rown'd him like a Catt let out of a Baskett. At last, like the creature Balaam Rode on, he opened his mouth and said: have You any Ribinen for Hatbands to sell I pray?   (pp. 41-42)

Another curious character is a guide whose "shade on his Hors resembled a Globe on a Gate post." Hearing "Adventurs he had passed by late Rideing, and eminent Dangers he had escaped," Madame Knight, "Remembring the Hero's in Parismus and the Knight of the Oracle," imagined that she may have "mett wth a Prince disguis'd" (p. 4).

In another entry the magical transformation was malignant:

The post encourag'd mee, by saying wee should be well accommodated anon at mr. Devills, a few miles further. But I questioned whether we ought to go to the Devill to be helpt out of affliction. However, like the rest of Deluded souls that post to ye Infernal denn, Wee made all posible speed to this Devill's Habitation; where alliting, in full assurance of good accommodation, wee were going in. (p. 20)

Unfortunately Madame Knight was not able to get lodging there, and so warned her readers in one of the several original poems integrated in the diary:

May all that dread the cruel feind of night
Keep on, and not at this curs't Mansion light.
'Tis Hell; 'tis Hell! and Devills here do dwell:
Here dwells the Devill—surely this's Hell.
Nothing but Wants: a drop to cool yo'r Tongue
Cant be procur'd these cruel Feinds among.
Plenty of horrid Grins and looks sevear,
Hunger and thirst, But pitty's bannish'd here—
The Right hand keep, if Hell on Earth you fear!   (p. 21)

The quality of accommodations was just one of the hazards Knight faced. In one entry she encountered a dangerous ford at night:

Hee [her guide] told mee there was a bad River wee were to Ride
thro', wch was so very firce a hors could sometimes hardly stem it: But
it was but narrow, and wee should soon be over. I cannot express the
concern of mind this relation sett me in: no thoughts but those of the
dang'ros River could entertain my Imagination, and they were as
formidable as varios, still Tormenting me with blackest Ideas of my
Approching fate—Sometimes seing my self drowning, otherwhiles
drowned, and at the best like a holy Sister Just come out of a Spiritual
Bath in dripping Garments.   (pp. 10-11)

Her anticipation of danger was enhanced as her imagination
heightened the sense of anxiety: "The only Glimering we now
had was from the spangled Skies, whose Imperfect reflections
rendered very Object formidable. Each lifeless Trunk, with its
shatter'd Limbs appear'd an Armed Enymie; and every little
stump like a Ravenous devourer" (p. 11). Rallying her courage, Madame Knight proved equal to the task: "Knowing that I
must either Venture my fate of drowning, or be left like y^e
Children in the wood . . . I gave Reins to my Nagg; and sitting
. . . Stedy . . . got safe to the other side" (pp. 12-13).
    Many commentators on the Knight diary center their atten-
tion about her personal character, emphasizing that her journey, arduous even for a man, was an exceptional achievement
for a woman. Certainly she showed courage, but this is not the
quality which her diary stresses. By her own record her distinction lay in her ability to use intellect rather than will to
transmute her achievement to heroism by a process of the
mind that was inaccessible to those around her. Her achievement as she would have it perceived through the diary was
inaccessible to the ordinary fools around her by virtue of their
folly. They could not recognize the creative possibility which
allowed heroism to exist. Triviality, ignorance, and greed were
the more culpable, because they destroyed the individuals
who displayed them. Our amusement is more important as a
reaction to her descriptions than any grave consideration
could ever be, because it offers the most appropriate censure
possible of the fool. It is this attitude toward vice which would
become part of the American adaptation of eighteenth-century
English satire. When we read in John Adams's diary of the
created "character" of an old man who as a youth had wasted
his efforts in condemning vice but had "at last obtained a settled Habit of making [himself] . . . merry at all the Wickedness

and Misery of the World" until he became "the most tittering, giggling Mortal you ever saw," we should think of Madame Knight's achievement. Essentially this achievement was the artistic integration of the values of her society.

II   *Dr. Alexander Hamilton (1712-1756)*

Although America in 1744 still had clearly defined social classes, these distinctions were being broken down. The isolation, the increased importance of talent, the ready availability of cheap land, and certain egalitarian aspects of many of the major religious movements all contributed to its decline. This decline was, of course, more apparent on the frontier than in the more established settlements, but it was also more rapid in the North than in the South, where the climate and other factors favored the existence of large landholdings. An extreme example of this situation can be seen in the following excerpt from David McClure's journal in which he recounted an incident told him about the experience of a man sent as a messenger to Jonathan Law who, at the time of Hamilton's journey, was governor of Connecticut:

He knocked at the door and was let in by a man in the plain dress and appearance of a common farmer. He concluded he was a labourer or a servant of the Governor, and asked him if Gov. Law was at home. He was a little surprised to find that he had made a mistake and that it was the Governor whom he was addressing. . . . He was invited and urged to stay and dine. A large boiled dish was placed on the table, around which the family and labourers were seated and each one helped himself. A lad came into the room and told the Governor that his father wanted to borrow his spade. He directed his son to go and get it.[2]

In traveling into an area where such a leveling of social classes could take place, Hamilton was symbolically moving ahead in the history of American society; and, as Carl Bridenbaugh wrote in his introduction to the diary, "Alexander Hamilton was witnessing in the American colonies the beginnings of one of the greatest revolutions of modern times—the breakdown of the medieval class structure and the liberation of the common man."[3]

In Pennsylvania, seeing a fight between a master, "an unweildy pott-gutted fellow" and his servant, "muscular, raw-bon'd, and tall," he sensed the irony of a situation in which ability was so at odds with station (p. 24). In New Jersey he found that the "Proprietor of most of the houses in the town . . . milks his own cow, dresses his own vittles, and feeds his own poultry" (p. 38), while in Connecticut a woman who, though "the homliest piece bothe as to mein, make and dress," assumed a genteel title (p. 164). Hamilton attributed this slurring of class to the scarcity of true gentlemen in America which he felt deprived America of the chance to "know what it is that really constitutes that difference of degrees" (p. 186).

Among the features of this social revolution was the common assumption of a right to familiarity. In the following excerpt Hamilton took the opportunity to use his own education to poke fun at a man who he felt was presumptuously inquisitive:

His questions were all stated in the rustick civil stile. "Pray sir, if I may be so bold, where are you going?" "Prithee, friend," says I, "where are you going?" "Why, I go along the road here a little way." "So do I, friend," replied I. "But may I presume, sir, whence do you come?" "And from whence do you come, friend?" says I. "Pardon me, from John Singleton's farm," replied he, "with a bag of oats." "And I come from Maryland," said I, "with a portmanteau and baggage." "Maryland!" said my companion, "where the devil is that there place? I have never heard of it. But pray, sir, may I be so free as to ask your name?" "And may I be so bold as to ask yours, friend?" said I. "Mine is Jerry Jacobs, att your service," replied he. I told him that mine was Bombast Huynhym van Helmont, att his service. "A strange name indeed; belike your a Dutchman, sir,—a captain of a ship, belike." "No, friend," says I, "I am a High German alchymist." "Bless us! You don't say so; that's a trade I never heard of; what may you deal in sir?" "I sell air," said I. "Air," said he, "damn it, a strange commodity. I'd thank you for some wholesom air to cure my fevers which have held me these two months."   (p. 124)

In another form this familiarity was a naive openness which Hamilton could describe sympathetically. In one entry Hamilton came to a ferry just as the ferryman and his family were about to have dinner. They invited him to join them but he declined, noting in the diary that they lacked not only a tablecloth and napkins but even forks, spoons, and plates. He appears to have been sympathetic to the poor family that had welcomed him: "I looked upon this as a picture of primitive simplicity practiced by our forefathers long before the mechanic arts had supplied them with instruments for the luxury and elegance of life" (p. 8). His sympathy was not for their poverty, but for a goodness of spirit which was not rewarded by material advantages.

For Hamilton material possessions were overvalued in American society and used in place of inner qualities as a basis for a claim to gentility. Hamilton admitted that he, as many other "gentlemen," did get caught up in the outward signs of breeding such as codes of dress. In one entry he wrote:

I dined with Mr. Fletcher in the company of two Philadelphians, who could not be easy because forsooth they were in their night-caps seeing every body else in full dress with powdered wigs; it not being customary in Boston to go to dine or appear upon Change in caps as they do in other parts of America. What strange creatures we are, and what triffles make us uneasy! It is no mean jest that such worthless things as caps and wigs should disturb our tranqulity and disorder our thoughts when we imagin they are wore out of season. I was my self much in the same state of uneasiness with these Philadelphians, for I had got a great hole in the lappet of my coat, to hide which employed so much of my thoughts in company that, for want of attention, I could not give a pertinent answer when I was spoke to.   (p. 134)

Ultimately for Hamilton, gentility required an ability to react appropriately in all situations and among the members of any class. The ultimate test of this skill was when tact required him to satisfy the needs of others in ways contrary to his own sense of propriety. For example, in one incident, having complimented his host's daughter's playing of the spinet as the best he had heard in America, his host bluntly asked if Hamilton "could pay her no other compliment but that." Hamilton remarked in the diary that this request "dashed me a little, but I soon replied that the young lady was every way so deserving and accomplished that nothing that was spoken to her in commendation could in strict sense be called a compliment." Hamilton seems glad to have pleased others, but he was aware that with this false flattery he had "talked nonsense" (p. 138). The reader of the diary is allowed to see the multiple levels of such words and actions, and Hamilton demonstrated this skill effectively in veiled satire such as the following response to a Boston woman's comment about his "odd" appearance:

I desired [a friend] . . . to give my humble service to the lady and tell
her that it gave me vast pleasure to think any thing particular about
my person could attract her resplendent eyes . . . and that I intended
to wait upon her so that she might entertain her opticks with my od-
dity, and mine with her unparalleled charms.   (p. 139)

Hamilton's sensibility was most offended by persons who
claimed superior station without desert. In the diary such
people were exposed, not by attack or invective, but by skillful
satiric portraits. A good example comes early in the diary in a
passage describing "a very rough spun, forward, clownish
blade, much addicted to swearing, att the same time desirous
to pass for a gentleman; notwithstanding which ambition the
conscientiousness of his naturall boorishness obliges him frequently to frame ill tim'd apologys for his misbehavior which
he termed frankness and freeness." Hamilton next proceeded
to portray an incident in which this clown railed at a landlady
who failed to serve him as a gentleman and then attacked
Hamilton's own Maryland saying, "Damn my blood if ever I
come into that rascally province again if I don't procure a
leather jacket that I may be in a trim to box the saucy jacks and
not run the hazzard of tearing my coat." Hamilton reserved his
comment for the reader, writing, "This showed, by the bye,
that he payed more regard to his coat than his person, a remarkable instance of modesty and self denial" (pp. 13-14).
      These passages show those features characteristic of Hamil-
ton's character sketches. His introduction frequently undercut
the subject with an acid physical and character description,
while the success of the body of the piece hinges on Hamilton's memory for the details of an incident, especially his re-
construction of the dialogue. Typical of these features are:
Hamilton's introduction to "one Dr. Mcgraa, a pretended
Scots-man but by brogue a Teague," who had "an affected way
of curtseying instead of bowing when he entered a room" (p.
83); and his eavesdropping on the professed poet Major Spratt
who announced, "Pray take notice of the concisest, wittiest,
prittiest epigram or epitaph, call it what you will you ever
heard. Shall I get a pen and ink to write it down? perhaps you
mayn't remember it else. It is highly worth your noting. Pray
observe how it runs, –

> Here lyes John Purcell;
> And whether he be in heaven or hell
> Never a one of us can tell."   (p. 81)

Hamilton's work was not limited to character sketches. He devoted considerable space to the physical description of the towns and countryside, and included details such as the nature of the fortifications, the price of the ferry tolls, and the size of the local onions. However, nothing comes close to occupying the position in the diary of his concern for character, and it is this concern that Hamilton himself declared was the unifying feature of the diary. In his conclusion he wrote that in the 1,624 miles of his travels he found variety in "constitutions and complexions, air and government," but that he "found little difference in the manners and character of the people in the different provinces" (p. 199). He did not attempt to identify what the nature of these manners and character was, but from the diary we can infer that he would have included intense energy which, combined with an uncertainty about social station, resulted in unwarranted pride and familiarity. It was a judgment similar to that expressed almost a century later by another traveler, Alexis de Tocqueville, who wrote: "In democracies everybody's status seems doubtful; as a result there is often pride but seldom dignity of manners." In such a situation Hamilton found that the best expression of this colonial character was in its individuals.

III   *Philip Vickers Fithian (1747-1776)*

Despite the fact that Fithian's term as tutor to the children of the Carter family in colonial Virginia lasted almost a year, his record of the experience is appropriately classified as a travel diary. Throughout his extended visit Fithian not only held the conviction that his stay would be temporary, but also preserved the attitude of an outsider. Unlike Hamilton, who almost thirty years earlier had asserted the existence of common characteristics between colonists in the North and South, Fithian preserved his initial perception of a great gulf between the cultures of Virginia and his native New Jersey. Toward the end of his stay he wrote to a young man who had been a fellow student in the North and was now planning to go to Virginia as a tutor. Fithian's letter outlining the differences the young man would encounter included the following advice: "You come here, it is true, with an intention to teach, but you ought to likewise have an inclination to learn."[4] This injunction might serve as the motto for Fithian's diary, because that work is devoted more to Fithian's "education" in the culture of Virginia than to his own actions and ideas.

In a New Year's reminiscence Fithian wrote of the anxieties he felt in leaving for a "strange province" and how his interest in gaining "a more general acquaintance with the manners of Mankind and a better knowledge of the soil and commerce" of other states overcame the warnings of friends and relations (pp. 46-47). What he encountered clearly fulfilled his hopes for new experiences. Fithian devoted several pages to descriptions of the magnificence of the Carter home, Nomini Hall, including not only his impression of its size and general appearance, but even details like the number of its window-panes.

Yet more impressive, both in terms of its impact on the reader and its importance in the diary, is the quality of life which Fithian found on the Virginia plantations. "The *Balls*, the *Fox-hunts* and the fine *entertainments*" made a strong impression on the young man. The following excerpt from an entry describing a ball offers an excellent portrait of Virginia society:

The Ladies dined first, when some Good order was preserved; when they rose, each nimblest Fellow dined first—The Dinner was as elegant as could be well expected when so great an Assembly were to be kept for so long a time.—For Drink, there was several sorts of Wine, good Lemon Punch, Toddy, Cyder, Porter &c.—About Seven the Ladies & Gentlemen begun to dance in the Ball-Room—first Minuets one Round; Second Giggs; third Reels; And last of All Country-Dances; tho' they struck several Marches occasionally—The Music was a French-Horn and two Violins—The Ladies were Dressed Gay, and splendid, & when dancing, their Silks & Brocades rustled and trailed behind them!—But all did not join in the Dance for there were parties in Rooms made up, some at Cards; some drinking for Pleasure; some toasting the Sons of america; some singing "Liberty Songs" as they call'd them, in which six, eight, ten or more would put their Heads near together and roar, & for the most part as unharmonious as an affronted—.... (p. 57)

But such life was not for Fithian, who ended this entry with the conclusion that it was better for him to be in his room with a warm fire than "to be at the Ball in some corner nodding and awakened now & then with a midnight Yell" (p. 57)

Fithian's writing was by no means limited to descriptions of physical appearance and social customs; his ability to characterize those he encountered is one of the most engaging features of the diary. Insights gained through such examinations of character contributed greatly to Fithian's "education" in Virginia. In several entries he revealed the Carters to be appropriate characters for a comedy. Some of the children might be impetuous, clumsy, or wrathful, but such failings were usually moderate or tempered by excusing virtues. However, while Fithian learned to appreciate the charming ways of these genteel Virginians, he also found material for a serious subplot which undercut the generally light tone of the diary.

This subplot involves the institution of slavery, and Fithian as an outsider was able to face the fact that as the Carters' way of life was based on slavery, their happiness had been paid for by moral corruption and fear. The refusal of the slave owners to allow their slaves to marry, "thinking them improper Subjects for so valuable an Institution," constituted a self-contained irony (p. 59). This judgment can also be applied to Mrs. Carter's admission to Fithian that the cost of the slaves could not be justified by their productivity. Left unsaid were the noneconomic reasons for the perpetuation of the institution.

Just as the financial expense seemed not justified by income so, as Fithian showed, the social "benefits" were not worth their cost. Although his work is rarely propagandistic and more often humorous than serious, his message comes across. The careful reader will see the dark fear behind a Virginian's jests about miscegenation and the chain of fear on the gentleman who chained his driver to the coach so he could not run away: "In the Language of a Heathen," wrote Fithian, "I query whether cunning old *Charon* will not refuse to transport this imperious, haughty Virginian Lord when he shall happen to die over the Styx to the Elysian Gardens; lest his Lordship in the passage should take affront at the treatment, & attempt to chain him also to the Stygean Galley for Life!—Or, in the language of a Christian, I query whether he may be admitted into the peaceful Kingdom of Heaven where meekness, Holiness, & Brotherly-Love are distinguishing Characteristicks?—" (p. 85).

Even the Carters, whom Fithian found "considerate" slaveholders, were portrayed as guilty by association with the system. In one instance a slave told Fithian "that excepting some favourites . . . their weekly allowance is a peck of Corn, & a pound of Meat a Head!" Fithian continued this account by giving a more extreme example of the treatment of slaves by professed "Christians":

—When I am on the Subject, I will relate further, what I heard Mr. George Lees Overseer, one Morgan, say the other day that he himself had often done to Negroes, and found it useful; He said that whipping of any kind does them no good, for they will laugh at your greatest Severity; But he told us he had invented two things, and by several experiments had proved their success.—For Sulleness, Obstinacy, or Idleness, says he, Take a Negro, strip him, tie him fast to a post; take then a sharp Curry-Comb, & curry him severely til he is well scrap'd; & call a Boy with some dry Hay, and make the Boy rub him down for several Minutes, then salt him, & unlose him. He will attend to his Business, (said the inhuman Infidel) afterwards!—But savage Cruelty does not exceed His next diabolical Invention—To get a Secret from a Negro, says he, take the following Method—Lay upon your Floor a large thick plank, having a peg about eighteen inches long, of hard wood, & very Sharp, on the upper end, fixed fast in the plank—then strip the Negro, tie the Cord to a staple in the Ceiling, so as that his foot may just rest on the sharpened Peg, then turn him briskly round, and you would laugh (said our informer) at the Dexterity of the Negro, while he was releiving his Feet on the sharpen'd Peg!—I need say nothing of these seeing there is a righteous God, who will take vengeance on such Inventions!—   (pp. 38-39)

One penalty which the slaveholders incurred was the fear of murder by rebellious slaves. Fithian too slept in fear behind bolted doors and windows after three Negroes were seized for the attempted murder of their owner. This attempt Fithian excused, writing, "The ill Treatment which this unhappy part of mankind receives here, would almost justify them in any desperate attempt for regaining that *Civility*, & *Plenty* which though denied them, is here, commonly bestowed on Horses!—" (p. 187). Ironically soon evidence came to light indicating that the Negroes were blameless and that the act was really arranged by the intended victim's own brother. Again it is slaveholder and not slave who in the diary is shown to possess a dark nature.

Such entries yoked to scenes of beauty and elegance create the essential energy of the diary. The reader like the author will be attracted by the lighthearted behavior and luxurious life of the Carters and then repelled by lines which recall the slavery which made that society possible. On the other hand, the reader may, like Mrs. Carter, find Fithian "grave," yet prefer that gravity to the price of the Carters' gaiety.

Fithian's sense of larger patterns in the situations and actions he observed is visible in his other diaries which cover his travels as a Presbyterian minister from the recently settled sections of central Pennsylvania through the Shenandoah Valley of Virginia and his period of service as a chaplain in the Continental Army during the battles for New York and the surrounding region. The first diary runs from May 1775 through February 1776; the second, from July 1776 until Fithian's death from dysentery in October 1776.[5]

Traveling over a wide area, Fithian did not give as detailed or unified a portrait of frontier society as he did of that at Nomini Hall, but the controlling focus of this section is more inward than outward. It was Fithian's concern here to develop his character and prepare his reputation. The wilderness through which he traveled was, he concluded, a buffer against *"Idleness Levity* [and] undue *Experiences"* which might have destroyed his "delecate Reputation, which is at present, like a Virgin's Character, which like the driven Snow, is easily soiled—" (p. 98). Fithian's danger in this regard is revealed in his controlled attraction to feminine beauty and his fondness for flowery passages on life and nature. But this youthful exuberance contributed to the diary's attractiveness, and Fithian's attempt to control it provided much of his work's dramatic force.

Fithian's military diary of 1776 has many interesting entries, but it was not sustained long enough to develop a coherent identity. It is through the earlier two diaries that Fithian's reputation as a diarist will be best established.

IV *Dr. John Morgan (1735-1789)*

John Morgan was to become the first Professor of Medicine in America and Director General of Military hospitals and

Physician in Chief of the Continental Army during the American Revolution,[6] but in 1764 Dr. Morgan was a young man who, having completed medical studies in Edinburg, was making a grand tour of Europe. His diary kept on this tour is lucidly written and offers descriptions of many interesting events,[7] but Morgan took too little control over the diary to mold it into a really important work. Nevertheless the work is pleasingly light, giving a good picture dependent more on the age and situation of its author than of its place in time and space.

Although at twenty-eight a man of the mid-eighteenth century might be expected to assume a mature position, Morgan on his tour was clearly the "young" man caught between his education and his adult role. His beliefs and attitudes do not seem firmly defined, yet he quickly reacted to or formed strongly expressed opinions of everything. He became suddenly indignant when a customs officer, who had been incorrectly bribed, "unpacked every bundle" in a search for dutiable items[8] and found it "irksome" when in Italy he saw an English comedy badly acted. Thus one cannot be sure whether it was irritation or amusement which prompted him to write in his entry for August 22, 1764, this account of a secretary brought in to translate a letter into Italian which Dr. Morgan had written:

[The secretary] having perused my letter, desired he might before transcribing it, be allowed to go home, being two or three doors off, for his hat and sword, which he had come away in such a hurry as to leave behind. I begged he would not stand upon ceremonies, told him nobody should come into the room before he had finished the translation, which could take up little time, and I was confident the transcription would be as well performed without them, as with them. By no means however could I prevail. I did not know what to think of this; but conjectured that his hat and sword were as necessary to his making a good composition, as they are sometimes to a fribble, to display his person and accomplishments to the fair, or as a pinch of snuff is to the poet or philosopher, when any sublime or knotty subject is to be treated of by them. Another suggestion which does not appear improbable, was, that if he transcribed for me without hat or sword, I might look upon him as a common scribbler, but thus appareled, he would be a person of more consideration, and this would enhance the merit of the performance. In the same way, it is that a physician, who appears before his patient in a plain manner, with a common apparel, in the eyes of the world must be ignorant in his profession, whilst one with a monstrous paraphinalia of dress, enormous wig, and appropriate grimace, is estimated a second Hipocrates.

In this passage the incident was converted into an opportunity for Morgan, whose European training had given him far greater and more current knowledge than most physicians he would meet on his return to America, to express his concern for the attitudes he might expect.

Dr. Morgan had the good fortune to meet significant people, a situation which, whether the result of luck or personal manipulation, must be an asset in a diary.[9] One of the most interesting encounters recorded in his diary was his visit at the home of Voltaire. This diary section, the only one published thus far, forms an almost self-contained unit, because Morgan made himself an observer by avoiding extensive comment. This avoidance was an advantage, because Morgan's naiveté was such that he seems to have missed the significance of many points Voltaire made and to have taken the greatest notice of insignificant items such as Voltaire's pronunciation of English. However, Morgan was a faithful recorder, and his subject speaks for itself.

The visit began as Morgan and his friend Mr. Powel were greeted by Voltaire, who introduced them to a group of his friends. Morgan turned the conversation to medicine, but Voltaire quickly changed the subject:

A little dog happening to cross the room stopped before Mr. Voltaire. He wagged his tail and seemed to notice him very attentively. On which Mr. Voltaire turned to Mr. Powel, and as I thought a little abruptly asked him, what think you of that little dog; has he any soul or not? and what do the people in England now think of the soul. This question so unexpected and before company some of whom Mr. Powel was very sure, at least of Mr. Voltaire, that they entertained sentiments concerning the soul very different from himself and the bulk of mankind who have been taught at all to reason about the soul—was a little startled at this question put so mal ä propos. To show that he was not desirous of enlarging upon this topic, his answer was that the people of England now as well as heretofore entertained very different notions from each other concerning the soul.[10]

Voltaire would not yield to Powel's evasions and returned to his subject with a discourse on Bolingbroke:[11]

He has done essential service to mankind, but there would have been still greater had he given the same matter in fewer words; of these he is so profuse that he frequently renders the subject he handles obscure from being too copious in his expression. Have you not read this valuable author? another question as little to Mr. Powel's gout as the former. But without hesitation he told him what appeared to me sufficiently spirited—whatever his merit may be I own I have never read him.

Voltaire advised him to do so, then added:

The English . . . have some fine authors, they are, I swear by God himself, the first nation in Europe; and if ever I smell of a resurrection, or come a second time to earth, I will pray God to make me be born in England, the land of liberty. There are four things which I adore that the English boast of so greatly—with the forefinger of the right hand counting them up, and naming each distinctly and with an emphasis,—Liberty, Property, Newton and Locke.   (p. 46)

It is important to note in this conversation how Morgan's attitudes and limitations appear, although he must not have intended to make such a betrayal. He seems to have been concerned and pleased that his friend's admission of not having read Bolingbroke was "sufficiently spirited," as if Voltaire's suggestion was an impertinence which must be countered, and seems to have missed the humor in the way Voltaire listed Newton and Locke with Liberty and Property.

Although his own religious views were less formal than those prevailing in his society, Morgan attempted to avoid "being hooked into any seeming dispute about the soul" (p. 46) by striking up a conversation with another individual, but Voltaire controlled this section of the diary both as central character and unifier of topic with a force that provided the artistic integrity of the section. Introducing other minor themes—the virtues of freedom, nature, and literature—Voltaire, with each utterance, revealed ample information about his own life, his writing, his home, and his family. However, his major theme was his hatred of formal religion:

Where my Chateau is, says he, there were churches and chapels, I bought all and pulled them down to build my chateau. I hate churches and priests and masses. You gentlemen have been in Italy; you have been at Rome. Has not your blood often boiled to see shoe-

scrapers and porters saying mass in a place where once a Cicero, a
Cato, and a Scipio have thundered in eloquent harangues to the
Roman people. His soul seemed to be moved with indignation whilst
he spoke it, and he accompanied this with a vehemence of action that
showed to what a degree he abhorred masses and the religions. How
often when one would go fast do these fellows detain you, says he; If
you ask where is the postillion he is gone to mass, and you must await
with patience for a half an hour till he has done.   (p. 48)

Appropriately the section ends with Morgan's mention of Voltaire's declaration inscribed over the door of his chapel, "Deo
erexit"—God is dead—and the graffiti in a nearby tavern, "Behold the pious work of vain Voltaire / Who never knew a God,
or said a prayer" (p. 50).
   Despite the apparent control of author by subject, Morgan's
diary hints at the possibility that he deserves greater credit
than we might give him credit for. If he was so little concerned
with shaping his narrative and so unmoved by the ideas of his
subject, how was it that he remembered the details, the very
words, so well? Then too, how was it that in this brief visit
Morgan managed to encounter and record so many of the
major concerns of Voltaire? The shaping of the section appears
too well done to have been wholly the result of coincidence.

V *Governeur Morris (1752-1816)*

   Because the period covered by this volume ended so soon
after the declaration of America's independence, there were
few diplomatic diaries produced of sufficient merit to warrant
consideration, but when such limitations are taken into account it becomes clear that American diplomats were prolific
diarists and that their works are notable for literary quality.[12]
There are several factors which combined have produced this
excellence. One is the background of those chosen for diplomatic posts; such men were likely to be cultured and well
educated. Of course diplomats have not always been wisely
chosen, but effective diplomats are likely to be those who are
insightful and able to manipulate situations and language.
Moreover, their jobs require an insight into the society and
leaders of the country in which they serve.
   Diplomats are travelers in the sense that they are foreigners

analyzing their surroundings as requiring adaptation and
analysis, and although they are more stationary than tourists,
their activities provide them with a constant flow of new
sights and situations. Few diplomats in America's early years
spent sufficient time to make them feel at home. Like other
travelers and explorers, most expected that they would be returning to their own land, at which time their diaries would
prove valuable possessions.

Governeur Morris's work is a superior mixture of personal
and public themes, making it one of the best diplomatic
diaries. On one hand we have the social life of the decadent
court of Louis XVI highlighted by Morris's affair with a
French countess, and on the other hand we have the political
upheaval of the French Revolution from the period before the
storming of the Bastille to that just prior to the beheading of
the king, when there was a significant hiatus in diary production. The greatness of the diary stems from the successful
interplay between these two themes. The reader sees "all
Paris . . . in a Tumult" and Morris going to dinner with his mis-
tress; the Bastille falling and Morris writing humorous verse.
Such juxtaposition does not diminish the importance of either
of the themes; rather, it enhances both. Morris's diary offers
the age-old mixture of romantic passion and grand conflict that
we find in *The Iliad* or *Antony and Cleopatra*.

While both love and politics are crucial to Morris's diary, he
showed them to be less noble activities than they have been
pictured as in romances; in a world peopled by Lafayette and
Jefferson, Mirabeau and Necker, society turned the pursuit of
exalted ends into a catastrophe. Morris was constantly exposing the fact that the failure of French society in this era was
dual. It could neither treat serious matters with calmness and
reason nor treat trivial ones with delight and frivolity. The result of this imbalance of values was a storm in which "Man,
turbulent like the Elements, disorders the moral world"; only
God, Morris declared, could direct it and "bring Order from
Confusion."[13] Nothing serves so well to show Morris's vision
of these disorders than his advice to an artist who was at work
on a painting with a classical subject:

I tell him he had better paint the Storm of the Bastile, it will be a
more fashionable Picture, & that one Trait will admit of a fine Effect.

It is one of the Gardes Françaises who, having got Hold of the Gate and unable to bring it down, cries to his Comrades of the Populace to pull by his Legs, and the Man has the Force and Courage to hold while a dozen of them pull him like a Rope and bring down the Gate, so that he actually sustains the Rack. To represent him drawn out of Joint with his Head turned round, encouraging them to draw still harder, must I think have a fine Effect.   (I, p. 155)

The proposed painting might be interpreted as French society, in its zeal for democratic revolution, tearing itself apart; it would not be a painting of man's courage, but of his folly.

Morris's view of love was no less anticonventional than his view of politics. He accepted love as real, but contrary to the opinion of most of mankind he assumed that it must be of short duration. For Morris, the essential quality of love was the couple's mutual desire to render each other happy, a condition which he found generally wanting in marriage. Believing as he did and being in a society in which affairs were so common and socially acceptable, it is understandable that Morris should have involved himself in one. Morris included in the diary an account of his affair with the Comtesse Flahaut; however, while he even recorded instances of the relationship's consummations, the diary is not for those seeking voyeuristic pleasure. This situation is not merely because the details of the sexual encounters were tactfully replaced with euphemistic expressions such as: "we perform the Rites of the Cyprian Goddess" (II, p. 81) or that Morris's humor dominated such entries, but the incidents were woven into the fabric of the narrative so that, as in the following entry, features more important to the general development of the relationship and the diary predominated:

Go to the Louvre. Madame is still suffering. She has followed my Prescription but hitherto unsuccessfully. After being with her a few Minutes I exhibit another Medicine which works Wonders. The Roses blush on her Cheek, her Eyes sparkle; she assures me repeatedly that she is very well. We go to her Convent and visit her Religieuse. The old Lady admires her Looks and will not believe that she is indisposed. We return and celebrate again the Cyprian Mystery. I then leave her to receive the Bishop. She drops an expression for the first Time respecting him which is a Cousin German to Contempt. I may if I please wean her from all Regard towards him. (I, p. 261)

In the context of the diary this entry holds the reader's special attention, because Morris's boast of his success as a lover provides an example of his egotism, because the convent visit coming between two adulterous encounters highlights the moral hypocrisy of the French society, and because the Bishop about whom the Comtesse made a contemptuous remark was (position notwithstanding) one of her lovers and so was significant in Morris's battle to win sole possession of the lady's affections.

While the Comtesse, who could juggle three lovers and a husband, played a game with Morris using "all the Arts of wily Woman" (I, p. 244), Morris proved equally capable of manipulation. Both seem to have enjoyed deceiving and being deceived, as in the following scene in which self-conscious melodrama becomes comic. It begins with Morris's refusal to wear a ring as a promise to marry her if she ever became free. Madame de Flahaut replies with "Tears. A Countenance of Anguish, broken Expressions and all other due accompanyments of an agonizing Spirit." Vowing "eternal Fidelity" she swears that she will go anywhere with him. He counters, "Will you go to England next Monday?" She answers, "I do not think you capable of ruining me but if you command I obey. I am yours," and Morris submits—for the time being (I, pp. 244-45).

Morris had been warned that the Comtesse was a coquette but had concluded that while he "gives her Liberty to do as she pleases her Coquetry can answer but little Purpose" (I, p. 243). Even when he appeared to have been displaced in her affections by the Bishop, his ability to appear detached was the means by which he expected to "reverse" the situation (II, p. 55). He could assume for the moment "the Timidity of a young Lover who feels for the first Time," and then mortify her by leaving her to the attentions of his rival as if he did not care (II, p. 57). Again and again he alternated between expressions of "my deep Regret that I must see her no more," and attentions which "leave her convinced that I love her to Distraction" (II, p. 70). This toying with affections would seem cruel if it were not abundantly clear that the game was played and enjoyed mutually.

Morris's affair with Madame de Flahaut was only one part of his portrait of the social life of the French capital, but all this is secondary to the main subject of the diary, the political and social upheaval of the French Revolution. Morris portrayed the revolution not through history-book descriptions of the major events, but as a gradual unfolding of incidents and disclosures revealed entry by entry. Truth gradually emerged from falsehood, fact from rumor, as the diary progressed. All elements were tied together as Morris attempted to analyze, predict, and influence the actions of those directly involved.

As American ambassador, Morris had access to important people and information; as an outsider, he was able to be more objective than those directly affected. When, early in the revolution, the nobles expected "a World of Triumph" (I, p. 120), Morris correctly assessed that they had "less Cause for Exultation than they imagine" (I, p. 121). Of their antagonists in the National Assembly, Morris showed that although they considered themselves "modern Athenians," they were so "entangled from Want of Judgment" (I, p. 232) that it was doubtful that the democracy they were struggling to create could endure.

Morris's skepticism about French democracy stemmed from his beliefs that "every Country must have a Constitution suited to its Circumstances" (II, p. 72), and that while the French desired an American Constitution, they lacked "American Citizens to support that Constitution" (I, p. 136). For Morris, one of the authors of that American Constitution, democracy and liberty did not always support one another, and of the two Morris preferred liberty. It was not that Morris was against democracy, although he approved the existence of a nobility, but rather that he showed the distrust of unlimited democracy shared by many American Federalists. Indeed, Morris was skeptical of anything taken to excess, recording in his diary that he had "steadily combated the Violence and Excess of those Persons who, either inspired with an enthusiastic Love of Freedom or prompted by sinister Designs, are disposed to drive every Thing to Extremity" (I, p. 136).

Morris's diary includes numerous instances of such violence. "Paris," he wrote, "is perhaps as wicked a Spot as exists. Incest, Murder, Bestiality, Fraud, Rapine, Oppression, Baseness, Cruelty; and yet this is the City which has stepped forward in the sacred Cause of Liberty. The Pressure of incumbent Despotism removed, every bad Passion exerts its peculiar Energy" (I, p. 266). Two days before the fall of the

Bastille Morris described an encounter he had just seen in which a mob attacked with a "Shower of Stones" an armed cavalry unit, and recorded another between "a large Body of the Gardes Françoises" and an armed mob "employed in breaking open the Armorers' Shops." He concluded the entry by commenting prophetically that "the little Affray which I have witnessed will probably be magnified into a bloody Battle before it reaches the Frontiers" (I, pp. 144-45). Ten days later he wrote:

In this Period the Head and Body of M^r. de Foulon are introduced in Triumph. The Head on a Pike, the Body dragged naked on the Earth. Afterwards this horrible Exhibition is carried thro the different Streets. His Crime is to have accepted a Place in the Ministry. This mutilated Form of an old Man of seventy five is shewn to Bertier, his Son in Law, the Intend^t. of Paris, and afterwards he also is put to Death and cut to Pieces, the Populace carrying about the mangled Fragments with a Savage Joy. Gracious God what a People! (I, pp. 158-59)

Even second hand, Morris's descriptions in the diary have a vividness lacking in most historical accounts. He wrote of the September massacres which followed a proclamation that enemy troops were outside Paris:

Sunday 2^d.–[September 1792] . . . I observe that this Proclamation produces Terror and Despair among the People. This Afternoon they announce the Murder of Priests who had been shut up in the *Carmes*. They then go to the Abbaie and murder the Prisoners there. This is horrible.
Monday 3^d.–The murdering continues all Day. I am told that there are about eight hundred Men concerned in it. The Minister of Parma and Embassadress of Sweden have been stopped as they were going away.
Tuesday 4.–The Murders continue. The Prisoners in the Bicetre defend themselves and the Assailants try to stifle and drown them. (II, p. 537)

Such violence supported Morris's belief that the French were not ready for democracy and made him increasingly favor the cause of the nobles.

Morris had long pitied the king as an "unfortunate Prince! The Victim of his Weakness, and in the Hands of those who are not to be relied on even for Pity" (I, p. 246). To Morris the king was a tragic figure whose good intentions were flawed by an inability to act, "an honest Man . . . [who] wishes really to do Good, but . . . has not either Genius or Education to shew the Way towards that Good which he desires" (I, p. 136). Faced with conflicting advice from "bad company" that Morris believed made it "impossible that he should not act wrongly" (I, p. 154), the king made, then retracted, decisions or followed an indecisive middle course until he was executed.

Morris first tried to aid the king by offering advice to anyone who would listen, and it was a sign of both Morris's ego and effectiveness that he offered it to many of the most prominent men in France and they did listen. Later he became more actively involved, assisting in the transfer of funds and hiding nobles who were allied with the monarchy. It was Morris's involvement that eventually forced him to end his diary. As its final words explain: "The Situation of Things is such that to continue this Journal would compromise many People, unless I go on in the Way I have since the End of August, in which Case it must be insipid and useless.[14] I prefer therefore the more simple Measure of putting an End to it" (II, p. 598). These words also tell us of the great attachment between a man and his diary that can prompt faithful attention when so many other things vie for his time and effort.

CHAPTER 4

Diaries of Romance and Courtship

ROMANCE and courtship are important concerns in many diaries in which other aspects are dominant and so prompt their placement in other categories. The brief but crucial courtship period included in Michael Wigglesworth's spiritual journal and the extended thematic concern with a romantic separation in Fithian's travel diary may serve as examples of the diverse roles such a stage or event can play in a diary. There are, however, certain diaries in which the concerns of romance and courtship are not merely important, but central.

The frequency with which romance and courtship appear in diaries should not seem surprising when one considers that together they constitute one of the most common and affecting experiences in human life. These experiences may come late in life, as in the courtships Samuel Sewall recorded in his diary when aged; however, it is for the young that romance and courtship are most likely to dominate other life activities, becoming the impetus for and central focus of a diary. Not only is this a period in which a diarist is less established in other activities, but also a period of uncertain ties and supports. The dominance of the parents has ended, or at least is beginning to weaken, yet the support of the family in which the individual will be a parent has not yet been established. Friends may be important as confidants to one facing the problems of this period, yet the confidential nature of intimate feelings frequently precludes such confidences. It is not surprising that many people who keep no other such record turn at this time to find a sympathetic audience in a diary. Such surely was the case with John Smith in his anxious courtship of Hannah Logan and with Anne Home Livingston as she helplessly watched the end of all hopes for a successful marriage and the loss of the man she loved.

Not all diaries of romance and courtship are serious, agonized searches of the writer's soul. Sally Wister's epistolary diary of flirtations with young American officers during the Revolution offers the lighthearted behavior of a sixteen-year-old girl. Yet even in Miss Wister's diary the reader will notice anxieties and uncertainties: Will she prove as popular as she hoped? Will her actions show a character worthy of mature consideration or will she appear childish? Such questions may not seem as serious as those faced by Mrs. Livingston, but they are sufficiently crucial to this stage of development to move the focus of the diary away from the very real threats of war and toward the concerns that mark a developmental stage and an identifiable diary type.

I   *John Smith (1722-1771) and William Black*

Published under the title *Hannah Logan's Courtship*, John Smith's diary does deal with other events, but its concern with the courtship is central. Even without this title the reader would quickly recognize that its essential function was to aid its author's suit. Indeed, at times the romantic elements of the diary seem excessive, but people in love are excused excesses in emotion and language not extended to them when engaged in any other endeavor. In one entry displaying this "excusable" effusiveness Smith wrote:

Spent part of the Even^g . . . at Wm Logan's with that dear Creature H. L., the Charm of whose Conversation Excells, if possible, those of her person. Her discourse seemed more Agreeable than Common this Even^g after being pestered with much Impertinence in the afternoon. Oh, could I be Blest with the favour of Retiring to it upon every occasion—
    Soft Source of Comfort, kind Relief from Care,
    And 'tis her least Perfection to be fair.[1]

As he exalted Hannah he debased his own worth, eventually calling her acceptance of his proposal a condescension made possible only by the "unmerited kindness of God" (p. 183).

Smith's suit was not quickly accepted, and the near losses of

Hannah's favor and delays in her responses allowed Smith to play the role of despairing lover. At first he even refused to go where she might be, "Least it should disoblige my dearest Hannah," and when "love prevailed" and he went to see her, he was racked by the thought that "she did not like my coming" (p. 117). When he finally made his suit, his words not only praised her but degraded his own merit:

Made proposals of waiting upon her at home & of Asking her parents' Consent if such attention was not Absolutely Disagreeable to her. I was in a good deal of Confusion, but her Good Nature Bore with it, without Endeavouring to Encrease it, And Though I could not perceive that she was willing I should take that Step; she Consented to receive another Letter from me upon my promising not to take that for any Encouragement &c[a]. Many were the Revolving thoughts with which my mind was Crowded after this Conversation, & yet upon the whole I found my Affection Encreased by her Generous behaviour & was thankful for the opportunity I had of so much Conversation with her. I pray God to pour down his Choicest Blessings upon her head.   (pp. 142-43)

Smith was a devout Quaker, and as he waited for his suit to be accepted or rejected, his hopes were sustained by a firm belief in the unity of divine providence and romantic love. Even his letters to Hannah were frequently religious in nature. He prayed to God:

O gracious & Infinite God, be thou pleased to help my weakness, Strengthen my feeble desires to Love and serve thee above every other Consideration, pardon my former Errings & Strayings, and Oh, make me Every Whit Clean. Let Thy pure Love guide and protect me . . . until I am made compleat in thy Beloved Son. And as thou has favoured my dear Hannah and me with a degree of thy uniting Love, Blessed and Holy Father, Encrease it I pray thee, that we may be truly and forever one another's Joy in thee, – that thou may always be our God, and may we never deviate from thy ways. Then wilt thou Continue to Own us with the Bedewings of Celestial rain, the sweet Overshadowings of divine Goodness, through time, and at last admit us through Infinite favour to join the Heavenly Host in never-ceasing Songs of praise to thy High, Holy and Ever worthy name. (pp. 184-85)

Smith even sought God's guidance in determining actions of his courtship. In one early entry he described his attendance at a Quaker meeting where he "waited for a sence whether it would be suitable for me to renew my visits to dear Hannah Logan; and in my waiting my mind was filled with sweetness, and enlarged in pure Love & a particular openness & freedom so that I determined in the affirmative" (p. 216).

Yet, divine guidance was not sufficient to avoid uncertainties and changes in Hannah's attitude. Through the diary the reader can share Smith's reactions to setbacks in his suits before the lovers were finally engaged and married. Religiously serious, yet romantically emotional, the diary maintains the reader's concern for its central characters.

William Black's diary is a useful supplement to that of John Smith. Written in Pennsylvania while Black was secretary to a group of commissioners from his native Virginia appointed to treat with the Iroquois Indians, Black's diary is itself a travel diary made especially interesting by a tendency toward emphatic images. In one entry he was welcomed "with a Bowl of fine Lemon Punch big enough to have Swimm'd half a dozen of young Geese."[2] He had a good eye for details of new sights but spent a good portion of his attention on frivolous pursuits such as billiards and banqueting. He also had an eye for "the pretty Creatures, the young Ladies" (p. 405). Among those that caught his eye was Hannah Logan, of whom he wrote:

I was really very much Surpriz'd at the Appearance of so Charming a Woman, in a place where the seeming Morosness, and Gratified Father's Appearance, Promised no such Beauty, tho' it must be allow'd the Man seem'd to have some Remains of a handsome enough Person, and a Complection beyond his years, for he was turn'd off 70: But to return to the Lady, I declare I burnt my Lips more than once, being quite thoughtless of the warmness of my Tea, entirely lost in Contemplating her Beauties.

She was tall, and Slender, but Exactly well Shap'd her Features Perfect, and Complection tho' a little the whitest, yet her Countenance had something in it extremely Sweet, her Eyes Express'd a very great Softness, denoting a Compos'd Temper and Serenity of Mind, Her Manner was Grave and Reserv'd, and to be short, She had a Sort of Majesty in her Person, and Agreeableness in her Behavior, which at Once Surprized and Charmed the Beholders. (p. 407)

Hannah was not the only woman given such attention in Black's diary; far more extensive comment was reserved for Miss Mary (Molly) Stamper. Black began by saying that she, Molly, "Seem'd to enter the Room like a Goddess, Smiling and all Cheerful, as I always found her; I am No Painter, Neither do I pretend to any thing in that way, yet I cannot pass by this Lady, without giving you a Rough Draught of her" (p. 44). After continuing with a detailed physical description replete with figurative language, Black concluded:

My Eyes was my Greatest Sense; when I view'd her I thought all the Statues I ever beheld, was so much Inferior to her in Beauty that she was more capable of Converting a man into a Statue, than of being Imitated by the Greatest Master of that Art, and I Surely had as much delight in Surveying her, as the Organs of Sight are Capable of Conveying to the Soul: as usual I seed her Safe home, and Return'd to Mine, and about 11, went to Bed full of pleasing Reflections.   (p. 45)

With his romantic temperament, Mr. Black made his brief diary an entertaining picture of the life of a young southern gentleman in the mid-eighteenth century. Unfortunately the diary was not continued long enough to portray more than the moment of careless youth. Had it been continued the record might have matured with him.

II *Sally Wister (1761-1804)*

Second-Day Afternoon.
The General and officers drank tea with us, and stay'd part of the evening. After supper I went into aunt's where sat the Gen'l, Col. Line, and Major Stodard. So Liddy and I seated ourselves at the table in order to read a verse-book.
The Major was holding a candle for the Gen'l, who was reading a newspaper. He look'd at us, turn'd away his eyes, look'd again, put the candlestick down, up he jump'd, out of the door he went.
"Well," said I to Liddy, "he will join us when he comes in."
Presently he return'd, and seated himself on the table.
"Pray, ladies, is there any songs in that book?"
"Yes, many."
"Can't you fav^r me with a sight of it?"
"No, Major, 'tis a borrow'd book."
"Miss Sally, can't you sing?"

"No."
Thee may be sure I told the truth there. Liddy, saucy girl, told him I cou'd. He beg'd and I deny'd; for my voice is not much better than the voice of a raven. We talk'd and laugh'd for an hour. He is very

clever, amiable, and polite. He has the softest voice, never pro-
nounces the *R* at all.
. . . .
    Dr. Diggs came Second-day; a mighty disagreeable man. We were
oblig'd to ask him to tea. He must needs prop himself between the
Major and me, for which I did not thank him. After I had drank tea, I
jump'd from the table, and seated myself at the fire. The M—— followed my example, drew his chair close to mine, and entertain'd me
very agreeably.
    Oh, Debby; I have a thousand things to tell thee. I shall give thee
so droll an account of my adventures that thee will smile. "No occasion of that, Sally," methinks I hear thee say, "for thee tells me every
trifle." But, child, thee is mistaken, for I have not told thee half the
civil things that are said of us *sweet* creatures at "General
Smallwood's Quarters." I think I might have sent the gentlemen to
their chambers. I made my adieus, and home I went.[3]
    I have a vast deal to say, and shall give all this morning to my pen.
As to my plan of writing every evening the adventures of the day, I
find it impracticable; for the diversions here are so very late, that if I
begin my letters after them, I could not go to bed at all.
    We past a most extraordinary evening. A *private* ball this was
called, so I expected to have seen about four or five couple; but Lord!
my dear Sir, I believe I saw half the world! Two very large rooms
were full of company; in one, were cards for the elderly ladies, and in
the other, were the dancers. . . .
    The gentlemen, as they passed and repassed, looked as if they
thought we were quite at their disposal, and only waiting for the honour of their commands; and they sauntered about, in a careless indo-
lent manner, as if with a view to keep us in suspense. . . .
    Not long after, a young man, who had for some time looked at us
with a kind of negligent impertinence, advanced, on tip-toe, towards
me; he had a set smile on his face, and his dress was so foppish, that I
really believe he even wished to be stared at; and yet he was very
ugly.
    Bowing almost to the ground, with a sort of swing, and waving his
hand with the greatest conceit, after a short and silly pause, he said,
"Madam—may I presume?"—and stopt, offering to take my hand. I
drew it back, but could scarce forbear laughing. "Allow me, Madam,"
(continued he, affectedly breaking off every half moment) "the honour and happiness—if I am not so unhappy as to address you too
late—to have the happiness and honour—"
    Again he would have taken my hand, but, bowing my head, I
begged to be excused, and turned to Miss Mirvan to conceal my laughter.[4]

The first of these two quotations is from an entry in *Sally Wister's Journal* written in 1777; the second is from *Evelina*, an epistolary novel published in 1778 and written by Fanny Burney, famous as a diarist as well as a novelist. The similarities in style and attitude of the two excerpts are a tribute to both writers for they show the accuracy with which Burney, the novelist, captured in fiction the views and tone of a young gentlewoman of the country writing about an early exposure to the pleasures and discomfitures of courtship, and they show the skill of a sixteen-year-old diarist in so capturing the charm and humor of a real situation to the extent that a comparison with an excellent novel is not ridiculous.

Epistolary diaries such as Sally Wister's are different from other types of diaries; they are equally distinct from most collections of letters. The essential situation in their creation which causes their distinction from regular letters is that the work (or a large section of the work) is completed before any letter or other feedback is received from the party to which the work is addressed. Therefore, it spends no time in response to such information. The diarist is, thus, able to impose his or her conception of the addressee's reaction. As a result, the diary as audience increasingly becomes a creation of the diarist's mind and decreasingly becomes an accurate approximation of the real person addressed. Just as a person separated from a friend or relative may picture that acquaintance as he or she was at their last meeting and may even temper that picture according to personal fancy or fantasy, so the author of an epistolary diary may create the intended recipient with much of the freedom that a novelist has in creating a character.

Sally Wister wrote her epistolary diary to her school friend Deborah Norris, but she also anticipated another reader, Sally Jones.[5] In her opening statement to Miss Norris, Miss Wister claimed that the reason for the diary was that she "lacked the opportunity to send a letter" (p. 65), but from the same entry we may infer that the diary was also prompted by the excitement of the actions which suddenly surrounded her. The diary began two weeks after the battle of Brandywine, and Miss Wister had learned the previous day that the British army had forded the Schuylkill River on its way to capture Philadelphia. At this point rumor placed the British army as close as five miles away from the Wister home in Penllyn. In this situation the diary offered the opportunity for a sympathetic audience for Miss Wister's expressions of anxiety.

In the first two entries she poked fun at her fear, lessening it by humorously admonishing herself for cowardice and gullibility. In one early entry after a large troop of the Philadelphia militia "begged for a drink," several, including one soldier with a "mind to be saucy," forced their way into the house. Miss Wister's description of her subsequent panic also shows her courage:

> I then thought it time for me to retreat; so figure me (mightily scar'd, as not having presence of mind enough to face so many of the Military), running in at one door, and out another, all in a shake with fear; but after a while, seeing the officers appear gentlemanly, and the soldiers civil, I call'd reason to my aid. My fears were in some measure dispell'd, tho' my teeth rattled, and my hand shook like an aspen leaf.   (pp. 66-67)

In the next entry a neighbor brought a rumor and Miss Wister panicked again:

> This day, till twelve o'clock, the road was mighty quiet, when Hobson Jones came riding along. About that time he made a stop at our door, and said the British were at Skippack road; that we should soon see their light horse, and [that] a party of Hessians had actually turn'd into our lane. My Dadda and Mamma gave it the credit it deserv'd, for he does not keep strictly to the truth in all respects; but the delicate, chicken-hearted Liddy and I were wretchedly scar'd. We cou'd say nothing but "Oh! what shall we do? What will become of us?" These questions only augmented the terror we were in.   (pp. 67-68)

In the Wister diary we find an effective portrait not only of a young girl reacting to her world, but also of that world recreated in her mind. Her response to the handsome American officers gathered at the Wister house is a combination of naive romanticism and self-aware satire:

> How new is our situation! I feel in good spirits, though surrounded by an Army, the house full of officers, the yard alive with soldiers —very peaceable sort of men, tho'. They eat like other folks, talk like them, and behave themselves with elegance; so I will not be afraid of them, that I won't.
>
> Adieu. I am going to my chamber to dream, I suppose, of bayonets and swords, sashes, guns, and epaulets.   (p. 81)

Another entry shows her delight in hearing that the beauty of her cheek has captivated the "poor soul of an officer" (p. 167). Her quick wit easily gains the reader's assent to her deprecation of a Virginia officer whose chief subject of conversation was "how good turkey hash and fry'd hominy is" (p. 107), but she could also turn serious when that pose suited her subject, as it did when she wrote the following excerpt describing the manner of General Smallwood:

I declare this Genl is very, very entertaining, so good natur'd, so good humour'd, yet so sensible; I wonder he is not married. Are there no ladies form'd to his taste?

Some people, my dear, think that there's no difference between good nature and good humour; but, according to my opinion, they differ widely. Good nature consists in a naturally amiable and even disposition, free from all peevishness and fretting. It is accompanied by a natural gracefulness,—a manner of doing and saying everything agreeably; in short, it steals the senses and captivates the heart. Good humour consists in being pleas'd, and who wou'd thank a person for being cheerful, if they had nothing to make them otherways. Good humour is a very agreeable companion for an afternoon; but give me good nature for life.   (pp. 101-102)

Miss Wister was equally successful in giving a portrait of her own insecure position between adolescence and adulthood. Indicative of this situation are her comments on a moment when her elegant dress made her appear a mature woman:

I . . . put on a new purple and white striped Persian, white petticoat, muslin apron, gauze cap, and handkerchief. Thus array'd, Miss Norris, I ask your opinion. Thy partiality to thy friend will bid thee say I made a tolerable appearance. Not so, my dear. I was this identical Sally Wister, with all her whims and follies; and they have gain'd so great an ascendency over my prudence, that I fear it will be a hard matter to divest myself of them. But I will hope for a reformation. (p. 179)

Perhaps the best part of the whole diary is the series of entries centering on a cruel practical joke on one Mr. Tilly, who is first described in the following excerpt:

Now let me attempt to characterize Tilly. He seems a wild, noisy mortal, tho' I am not much acquainted with him. He appears bashful when with girls. We dissipated the Major's [Stodard's] bashfulness;

but I doubt we have not so good a subject now. He is above the common size, rather genteel, an extreme pretty, ruddy face, hair brown, and a sufficiency of it, a very great laugher, and talks so excessively fast that he often begins sentences without finishing the last, which confuses him very much, and then he blushes and laughs; and in short, he keeps me in perpetual good humour; but the creature has not address'd one civil thing to me since he came.　　　　(p. 122)

Miss Wister's fascination with Tilly seems to stem from the fact that she found him physically attractive and was hindered by his persistent bashfulness from developing her romantic fantasies. In one entry she described sitting at tea when Tilly returned from riding. "His appearance," she wrote, "was elegant; he had been riding; the wind had given the most beautiful glow to his cheeks, and blow'd his hair carelessly round his face." Unfortunately, while his appearance made her caution her heart to be secure, his behavior left it "without a wish to stray" (p. 123).

In contrast to the naive Tilly was the equally handsome Major Stodard, whom Miss Wister described as follows: "I verily believe the man is fond of the ladies, and, what is to me astonishing, he has not discovered the smallest degree of pride. Whether he is artful enough to conceal it under the veil of humility, or whether he has none, is a question; but I am inclined to think it the latter" (p. 125). It was Stodard who devised and gained Sally's assent to a plan to frighten Mr. Tilly with a six-foot statue of a British grenadier. After removing all weapons for safety, the Major and his accomplices placed this and another statue at the entry and had it announced to the company that someone was at the door. Tilly was the first to reach the entry, where "the first object that struck his view was a British soldier. In a moment his ears were saluted with, 'Is there any rebel officers here' in a thundering voice. Not waiting for a second word, he darted like lightning out at the front door, through the yard, bolted o'er the fence. Swamps, fences, thorn-hedges and plough'd fields no way impeded his retreat." Amid the general laughter at Tilly's discomfiture, Miss Wister imagined his plight: "Figure to thyself this Tilly, of a snowy even^g, no hat, shoes down at heel, hair unty'd, flying across meadows, creeks and mud-holes. Flying from what? Why, a bit of painted wood." After a while Tilly returned and Wister confessed, "The greatest part of my risibility turn'd to pity. Inexpressible confusion had taken entire possession of his countenance, his fine hair hanging dishevell'd down his shoulders, all splashed with mud; yet his fright, confusion and race had not divested him of his beauty. He smil'd as he trip'd up the steps; but 'twas vexation plac'd it on his features." Miss Wister did not in her "pity" stop Major Stodard and the others from teasing Tilly well into the next day (pp. 128-32).

Although Miss Wister lived close to the very real sufferings of the American camp at Valley Forge and was frequently frightened by false alarms regarding movements of the British, the teasing of Mr. Tilly is the closest thing to tragedy in the diary. But, although the diary is a comedy, it is a comedy that to a great extent occurred because of the war. This was true not merely because the events that took place would not have happened without the war, but also because much of the gaiety of the situation was a product of the dangers of war and the release of the tensions it created. Thus in placing this diary it is difficult to choose between the category of civilian responses to war and that of romance and courtship. There is evidence to show that the work draws force and unity from both areas. These elements contributed to the ability of a sixteen-year-old girl to write a diary with much of the charm and power of planned fiction.

III *Anne Home Livingston (1763-1841*, Neé [Nancy] Shippen)

In decided contrast to the happy courtship of John and Hannah Logan Smith and the lighthearted flirtations of William Black is the tragic self-portrait of Anne Home Livingston. Her diary was born out of a life crisis beyond her endurance, and it proved the prop to sustain her. When the diary began in 1783 Anne, age twenty, had just left her husband to return with her baby to her parents' home. To understand this moment we need to go back two years. In 1781 Nancy Shippen's situation seemed anything but tragic. The Shippens were a wealthy and socially prominent Philadelphia family. Nancy's father was a respected physician, and her mother was one of the Virginia Lees. Their home was visited by many of the important patriots of the Revolution. Nancy, then eighteen, was courted by several suitors. Among these were Louis Guillaume Otto (later Comte de Mosloy), Attaché of the French Legation, and Leftenant Colonel Henry Beekman Livingston of the Continental Army. Nancy fell in love with Otto and after a period marked by love poems and highly romanticized correspondence promised to marry him. Unfortunately for the two lovers, Nancy's father, perhaps influenced by the great wealth and social position of the Livingston family, forbade Otto to visit and influenced his daughter to reverse her choice. Livingston's success in obtaining his bride did not satisfy his jealousy of Otto. His anger and unfounded accusations grew until they finally caused the separation that gave rise to the diary.

The first entry contains many of the elements that characterize the diary, including romantic pseudonyms for the characters, a feature Mrs. Livingston adopted from her courtship correspondence with Otto:

After Breakfast rode out with Lord Worthy. Had a conversation about Lord B. & dear Leander. His sentiments corresponding with mine made me extremly happy—wou'd to God it was a happiness that wou'd last—but the die is cast—& my life must be miserable! Lord Worthy sees the consequencies of my unhappy choice too late—it is well for me he sees it at all.[6]

Lord Worthy was her father (Dr. William Shippen), Lord B. was her husband, and Leander was Otto. The choice of the name Leander was, perhaps, intended to associate the lovers with Hero and Leander from Marlowe's tragic poem of two lovers separated both by the woman's vow of chastity and the physical obstacle of the Hellespont; they could see each other across the strait of social convention, but they could be together only at great risk.

In entries such as the following, Mrs. Livingston described the sufferings of her marriage:

Miserable all day—in consequence of a letter from Lord B. He tells me—O what is it that bad he does not tell me! but what affect[s] me most is his accusing me of infedelity. Wretched Unhappy man—Nothing but your being jealous, & treating me ill in consequence of that jealousy, shou'd have tempted me to leave you—& now you say I left you because I loved another.—Had you not decieved me by so often swearing you loved me to distraction I shou'd not have been the wretch I am. O I'm wretched indeed! & the father too of my sweet baby—I'm almost distracted—   (p. 143)

Mrs. Livingston's attitude toward marriage was more liberal than those of most of her time and society. Reading Madame Maintenon's[7] "Advice to the D-- De B--g," she rejected the author's position that because her society established men as masters women must "suffer & obey with a good grace." Instead she answered in her diary that "I cannot agree with her that Women are only born to suffer & to obey – that men are generally tyrannical I will own, but such as know how to be happy, willingly give up the harsh title of master for the more tender and endearing one of Friend. Equality is the soul of friendship: marriage, to give delight, must join *two minds*, not devote a slave to the will of an imperious Lord" (p. 145).

While her husband sent letters of reproach, Mrs. Livingston had the consolation of the friendship of Otto, who praised her baby daughter and managed to make her life the happy one it appears in the following entry:

I heard in the Morning there was to be a very large Company. – I spent great part of the day in making preperation – I wish'd to look well. Sett off about six oclock – my glass told me I look'd well – was dressed in pink with a gause peticoat – an Elegant french Hat on, with five white plumes nodding different ways – a bouquet of natural flowers – & a white satin muff. Found a roomfull – & in the midst of them *Leander* – he told me what I believed – that I look'd like an Angel – shall I confess that I felt pleas'd to be approved of by him? Why? because he is my sincere friend – & was once (O! happy time!) my lover. I passed a most agreable even'ing – though a large company – which is seldom the case – a most admirable supper – excellent wine an elegant desert of preserv'd fruits & every body in spirits & good humor. – It is now late & I am sleepy. – Found my Child well. –   (pp. 141-42)

Although her former lover and her "angel child," as she calls her daughter, were the only things of value left to her, they were precisely the things Mrs. Livingston was forced to give up. Of her separation from Louis Otto she wrote:

Leander went past the window while we were at Tea – he look'd in – & his Eyes told me he wou'd be happy to join us – but I did not ask him – prudence firbid it – Why shou'd it? he is my friend – & I am his – but because he was once my lover I must not see him – Cruell custom – I have read or heard, I forget which, "that the best friendship is the child of love" – why am I not at liberty to indulge that friendship? Why? because it wou'd displease my husband.   (p. 150)

The social pressures and class expectations of eighteenth-century America were quite different from those of the present, but one must grasp them to understand Mrs. Livingston's actions, especially in her surrender of her child:

−Papa told me this morn[g] at breakfast that I must send my darling Child to its Grandmama Livingston; that she had desir'd Mrs. Montgomery to request it for me, as a particular favor. I told him I cou'd not bear the Idea of it, that I had sooner part with my life almost than my Child. He told me it was for the future interest of my baby, that its fortune depended on the old Lady's pleasure in that particular−beg'd me to think of it, & to be reconciled to it. If I know my own heart I never can. When will my misfortunes end! I placed my happiness in her! She is all−& I must part with her! cruel cruel fate−   (p. 145)

Although her ties to her child were unusually strong, Mrs. Livingston balanced her unhappiness against the child's loss of wealth and social position; her final consent was also influenced by her hope that it might be the means to a reconciliation with her husband:

My darling Child.−O I'm wrapt up in her! & if at last I shou'd be so happy as to have it in my power to remain with her−to find that she makes an impression in the heart of her father−that he will love her−O it will be a happy jaunt for me indeed!−What a sweet little mediator!−can he but relent when he sees her−his picture in miniature−will he not be glad to see me−fold me in his arms−& repent that he has treated me ill−wonder at my forgiveness & condescension−& become a new man.−happy prospect−I will immediately write to him−tell him that I am going to take our dear Child to his Mothers−tell him I will expect to see him before I arrive−ask him to meet us & conduct us to his Mothers−   (p. 153)

Unfortunately this hoped-for reconciliation was not to be. Mrs. Livingston's husband refused to see her; Louis Otto left for France; and her dear child, after less than a year's separation, forgot her. This last tragedy was played out in the following scene:

When first I enter'd the room I cou'd scarce see any body in it my Eyes so eagerly search'd every part of it for the dear object of my affections, but she was not there so I paid my respects to the family as well as I cou'd, & seated myself; M[rs]. L[ivingston] arose immediately after & said she wou'd go & fetch the Child. My heart leap'd for joy; &

I was in such an agitation that I cou'd hardly answer the questions of the family concern'g my health & that of my Parents, with any tolerable propriety. At length in came M^{rs}. L. with the dear Baby in her arms, but so much alter'd I should not have known her, had I seen her any where else; so much grown, so much more beautiful; I got up instantly that the door open'd, & ran to meet her & clasp'd her in my arms, but she had quite forgot me & told me to "get long." (p. 190)

It was only a month after this distressing incident that she learned of Otto's planned departure. The entries of this period help to reveal the true function of the diary, which was not to allow its author to avoid despair, but to sustain her in her suffering. Mrs. Livingston's extremes of hope and despair were signs of her involvement in life; when Otto left and she found it difficult even to get news of her daughter, her rejection of life brought a rejection of the diary.

Then in February of 1784, after the diary had sustained a significant lapse, Nancy received a letter from her husband offering hope for a reconciliation and stirring her to resume the diary:[8]

February 24th 1785—This is my Birth day. I intend from this time to continue my journal, which I have neglected doing for these (near) four Months past. I heartily pray that I may so spend my time as to make me here after happy in the reflection. but O! may I have a better motive for trying to act well. O that my principal aim may be to please God, & appear good in his sight. May I from this time never offend "Him" in act, word, or deed! May I be duly mindful of every duty so as to be acceptable to God & approved of by virtuous people. Within these last three months my time has passed in a continual round of insipid amusements, & trivial occupations. I have however in the meantime, not long since, seen my husband, after an absence of three years; he came to this City upon business. I contrived however to see him, and thank God am reconciled to him. I have now a prospect of living happily with him & my darling Child. (p. 226)

This hope and its diary were shortlived, but after a second major lapse the diary resumed when she learned that Otto had returned from France:

This Morn'g I was disturbed again in my mind, by hearing that my Friend Leander is arrived from France in the honorable character of Secretary to the Embassy & chargé des affairs of France. Now must I be wretched in the reflection of what I have lost. O! had I waited till the obstacles were remov'd that stood in my Fathers way, then had I been compleatly happy. Now they are removed, but what is my unfortunate situation. — A wretched slave — doom'd to be the wife of a Tyrant I hate but from whom, thank God, I am separated.   (p. 233)

It is important when reading that Otto's return had "disturbed" the diarist to recognize that "disturbed" in this context did not mean to cause pain but to disturb her serenity, the calm that she had been able to maintain by withdrawing from life. Certainly this dairy was not a substitute for life, but a part of it.

From this point on the diary sputtered with each tragic possibility or foreclosure of possibility until Mrs. Livingston finally gave up a chance for divorce when it came with the precondition that she never see her child again. Otto left for France again and married. Two years later the diary had been virtually ended and received its last entry:

I have consider'd my life so uninteresting hitherto as to prevent me from continuing my journal & so I shall fill up the remainder with transcriptions — It is certain that when the mind bleeds with some wound of recent misfortune nothing is of equal efficacy with religious comfort. It is of power to enlighten the darkest hours, & to assuage the severst woe, by the relief of divine favor, & the prospect of a blessed immortality. In such hopes the mind expatiates with joy, & when bereaved of its earthly friends, solaces itself with the thoughts of one friend, who will never forsake it.   (p. 294)

The tension that the diary had helped its author endure was traded for the calmer comfort of religious faith.

CHAPTER 5

War Diaries

FOR most people, no event so disrupts the expected course of life as does war. Beyond changes in careers, locations, living situations, and so on, war changes reality itself, threatening or altering the very values which give life stability and direction. Since diaries are so frequently attempts to preserve or restore order to an individual's subjective world, wars give rise to the inception or alteration of a large number of diaries. In America during the seventeenth and eighteenth centuries there were two major war periods: the French and Indian Wars, a group of conflicts running from 1689 to 1763, and the American Revolution, 1775-1783. The French and Indian Wars produced a number of diaries including a large group dealing with the siege of Louisbourg in 1745, but except on the frontier the major effects of war were remote from American life. Among the better diaries of this period are those of Major Robert Rogers,[1] leader of a party of rangers on the frontier, and an early part of the diary of George Washington.[2]

Until the Civil War nothing so affected American life as did the Revolution. Consequently, it is not surprising that this event inspired large numbers of diaries, including a sufficient number of quality to overshadow the war diaries of earlier conflicts. Not only were large numbers of new diaries started during this period, but also, because of the historical importance of the Revolution, a larger than usual number of those diaries have survived and become public.

In assessing the nature and value of this body of literature it is necessary for the reader to move from the vision of the Revolution as it appears in most histories—as a national struggle presided over by a few significant politicians and military commanders—and, instead, to see it as an anthology of individual stories. After all, isn't this the way most of us view life, not as a grand epic in which we play a small part, but rather as a tragic or comic drama of lesser scope in which we are the hero or heroine? I would not suggest that these diarists were uninvolved with the wider drama of the war as a whole, but it was the background of their lives and in weak focus. An individual agony viewed nearby affects more forcefully than an account of widespread suffering reported from a distance.

This focus is only partly the result of the diary form's concern with self; autobiography shares that concern but is far more conducive to a broader focus. Periodic entries offer another explanation; they pressure a writer to organize into small units, prompt a constantly shifting perspective, and diminish the time available to consider an individual event's relationship to the whole. Moreover, the autobiographer, having allowed the passage of time, can count on the greater stability of his judgments; the diarist too often finds his "facts" and opinions quickly controverted in a subsequent entry. The diarist of a war period who takes much time considering the broader truth of the conflict is likely to find the day slip away without an entry. A diarist may be vitally concerned with the broader significance and context of events, but he or she must, like the Puritan spiritual diarists, trust that individual events follow a higher plan and that apparent contradictions in the truth of the moment will be shown later to be part of a unified truth.

The reader of a war diary can look for the broad but still personal truths in the diary's view of the struggle. As in a realistic drama abstract truths are more trustworthily depicted by the events that occur than by a straightforward pronouncement from one of the characters, so in the diary the observations and events taken as a whole form a more acceptable indicator of truth than does an individual prophecy or conclusion by the diarist. The most difficult task for a reader is to sense the pattern from the events, a task made easier when the diarist makes those events vital and hence memorable. This achievement is more likely when a diarist responds strongly to individual experiences than when he or she tries to emphasize context.

I *Military Diaries*

Few diarists of the Revolution were concerned with the creation of literary art; the tension and significance of the event moved many to suddenly begin diaries who lacked the interest and experience in writing that is such an asset to a diarist. Thus, as one might expect, the large number of these diaries does not mean that a proportionally large number of them have literary merit. However, not all common-sense assumptions about such diaries are true. For example, one might expect that although important and exciting events do not automatically assure good diaries, many if not most of the best diaries of the war would be those produced by writers stimulated by the excitement and danger of the combat experience. The reverse appears to be true. Several of the better diarists of the period are civilians, and the best diaries written by men in the military are by individuals with little or no combat role.

The reason so few of the best diaries of the Revolution were kept by combat soldiers is not attributable to a lack of skill or interest in writing on their parts. Many of these men had backgrounds which would have promised better works, and some kept diaries before and/or after the period of their military service. Certainly time was a factor. The urgency of battle and the rapid marches between engagements and encampments were not conducive to the production of literature, yet explorers, facing the hardships of the wilderness, have maintained excellent and extensive diaries. Constant travel and subjection to perpetual danger do not appear to have diminished significantly their capacity for or interest in the keeping of a literate record of their experiences. Another unsatisfactory explanation is the interference factor—the common neglect of a diary when its author faces those events which alter his or her life. Not only are military diaries born of such events, many of them are extensive; their lack is in quality, not in quantity or frequency of entry.

The best answer suggested by the evidence is that the crucial factor is the value system of the diarist himself as it relates to the nature of war. Few of the American participants in the Revolution were career soldiers; most were farmers or merchants. Most were religious in an era when religion was a vital factor in many areas of human life. Even those soldiers who kept quality diaries indicated that they felt the experience of war was too important and too different from their former lives and values to be easily subordinated to the systematization of personal philosophy, and was too close, too immediate, to be organized conveniently according to their visions of history.

As a result of these pressures, the better noncivilian diaries of the war were written by those whose personalities were so strong that almost any experience might be subordinated to them, or those who held noncombatant roles, such as surgeon or chaplain, and so could more easily integrate their war roles with their civilian lives.[3] Thus among the best military diaries of the war are those of Dr. Lewis Beebe, Dr. Albigence Waldo, and Dr. James Thacher, all military surgeons; Charles Herbert, an imprisoned sailor; and Josiah Atkins, an infantryman who, within months of enlistment, left combat service to become a surgeon's mate.

II *Dr. Lewis Beebe (1749-1816)*

Nowhere are we likely to see a more clear example of the imposition of a forceful personality on a diary than in that of Dr. Lewis Beebe. The dominant pattern of the diary is the counterpoint between two themes: the tragic suffering of the troops in General Sullivan's expedition against Quebec, and Beebe's own sarcastic vision of the incompetence of the American officers. It is in this sarcasm that the particular excellence of this diary lies, for it exposes the writer as readily as it does his subject. A historian would, because of the extremity of Beebe's attack on almost every individual he encounters as well as on the army in general, rush to other sources to confirm or contradict the statements in the diary; but, in reading a diary as an intrinsic form, we are less likely to be seeking elsewhere for our interpretation of truth. This is not to say that the reader of a literary work is not concerned with truth. When one reads a novel in which the narrator is also a character, a skilled reader will be careful to consider the possible biases or deficiencies of intellect or character of the narrator before assessing the truth of his or her statements. However, this truth is subjective and dependent on the premises of the work and not the objective truth of history. Thus in our analysis of Beebe's diary, we can use internal consistency as a standard for truth.

Some of Beebe's strongest condemnations were aimed at Benedict Arnold, who at the time of the diary, the spring of 1776—three years before he began his treasonous negotiations with the British—was an American hero. Basing his conclusions on inaccurate second-hand information,[4] Beebe blamed Arnold for collusion with the British, exclaiming in the diary, "Let execretions be multiplied and accumulated upon that infamous, villanous traitor, by all future generations."[5] Although the label "traitor" used in this entry interests us as readers because it was strangely prophetic, the entry is less important to our understanding of Beebe and his diary than are those opinions which he based on personal observation and knowledge, because they better reveal the diarist's mind and behavior.

Subtle stylistic features can be as vital or more vital than facts in analyzing a diary. For example, in the following excerpts, even if his evidence is second hand as in that above, Beebe's sarcastic tone and concise turn of phrase do more to gain our assent to his opinion than more extreme direct denunciations less skillfully articulated:

No intelligence of importance comes to hand this day; except orders, from the great Mr. Brigadier Genl. Arnold, for Colo. Poor with his Reg.^{t} to proceed to Sorrell immediately: Is not this a politick plan, especially since there is not Ten men in the Reg.^{t} but what has either now got the small pox; or taken the infection. Some men live to command, however ridiculous their orders may appear. But I am apt to think, we shall remain in this Garrison for the present.   (p. 333)

The great Genl. Arnold arrived here yesterday and began to give his inconsistent orders today & for his great pity and Concern for the sick; in the first place gave particular orders that every Sick man, together with everyone returned not fit for duty should draw but half allowance. In this Order is discovered that Superior Wisdom, which is necessary for a man in his exalted Station of life to be possessed of.   (p. 334)

Beebe's style is so captivating that it stifles our inclination to search for evidence to support his opinions; like a good novelist, he created a rapport with his readers which makes them accept whatever he says. Thus in reading the following entry the reader is unlikely to pursue the justice in Arnold's arrests of the colonels:

Genl. Arnold is very busy in making experiments, upon the field officers and others; within 2 days he has arrested Colo. Hazen, & Colo.
Dehose, together with 5 or 6 Captains; but for what offense I know
not. I heartily wish some person would try an experiment upon him,
(viz) to make the sun shine thro' his head with an ounce ball; and
then see whether the rays come in a Direct or oblique direction. (pp.
341-42)

Arnold was not Beebe's only target; officers as a class were
constantly being attacked in the diary. The following excerpt,
coming after a section in which Beebe criticized the American
decision to retreat from Crown Point to Ticonderoga, is similar
in tone to his earlier attack on Arnold:

My Sentiments respecting some of our Genl. officers, have been in-
variably the same, since I came into this department; their Conduct
hath been all of a piece; and hath spoke Villany, treason, & murder;
let their Characters be represented with all those Stains and blots
with which they are Blackened; and may all future Generations Read
their treachery, and Load them with Execrations. (p. 341)

Again, such direct attacks form an important part of the diary, but far more effective and significant in the overall diary
are sarcastic ones such as the following excerpt: "But being
favored with such Superiour Men for Generals . . . Glory, must
attend us" (p. 335).

Lest we think that Beebe was totally hostile to all men, we
should perhaps remember the context of his situation. The
army to which he was attached was still in the process of pulling back from Canada after an invasion attempt almost un-
equaled by any other American operation in the war as an
example of military bungling. It is therefore understandable
that Beebe should have so quickly suspected the competence
of this group of officers. There is evidence that Beebe did not
distrust all American officers, but those he praised were distant:

After Breakfast, 18 drums & as many fifes Paraded about 1200 men,
who went thro part of the manuel exercise, and many of the man-
oevres, with Surprising dexterity and alertness; had we a W-n, or a
Lee, to take the command from a Sett of Haughty, ambitious aspiring
miscreants, who only pride in promotion & honour, we might have
hopes of regaining Quebeck, notwithstanding the numerous difficulties which at the present attend us. (p. 331)

This observation of a self-serving attitude on the part of the American officers was particularly distressing to Beebe, for it showed that their professed patriotism was often superficial:

A spirit of pride and ambition appears more & more evident, in our army; which I fear will yet prove our ruin. Genl. Gates, Superceeding Gen[l]. Sullivan, I find gives universal uneasiness to all the New England officers, and most likely will finally cause them to resign their Commissions; then we Shall be in a fine pickle to meet the enemy. A man that is engaged in the Service, and often promoted is zealous indeed. But Neglect him for a moment, and let another come even sides with him, without his being advanced; and he appears very different from what he did before; then he was all life and zeal, but now he is totally indifferent how matters go; 'tis nothing to him whether England, or America Conquers.   (p. 340)

Such an attitude angered Beebe, because he saw the war as a battle for moral principle rather than for personal advantage. While Beebe did not often write in his diary about principles behind the Revolution, he effectively showed his own motives by exposing the self-serving ones of others. Further experiences in the army did nothing to change Beebe's view but rather prompted an expanded pessimism about the motivation of most American soldiers:

I find by experience, and many other ways, that the general principle, upon which our army act, whether they are taken as a body or as individuals, is entirely self. yet doubtless their sinister views, run in very different channels. Some are in persuit of money, some of promotion & honor. But was we free from all; except those who have the cause of Liberty nearest their heart; and who engage, principly with a view of defending, and transmitting, those inestimable prividledges, to posterity; for which our Ancestors Left their native land, and fled to this a howling wilderness, encountering every danger. I say was we free from all, except those who act upon this principle; our army would be reduced to a small number.   (p. 351)

More serious to Beebe than the army's lack of patriotic motive was its lack of personal morality, and he took every opportunity to expose and condemn the follies of his fellow soldiers. His attack was not limited; he found all ranks deficient and attacked each with an equal hand:

The Gen[ls] have their hands full in riding about camp—prancing their

Gay horses The Field officers, set much of their time upon Court marshals. The Capts. & Subs may generally be found at the grog shops. the Soldiers either sleeping, swiming, fishing, or Cursing and Swearing most generally the Latter. (p. 339)

As was typical in his diary, rather than directly condemning such behavior, Beebe resorted to a sarcastic praise:

Maj^r. Silly, who is rightly named is a very silly man: yet the fool, has learned to swear & damn by rule: to such a degree of perfection, that his equal is scarcely to be found in the Camp. Surprising genius! Our officers & soldiers in general, are remarkably expert in the swearing way. nothing comes more handy, or gives such power and force to their words, as a Blasphemous oath. In general the Reg^t. is composed of Deists, Arminians, and a few who ridicule the Bible, and every-thing of a sacred nature. In short they Laugh at death, mock at Hell and damnation; & even challeng the Deity, to remove them out of this world by Thunder and Lightning. (p. 352)

When two days later these officers had a drunken party, Beebe explained:

Drunkenness, is a great beauty, and prophanity an ornament in an officer. And in this light, we can Justly view the characters of most of our officers as shineing with a Superior Lustre. (p. 353)

When, unlike the case of Major Silly, those whom Beebe would have condemned lacked surnames that fitted his per-ception of them, Beebe was willing to provide them with de-scriptive nicknames. The character in the following anecdote in later entries became Mr. Coxcomb:

I accidentally met, near night, a little, great, proud self conceited foppish Quack; the coxcomb appeared very haughty & insolent. But after some time in a stiff, starched and a most exalted manner, says how do you do Mr. Beebe; after a few Complements had passed be-tween us, I asked if he could let me have a little Physic; says he, I have a plenty of physic but God Damn my soul if I let you have an atom. here our conversation ended. (p. 332)

Mr. Coxcomb was soon joined by another typed character, "Mr. Blacksnake":

M^r. Coxcomb this evening is taken very violently with the dysentery. Mr. Blacksnake is much better, so that he is able to crawl about and lurk under old Logs and in the weeds, watching an opportunity to spit his venemous, and Serpentine poison at some harmless and innocent person.   (p. 355)

Beebe was aware that his attacks on individuals might be excessive, but he only rarely let this awareness stand in his way. In one such instance, when Mr. Coxcomb was sick, we find Beebe catching himself: "M^r. Coxcomb, is a little poorly, I almost wish sometimes, that he was a good deal so, but this I know does not discover a good disposition" (p. 350). Certainly this self-admission does not seem to have had any permanent effect, for only eight days after learning that "Mr. Coxcomb cut his own throat" (p. 357), Beebe decided: "The character before mentioned by the name of Coxcomb ought to have been, Snipper Snapper" (p. 357).

Despite his distaste for the behavior of the soldiers Beebe had a real sympathy for their suffering, which as a regimental surgeon he saw almost daily:

If ever I had a compassionate feeling for my fellow creatures, who were objects in distress, I think it was this day, to see Large barns filled with men in the very heighth of the small pox and not the least thing, to make them Comfortable, was almost Sufficient to excite the pity of Brutes.   (p. 330)

Beebe conveyed in increasingly vivid language the "dirty stinking" quarters, the lack of assistance and provision "but what must be Loathed & abhorred by all both well & sick" (p. 333). It is easy to understand Beebe's sarcastic attacks when he found himself in a situation: "enough to confuse & distract a rational man . . . [with] nothing to be heard from morning to night, but Doct^r. Doct^r. from every side 'till one is deaf, dumb & blind, and almost dead" (pp. 333-34).

Beebe's ability to gain the interest and sympathy of the reader increases still further as he moves to more specific descriptions of the situation in which he found himself. If as Beebe claimed in the following entry "Language cannot describe nor Imagination paint, the scenes of misery and distress the Soldiery endure" (p. 336), few readers would wish a more vivid description than that which follows:

Scarcely a tent upon the Isle but what contains one or more in distress and continually groaning, & calling for relief, but in vain! Requests of this Nature are as little regarded, as the singing of Crickets in a Summers evening. The most shocking of all Spectacles was to see a large barn Crowded full of men with this disorder, many of which could not See, Speak, or walk—one nay two had large maggots, an inch long Crawl out of their ears, were on almost every part of the body. No mortal will ever believe what these suffered unless they were eye witnesses. (p. 336)

For Beebe the suffering in the army was the result of an act of divine Providence, and in the tradition of the Puritan spiritual journal Beebe looked to find a religious explanation for suffering:

Buried 4 this day, 3 belonging to our Reg^t. on the other side, they generally, Lose more than double to what we do here. Alas! what will become of our distressed army, Death reigns triumphant—God seems to be greatly angry with us, he appears to be incensed against us, for our abominable wickedness—and in all probability will sweep away great part of our army to Destruction.

'Tis enough to make humane nature shudder only to hear the army in General Blaspheme the Holy name of God. this sin alone is sufficient to draw down the vengeance of an angry God upon a guilty and wicked army. But what is still melancholy, and to be greatly lamented is, amidst all the tokens of Gods holy displeasure, we remain insensible of our danger, and grow harder & harder in wickedness, and are ripening fast for utter destruction. (p. 338)

Beebe conjectured that it might be because death had become such a frequent occurrence in the camp that the soldiers paid it so little regard. But he was surprised that it didn't even "prevent Cursing and Swearing in the same tent with the Corps[e]" (p. 339). For Beebe this cursing and swearing as a response to death was most to be lamented, because it was precisely the opposite of the divinely ordained response. We can see Beebe's view effectively in the following two entries:

Death is a Subject not to be attended to by Soldiers; Hell & Damnation is in allmost every ones mouth from the time they awake till they fall asleep again. (p. 332)

In contrast, six days later Beebe expressed the following self-admonition:

June this day compleats a year Since the departure of my dear Consort, the memory of whom will ever be sweet to me; O! fleeting time,
who dost make no delay, but with rapid force sweeps, all without
distinction to one common grave; therefore Let me remember, that
the same thing must take place with respect to me as it did to her—O!
that the noise and tumult of war, might not engage my mind so as to
forget my own mortallity; may the great things of futurity, the infinite
concerns of eternity, have their due weight upon my mind that they
might have a place still in my breast.   (p. 333)

This split between expectation and practice goes far to provide a thematic key to the diary. As a man of high and rigid
principles, Beebe was unable to countenance his fellow soldiers' extreme variations from what he considered a necessary
standard of behavior; as a surgeon faced daily with the extremity of suffering on the part of the same individuals he found
himself unable to condemn them completely for their actions.
The result was the "desperate" sarcasm of the diary, a comic
relief to retain hope in the midst of tragedy. This relief was the
diary's intended function.

Unfortunately for Beebe the sarcasm proved an inadequate
weapon, and by the time his service in the North was about to
end he had been brought to the edge of both faith and endurance: "I am almost Starved, have drew no bread for several
days, yet fare as well as the rest of my fellow Sufferors. We
must quit the camp soon, or [be] brot to the short allowance of
faith, which is poor provisions for a campaign" (p. 358). When,
in the last entry, Beebe returned home there was no indication
of victory, no expression of moral righteousness, not even an
expression of joy; instead there was only the sense of fatigue
and finality which gave the work a sense of unity and completeness rare in diaries: "Here my Journey and campaign
ends and I once more returned to my Fathers House" (p. 361).

III   *Dr. Albigence Waldo (1750-1794)*

Like Beebe, Albigence Waldo was a military surgeon in a
period of crisis. The period of suffering he witnessed at Valley
Forge was one of the few that could match that which Beebe
saw in the northern camps. We might therefore expect a strong
similarity between the two works, but such is not the case.

Perhaps the greater skill of the commanders and the more successful (or less disastrous) prior experience of the troops created a more positive atmosphere for Waldo than for Beebe, but these differences could not account for so great a contrast as exists between the two diaries.

Disagreements and envy among the officers were as great at Valley Forge as they were in the Canadian invasion. The period of Waldo's diary was the period of the "Conway Cabal," an alleged attempt, centering about General Thomas Conway, by members of both Congress and the military to defame Washington and have him replaced as commander of the American forces. Vicious rumors, personal attacks, and manipulation for advancement in "rank and precedence"[6] were certainly as prevalent at Valley Forge as in other areas. Waldo indicated in his diary that he was aware of these divisive elements, but he played down the conflict and praised those on both sides in the same paragraph:

The Marquis De la Fayette, a Volunteer in Our Army—& he who gave three Ships to Congress, is very agreeable in his person and great in his Character; being made a Major General—Brigadier Conway, an Irish Colonel from France, took umbrage thereat, and resigned—but is now made Inspector General of the Army—he is a great Character—he wore a Commission in the French Service when he was but ten years old. Major General Lord Stirling, is a man of a very noble presence,—and the most martial Appearance of any General in the Service— . . . —He is mild in his private Conversation, and vociferous in the Field. (p. 230)

The main reason for the contrast between Beebe's diary and Waldo's appears to have been the difference between the writers' personalities. Beebe presented himself as superior to others, while Waldo poked fun at himself and his own occasional failings. In one entry Waldo wrote: "Came home sulkey and Cross—storm'd at the boys—and swore round like a piper and a fool till most Night—when I bought me a Bear skin—dress'd with the Hair on: This will answer me to ly on" (p. 321).

Indeed, Waldo indicated that a release from emotional tension through honest self-examination in the diary was one of his main purposes in keeping it:

—it [the diary] serves to keep off those melancholly Ideas which often attend such a person, and who loves his family and wishes to be with them. If I should happen to lose this little Journal, any fool may laugh that finds it,—since I know that there is nothing in it but the natural flowings & reflections of my own heart, which is human as well as other Peoples—and if there is a great deal of folly in it—there is no intended Ill nature—and am sure there is much Sincerity, especially when I mention my family, whom I cannot help saying and am not asham'd to say that I Love. But I begin to grow Sober, I shall be home sick again.—Muses attend!—File off to the right grim melancholly! Seek no more an asylum in thine Enemy's breast!—Waft me hence ye Muses to the brow of Mount Parnassus! for to the summit, I dare not, will not presume to climb—. . . .   (p.321)

Waldo's personality alone was not sufficient to account for his sanguine reaction to the suffering he saw and experienced. The chief source of emotional strength and the element which most contributed to the thematic pattern of his diary was his personal philosophy, apparently a form of stoicism based on the perpetual mutability of fortune. Waldo began his revelation of this philosophy in his very first entry. Having met a British sea captain recently taken prisoner by the Americans, Waldo recounted the captain's recollection of a speech he made an hour before his capture:

His Majesty has made me commander of a fine ship—a packet too; I need not ever fight. I have nothing to do but transport gentlemen and ladies of the first rank. I have a fine stock of provisions aboard, hens, turkeys, geese, pigs, ducks, wine and cider. I have a good interest at home, and what is above all, an agreeable family. I am not troubled in my mind. In short, I've nothing to make me uneasy, and believe I am the happiest man in the world.   (pp. 299-300)

Reflecting that the captain "was now the unhappiest man in the world" (p. 300), Waldo did not condemn the fickleness of fortune, but rather the follies of men who, having seen such sudden reversals, still allowed themselves to be dependent on it. Waldo wrote:

A man of the least observation will find every state changeable, and while he considers this mutability of time and things, he will be better prepared to undergo the misfortunes of life and the disappointments inseparable from it. When a disappointment overtakes us unguarded by such reflections, it often throws us into a fit of anger

which vents itself on those connected with us in opprobrious words
against the Providence of God.   (p. 300)

Just as Waldo warned that reliance on the permanence of
good fortune makes men feel misfortune more acutely, so he
offered the solace that "the man who has seen misery knows
best how to enjoy good" (p. 308). Constantly trying to see such
a providential view of his misfortunes, he half joked that the
camp was "an excellent place to raise the Ideas of a
Philosopher beyond the glutted thoughts and Reflexions of an
Epicurian" (p. 306).

Sickness and hunger combined to become a severe test of
both Waldo's general good nature and his philosophy, but as
they did so he resorted to his diary as a means of both venting
his emotions through expression and controlling them by
submitting them to the creative process. The result was a series of long unified entries demonstrating an unusual stylistic
talent.

The following entry offers an excellent example of that talent. Waldo began impersonally with simple statements and
praise for the American troops:

Prisoners & Deserters are continually coming in. The Army which
has been surprisingly healthy hitherto, now begins to grow sickly
from the continued fatigues they have suffered this Campaign. Yet
they still show a spirit of Alacrity & Contentment not to be expected
from so young Troops.   (p. 306)

But with a suddenness that makes us feel that he was discard-
ing his original start as an unsuccessful attempt to disguise his
real discontent, he shifted in style and subject. The short
phrases punctuated by dashes indicate the extreme emotion
with which the piece must have been written:

I am Sick—discontented—and out of humour. Poor food—hard lodg
ing—Cold Weather—fatigue—Nasty Cloaths—nasty Cookery—Vomit
half my time—smoak'd out of my senses—the Devil's in't—I can't Endure it—Why are we sent here to starve and Freeze—What sweet
Felicities have I left at home; A charming Wife—pretty Children—Good Beds—good food—good Cookery—all agreeable—all har-
monious. Here all Confusion—smoke & Cold—hunger & filthy-
ness—A pox on my bad luck. There comes a bowl of beef soup—full of
burnt leaves and dirt, sickish enough to make a Hector spue—away
with it Boys—I'll live like the Chameleon upon Air.   (pp. 306-307)

Between this section and the following we have a more subtle shift than that described above. From the railing against
being sent to starve and freeze, Waldo made a transition toward humor and literary allusion. We can see that the diary
had already begun its work on the diarist as his consciousness
of the special demands of literary art induced him to bring his
emotions under control with his words. He became a character, an audience of his own diary personified as Patience, and
through its voice he tried to chide himself into accepting his
lot:

Poh! Poh! crys Patience within me—you talk like a fool. Your being
sick Covers your mind with a Melanchollic Gloom, which makes
every thing about you appear gloomy. See the poor Soldier, when in
health—with what cheerfulness he meets his foes and encounters
every hardship—if barefoot, he labours thro' the Mud & Cold with a
Song in his mouth extolling War & Washington—if his food be bad, he
eats it notwithstanding with seeming content—blesses God for a good
Stomach and Whistles it into digestion.   (p. 307)

The answer came not from Waldo but from an individual
who was a composite of all the suffering soldiers. This character took shape for the balance of his short life on the pages of
the diary:

But harkee Patience, a moment—There comes a Soldier, his bare feet
are seen thro' his worn out Shoes, his legs nearly naked from the
tatter'd remains of an only pair of stockings, his Breeches not sufficient to cover his nakedness, his Shirt hanging in Strings, his hair
dishevell'd, his face meagre; his whole appearance pictures a person
forsaken & discouraged. He comes, and crys with an air of wretched-
ness & despair, I am Sick, my feet lame, my legs are sore, my body
cover'd with this tormenting Itch—my Cloaths are worn out, my Constitution is broken, my former Activity is exhausted by fatigue,
hunger & Cold, I fail fast I shall soon be no more! and all the reward I
shall get will be—"Poor Will is dead."   (p. 307)

This passage and others in this section speak in a tone vague-
ly like that of some of the early chapters of *Moby Dick* as we
see "poor Lazarus there, chattering his teeth against the
curbstone for his pillow, and shaking off his tatters with his
shivering."
Concluding his entry, Waldo returned to a union of themes

frequently expressed in the diary—the lack of ability of those in comfortable circumstances to understand or be prepared for misfortune or to recognize the simple requirements necessary for worldly happiness:

People who live at home in Luxury and Ease, quietly possessing their habitations, Enjoying their Wives & families in peace, have but a very faint Idea of the unpleasing sensations, and continual Anxiety the Man endures who is in a Camp, and is the husband and parent of an agreeable family. These same People are willing we should suffer every thing for their Benefit & advantage, and yet are the first to Condemn us for not doing more!! (p. 307)

This final statement brings us back to the start of the entry defending the endurance of the young troops of the Continental Army against civilian attack.

A very similar theme and pattern can be seen in the combined entries of December 21 and 22. On December 21, after a factual statement, his own homesickness and physical suffering were hidden amidst the general misery of the camp:

Heartily wish myself at home, my Skin & eyes are almost spoil'd with continual smoke. A general cry thro' the Camp this Evening among the Soldiers, "No Meat! No Meat!" Immitating the noise of Crows & Owls, also, made a part of the confused Musick. (p. 309)

Following this sad chorus in dialogue and anecdote, we hear more of the sick humor of the camp:

What have you for your Dinners Boys? "Nothing but Fire Cake & Water, Sir." At Night, "Gentlemen the Supper is ready." What is your Supper lads? "Fire Cake & Water, Sir." Very poor beef has been drawn in our Camp the greater part of this season. A Butcher bringing a Quarter of this kind of Beef into Camp one day who had white Buttons on the knees of his breeches, a Soldier cries out—"There, there Tom is some more of your fat Beef, by my soul I can see the Butcher's breeches buttons through it." (p. 309)

On December 22 we hear the refrain of the previous day which Waldo personalized by integrating it with his own experience:

What have you got for Breakfast, Lads? "Fire Cake & Water, Sir." The Lord send that our Commissary of Purchases may live [on] Fire Cake

& Water, 'till their glutted Gutts are turned to Pasteboard. . . . I am ashamed to say it, but I am tempted to steal Fowls if I could find them, or even a whole Hog, for I feel as if I could eat one. But the Impoverish'd Country about us, affords but little matter to employ a Thief, or keep a Clever Fellow in good humour. But why do I talk of hunger & hard usage, when so many in the World have not even fire Cake & Water to eat.   (p. 310)

Having established the text for his sermon, Waldo could now speak at length of his philosophy with its emphasis on the "serenity" which comes from the experience of affections and the simple requirements for true happiness. Finally, as in the entry of December 24, the diary addresses a wider audience to convert the earlier complaints of the soldiers into a warning to civilians:

Ye who Eat Pumkin Pie and Roast Turkies, and yet Curse fortune for using you ill, Curse her no more, least she reduce your Allowance of her favours to a bit of Fire Cake, & a draught of Cold Water, & in Cold Weather too.   (p. 311)

Waldo's diary was obviously of great assistance in sustaining him in the face of deprivation as we may infer from the speed with which it deteriorated after January 8, when the furlough he had been seeking throughout much of the diary was finally granted. For its last week the diary became merely a list of travel expenses as Waldo returned home which, if the philosophy expressed in the diary worked for him, he was prepared to appreciate fully.

IV *Charles Herbert (1757-1808)*

At the time of his capture, Herbert was barely nineteen years old. Nevertheless, he possessed an exceptional maturity, which was revealed in the diary through the stability of his personality in the face of physical suffering; the activity of his intellect in the restrictive environment of prison; and most striking of all, in the resourcefulness of his imagination as a weapon against adversity.

When first in prison on board ship, Herbert's diet was adequate, but when he was transferred to Old Mill prison it was reduced to "a pound of bread, a quarter of a pound of beef, a pound of greens, a quart of beer and a little pot-liquor that the beef and greens are boiled in, without any thickening,—per day."[7] And even this scant allowance was frequently further reduced occasioning Herbert to write the following account:

We have trouble enough here, without hearing bad news; for it is enough to break the heart of a stone to see so many strong, hearty men, almost starved to death through want of provisions. A great part of those in prison, eat at one meal what they draw for twenty long hours, and then go without until the next day. Many are strongly tempted to pick up the grass in the yard, that have been laying in the dirt a week or ten days, and pound them to pieces and suck them. Some will pick up snails out of holes in the wall, and from among the grass and weeds in the yard, boil them and eat them, and drink the broth. Often the cooks, after they have picked over our cabbage, will cut off some of the but-ends of the stalks and throw them over the gate into the yard, and I have often seen, after a rain, when the mud would be over shoes, as these stumps were thrown over the gate, the men running from all parts of the yard, regardless of the mud, to catch at them, and nearly trample one another under feet to get a piece. These same cabbage stumps, hogs in America would scarcely eat if they had them; and as to our broth, I know very well hogs in America would scarcely put their noses into it.   (pp. 65-66)

But with spirit and imagination Herbert found a way to avoid such extreme misery. After only a few days on Mill Prison fare, Herbert concluded "that unless I take some method to obtain something more than my bare allowance, I must certainly suffer, if not die, and that soon" (p. 51). Instead of lamenting his situation as the unavoidable product of fate, Herbert resorted to his wits for a solution and "resolved to try to get something, and to-day when a carpenter came to put in a window at the end of the prison," Herbert entreated him to bring some wood so he could make a box for him (p. 51). The carpenter was so pleased with Herbert's work that he brought him more wood, and within two days of his original attempt at boxmaking, Herbert had organized a woodworking industry within the prison: "I have been busy all day making boxes, and some of the prisoners are making punch ladles, spoons, chairs, and the like; for which they, now and then, get a shilling" (p. 51). The pay for such work was meager, but it proved enough to make prison more endurable for Herbert than it was "with the pris-

oners in general who are obliged to live upon their allowance"
(p. 65).

Herbert's ingenuity in arranging this work also allowed him
to retain sufficient clothing to shut off the cold. He wrote:
"There are a great many in prison who have neither shoes nor
stockings for their feet, and scarcely a jacket or shirt for their
back: these must inevitably suffer, if not perish, this winter,
with cold, if not supplied with clothing. As to myself, I have
enough to keep me comfortable as to clothes, which is more
than two-thirds in prison have; for many have been obliged to
sell their clothes to buy provisions" (p. 78).

Later in the diary we learn that conditions at the prison
began to improve, but these improvements were not such that
we would normally look upon them with favor. It is a tribute to
Herbert's skill as a diarist that we can sense his exaltation at
the Spartan luxuries of Christmas dinner in prison:

Today our baker, who supplies us with bread, instead of brown bread,
sent us white, and our butcher, instead of beef, gave us mutton, and
instead of cabbage we had turnips; and the butcher's wife gave us
oatmeal to thicken our broth, and salt to salt it; so that on the whole,
we had not so hungry a Christmas as the last. I must confess I have a
very agreeable expectation, if my life is spared and the Lord pleases
to permit me, to sit down at my father's table next Christmas.   (p. 89)

As conditions became better our young entrepreneur
branched off into new projects and chronicled their development: "For a month past, I send out every few days and buy
half a pound of tobacco, and retail it out, so that I can afford to
sell better measure than can be bought at public market at the
gate, and thus oblige myself and my neighbors (pp. 89-90).
And, so that his time in prison may be profitably spent, Herbert purchased and read books and began to study navigation.

Herbert was not alone in his efforts at organized action to
improve his situation. In the diary he showed the unified action of the American prisoners both in improving their own
condition and in plotting escape. Given Herbert's skill in organization it is probably safe to assume that he played a major
role in such plans. Early in the diary he gave an account of the
"prisoner justice" which the Americans imposed on their fellows:

To-day the same lad who had stolen and run the gauntlet three times before, stole again; and we took another method with him. We tied him up, and our boatswain's mate gave him two dozen with the cat, on his bare back. At the least computation, in the three times which he run the gauntlet, exclusive of the punishment he received to-day, he must have had seven or eight hundred lashes, with hard nettles, on a bare back. (p. 38)

Such discipline may seem harsh, but when the thing stolen was a critical "allowance of bread and cheese" (p. 74) or when the culprit was a traitor who had betrayed those attempting to escape causing their confinement at half rations in the "black hole," it may be excused.

Ultimately, as Herbert showed, this impromptu justice became a "prisoner government" complete with its own laws and procedures for their enforcement (pp. 151-52). Not all of the prisoners submitted to these laws, and some even "threatened to take them down and destroy them" (p. 154). As violation of their government threatened their support by charitable Englishmen, the reaction of the organized prisoners was swift and severe:

This morning we found that our articles were abused, and we took three of the before-mentioned men and tied them up to a post in the prison, and poured cold water down their arms and neck, for the space of half an hour. One of the three was afterwards complained of to the agent, who ordered him to be put in irons, and separated from us. (p. 154)

Charitable acts by Britons were important to the comfort and sometimes even the survival of the prisoners. They began early in Herbert's imprisonment (on the warship the *Bellisle* he received a pair of socks from a sailor), and continued when Herbert was transferred to another ship, the *Tarbay*, where they ranged from "a handful of bread given to me by a woman which I *joyfully* received" (p. 29) to the extensive one described in the following excerpts:

To-day we had delivered to us, by the purser of the ship, bedding and clothes. I received a shirt, and bedding, consisting of a flock bed and pillows, a rug, and blankets. Some, who were almost naked, had nearly a whole suit given them. When they gave us the shirts, they told us to take off our old ones and throw them overboard, "lice and all".... Our beds are a great comfort to our sore bodies, after laying fifty-five nights without any—all the time since we were taken—sometimes upon hard cables, sometimes upon boards laid over the cables, and at other times on a wet deck, with nothing to cover us but the clothes on our backs. Now we have good bedding for our comfort, thanks be to God! and a good friend; for we are told that the captain of the ship, whose name is Boyer, gave us these clothes and beds, out of his own pocket.   (p. 31)

Such acts of kindness continued while Herbert was being treated for smallpox in the hospital where he wrote: "The nurses, ... are very kind to me. When I first came into this ward, I brought a little tea and sugar with me, which I obtained on board the ships, and after it was all expended, the nurses gave me out of their own stores, tea twice a day, or as often as they make it for themselves" (p. 43). After being sent to Mill Prison such charity was hindered by the act of Parliament which committed them to prison, but when the act expired British charity resumed:

No sooner is this very impolitic Act out, than our friends make themselves known to us, which before they dared not do. To-day we have sent to us a plum pudding, and a sixpenny white loaf, to each mess, as a new year's gift, which, with our allowance, was sufficient for one day. Some gentlemen, also, who are friends, came to see us, and among the number was one Mr. Hancock, a cousin of John Hancock, president of the Continental Congress. They inform us that upwards of 2800 sterling have been raised in London for the relief of the prisoners here, and that they are daily raising more. They further told us, that we should not want for any thing, so long as we are prisoners in England. Transporting words! We have found friends in adversity. "Friends in need, are friends indeed."   (p. 91)

Such charity by the British helps the reader to see that the Revolution was not the unanimous opposition of the people of one nation to those of another but an action of governments in which individuals involved themselves. Especially interesting is an early entry in which some British sailors first saw American prisoners: "Upon being pointed to where some of them stood. 'Why!' exclaimed they, 'they look like our people, and they talk English' " (p. 26). Through such entries a diary can return to history the human ambiguity and inconsistency lost in the important search for major trends and patterns.

The American prisoners were also charitable, and Herbert gave us further proof of their capacity for unified action through such "prisoner charity." For example, when a visitor contributed "half a quince to be drank by the prisoners," they decided instead "to divide it among the sick of the respective crews" (p. 158). And when the English wife and family of a fellow prisoner were "turned out of door wholly on account of his being in the American service," the prisoners set about raising funds to aid them (p. 169).

Vital to the spirit of unity among the prisoners was their patriotism. Denied newspapers by the British, the Americans sneaked access to them in order to follow the progress of the war. Though prevented by their incarceration from direct participation they were alternately saddened or cheered when they learned of the capture of Philadelphia by Howe or the surrender of Burgoyne to Gates. And though limited by their situation the prisoners took every opportunity to express their sentiments. When in a British hospital Herbert found a book of names headed "Upon such a day a ward was opened for the rebel prisoners," he risked punishment and "scratched out the word rebel and wrote American" (p. 40).

The following entries show a unified expression of patriotic spirit requiring great courage:

As it is two years to-morrow since the Declaration of Independence in America, we are resolved, although we are prisoners, to bear it in remembrance; and for that end, several of us have employed ourselves to-day in making cockades. They were drawn on a piece of paper, cut in the form of a half-moon, with the thirteen stripes, a Union, and thirteen stars, painted out, and upon the top is printed in large capital letters, "Independence," and at the bottom "Liberty or Death," or some appeal to Heaven. . . .

This morning when we were let out, we all hoisted the American flag upon our hats, except about five or six, who did not choose to wear them. The agent, seeing us all with those papers on our hats, asked for one to look at, which was sent him, and it happened to be one which had "Independence" written upon the top, and at the bottom, "Liberty or Death." He, not knowing the meaning of it, and thinking we were going to force the guard, directly ordered a double sentry at the gate. Nothing happened till one o'clock; we then drew up thirteen divisions, and each division gave three cheers, till it came to the last, when we all cheered together, all of which was conducted with the greatest regularity. We kept our colors hoisted till sunset, and then took them down.   (pp. 147-48)

The value of liberty had a special meaning for those in prison. Herbert had learned to live in the realities of the present rather than in either the memories of the past or the expectations of the future. While in prison he wrote about release: "Who knows but our redemption may come as suddenly and unexpectedly; so that I think it becomes us to put things on a medium, and make the best of a bad bargain; not to let our fears exceed our hopes, nor to put so much dependence on getting out, as to be disappointed of it (p. 99). Attempting to control his fortune rather than be controlled by it, Herbert and his fellow Americans were involved in several escape attempts. Some were successful, others were not. Herbert failed in his attempt at escape but succeeded admirably in allowing the reader to participate in it with him, sharing the expectations and the anxieties of each step.

Shortly after the escape attempt and after a little more than two years as a prisoner, his release was arranged, and in less than two weeks Herbert was in Paris standing at the house of Benjamin Franklin. In this happy ending we find Herbert displaying the same qualities of mind which made him both an interesting hero and narrator. While he had suffered greatly, his reaction to freedom occasioned expressions of interest in the experiences of the present, an opportunity to see the French monarchs and their court and to meet the American ambassadors Franklin, Adams, and Dean, rather than melodramatic pronouncements about the pain of his past imprisonment or the glory of his present freedom. Of course, freedom was important to Herbert. Indeed, he wrote of liberty as

a prize that is preferable to any other earthly enjoyment. I hope our days of trouble are nearly at an end, and after we have borne them with a spirit of manly fortitude, we shall be returned to a free country to enjoy our just rights and privileges, for which we have been so long contending. This will make ample satisfaction for all our sufferings.
(p. 110)

But Herbert in the course of the diary had learned that freedom is a thing of the living present. Free in France Herbert was true to his principles and faithful to the lessons of the diary.

V *Dr. James Thacher (1754-1844)*

Although the quality of the writing in Dr. Thacher's journal does not surpass that of the other military diarists of the Revolution, it stands out because its quality was sustained for a longer period than that of other such works, from a period just before the first shots at Lexington until the end of hostilities. There are other good diaries covering such a long period in the conflict for independence (among these is that of General William Heath, runing from June 1775 through the end of the war), but none of these maintained such a strong sense of immediate involvement in the present action. As the reader goes through Thacher's diary, there is no sense that the events described were past or their ramifications for the future decided. Even entries written after the fact are filled with the anxiety and hope that make us feel more like spectators than readers of history.

Thacher's entries were made irregularly. Occasionally he made daily entries, but usually they were separated by periods ranging from a few days to a few weeks. Frequently he would have only one entry to cover an entire month. Thacher clearly intended to keep a regular diary, as he indicated in excusing his lapses by noting the demand his duties made on his time; however, an excuse was rarely needed, for Thacher usually made up for his lapses with extensive entries covering the period omitted. Some were thousands of words long.

Thacher generally refrained from the notation of minor personal activity, trying instead to make his diary an account of the Revolution rather than the experience of one individual, but he did so by adding to his scope rather than depersonalizing his record. Moreover, he accomplished his task without losing the diary flavor of the work. One means by which he accomplished this end was by introducing a second-hand account with statements such as: "By intelligence from camp it

appears that Burgoyne has thrown up a line of entrenchments
in front of his camp and . . ." or "An express passed through
this city on his way to General Gates' head-quarters with the
information that . . ."[8] This technique allows us to feel that we
are the auditors of news that is alive and immediate. Thacher
also personalized such accounts by comments at the end of
such entries. For example, the two quotations above end:
"Our troops are panting for another opportunity of displaying
their valor, and another dreadful conflict is daily expected; alternate hopes and fears continually agitate our minds, and
create the greatest anxiety and solicitude. What can excite
ideas more noble and sublime, than impending military
events on which depend the destiny of a nation?" and "In
either event, the consequences must be exceedingly disastrous to our country. We tremble with apprehensions" (pp.
100-101).

Thacher did provide some episodes indicating personal involvement, such as an entry beginning with the following passage:

By reason of an extraordinary and unexpected event, the course of my
Journal has been interrupted for several days. At about twelve
o'clock, in the night of the 5th instant, I was urgently called from
sleep, and informed that our army was in motion, and was instantly to
abandon Ticonderoga and Mount Independence. I could scarcely believe that my informant was in earnest, but the confusion and bustle
soon convinced me that it was really true, and that the short time
allowed demanded my utmost industry.   (p. 82)

Then after describing the hurried loading of patients and hospital supplies on boats as the Americans began their escape
Thacher added material which, while secondary to the "plot"
of the entry, did much to aid in the characterization of its author:

The night was moon-light and pleasant, the sun burst forth in the
morning with uncommon lustre, the day was fine, the water's surface
serene and unruffled. The shore on each side exhibited a variegated
view of huge rocks, caverns and clefts, and the whole was bounded
by a thick impenetrable wilderness. My pen would fail in the attempt
to describe a scene so enchantingly sublime. The occasion was pecul-
iarly interesting, and we could but look back with regret, and forward
with apprehension. We availed ourselves, however, of the means of

enlivening our spirits. The drum and fife afforded us a favorite music; among the hospital stores we found many dozen bottles of choice wine, and, breaking off their necks, we cheered our hearts with the nectareous contents.   (p. 83)

By capturing this tranquil mood Thacher helped the reader to understand the emotions of the American troops when they suddenly found themselves threatened again:

Here we were unsuspicious of danger; but, behold! Burgoyne himself was at our heels. In less than two hours we were struck with surprise and consternation by a discharge of cannon from the enemy's fleet, on our gallies and batteaux lying at the wharf. By uncommon efforts and industry they had broken through the bridge, boom and chain, which cost our people such immense labor, and had almost overtaken us on the lake, and horridly disastrous indeed would have been our fate. It was not long before it was perceived that a number of their troops and savages had landed, and were rapidly advancing towards our little party. . . . [In a panic] we took the route to Fort Anne, through a narrow defile in the woods, and were so closely pressed by the pursuing enemy, that we frequently heard calls from the rear to "march on, the Indians are at our heels." Having marched all night we reached Fort Anne at five o'clock in the morning, where we found provisions for our refreshment.   (pp. 83-84)

Some of Thacher's entries discuss trivial matters. In one amusing anecdote he described how he and a fellow doctor who had challenged him to a shooting match missed the target and killed a horse belonging to an American general. However, most of the entries cover events of significance in the Revolution. Indeed, it is amazing how many major events Thacher either witnessed directly or was close enough to to be considered involved. While most diarists experienced only a few major events, Thacher was present in many of the most significant campaigns. In the fall of 1776 he, like Beebe, was in northern New York treating survivors of the Canadian Expedition; in the fall of 1777 he was in a hospital near Albany treating the wounded from the Battle of Saratoga (including Benedict Arnold, whom Thacher described as "peevish"). He was not at Valley Forge like Waldo, but in 1779 he was in the camp of Washington's army at Morristown, of which Baron DeKalb wrote: "Those who have only been in Valley Forge or in Middlebrook during the last two winters, but have not

tasted the crudities of this one know not what it is to suffer."9
Thacher was with the troops ordered to West Point when Arnold's treason was discovered and he was present at and recorded in his diary the execution of Major André:

Major Andre is no more among the living. I have just witnessed his
exit. It was a tragical scene of the deepest interest. . . . It was his earnest desire to be shot, as being the mode of death most comformable
to the feelings of a military man, and he had indulged the hope that
his request would be granted. At the moment, therefore, when suddenly he came in view of the gallows, he involuntarily started back-
ward, and made a pause. "Why this emotion, sir?" said an officer by
his side. Instantly recovering his composure, he said, "I am reconciled to my death, but I detest the mode." While waiting and standing
near the gallows, I observed some degree of trepidation; placing his
foot on a stone, and rolling it over and choking in his throat, as if
attempting to swallow. So soon, however, as he perceived that things
were in readiness, he stepped quickly into the wagon, and at this
moment he appeared to shrink, but instantly elevating his head with
firmness, he said, "It will be but a momentary pang," and taking from
his pocket two white handkerchiefs, the provost-marshal, with one,
loosely pinioned his arms, and with the other, the victim, after taking
off his hat and stock, bandaged his own eyes with perfect firmness,
which melted the hearts and moistened the cheeks, not only of his
servant, but of the throng of spectators. The rope being appended to
the gallows, he slipped the noose over his head and adjusted it to his
neck, without the assistance of the awkward executioner. Colonel
Scammel now informed him that he had an opportunity to speak, if he
desired it; he raised the handkerchief from his eyes, and said, "I pray
you to bear me witness that I meet my fate like a brave man." The
wagon being now removed from under him, he was suspended, and
instantly expired; it proved indeed "but a momentary pang." He was
dressed in his royal regimentals and boots, and his remains, in the
same dress, were placed in an ordinary coffin, and interred at the foot
of the gallows; and the spot was consecrated by the tears of thousands.
(pp. 226-28)

Although the entry is sentimental to the point of being melodramatic, it does show Thacher's eye for detail and memory for
dialogue, which keep the piece effective. Thacher did not
hurry his account as he might if he were concerned only with
facts; rather, he organized and paced the event to prepare his
reader to appreciate the unity of his conception.

On July 17, 1781, Thacher was transferred to a new select

corps of light infantry whose special task would be "to march in advance of the main army, constantly prepared for active and hazardous service" (p. 266). In this capacity he was among the troops Washington brought south with him for the siege of Yorktown. At this point in the diary Thacher's entries were written almost daily and most were extensive. While traveling to the area of the siege, Thacher, without seeming to have forced any facts into the natural context of his narrative, has given the reader a feeling for the history and geography of the region. He has reminded us of the importance of Virginia from the first settlement at Jamestown to her contribution of leaders to the Revolution, and he has described the situation of its towns, rivers, and crops. All of these details help to enhance a reader's sense of the epic quality of the battle that was about to begin.

Thacher also presented all the essential military facts, such as the number and disposition of troops and the names of the major officers; but all this we might expect from a history. What Thacher added are the details that taken separately would be too trivial for most histories but which taken together form the essence of history. These include the descriptions of and reactions to the shelling mentioned in the following excerpt:

Being in the trenches every other night and day, I have a fine opportunity of witnessing the sublime and stupendous scene which is continually exhibiting. The bomb-shells from the besiegers and the besieged are incessantly crossing each others' path in the air. They are clearly visible in the form of a black ball in the day, but in the night, they appear like a fiery meteor with a blazing tail, most beautifully brilliant, ascending majestically from the mortar to a certain altitude, and gradually descending to the spot where they are destined to execute their work of destruction. It is astonishing with what accuracy an experienced gunner will make his calculations, that a shell shall fall within a few feet of a given point, and burst at the precise time, though at a great distance. When a shell falls, it whirls round, burrows, and excavates the earth to a considerable extent, and bursting, makes dreadful havoc around. I have more than once witnessed fragments of the mangled bodies and limbs of the British soldiers thrown into the air by the bursting of our shells; and by one from the enemy, Captain White, of the seventh Massachusetts regiment, and one soldier were killed, and another wounded near where I was standing. (p. 284)

Unobtrusively Thacher offered inducements the reader to contrast the beauty of the shells in flight with the horror they created on impact, and with equal subtlety Thacher avoided seeming boastful as he mentioned his own exposure to danger. In another entry he praised Washington without an overt statement:

A considerable cannonading from the enemy; one shot killed three men, and mortally wounded another. While the Rev. Mr. Evans, our chaplain, was standing near the commander-in-chief, a shot struck the ground so near as to cover his hat with sand. Being much agitated, he took off his hat, and said, "See here, general." "Mr. Evans," replied his excellency, with his usual composure, "you had better carry that home, and show it to your wife and children."   (p. 280)

Thacher's objective was achieved by combining the tragedy of the first sentence with the comical anecdote that followed. The recognition of the real danger tempers the humour and keeps Washington's gesture from seeming frivolous. The fine line between humor and tragedy was also explored in the following anecdote, one of many that help to personalize the war and justify Thacher's presence in his own diary:

In the latter part of the night it rained severely and being in the open field, cold and uncomfortable, I entered a small hut made of brush, which the enemy had abandoned. Soon after, a man came to the door, and, seeing me standing in the centre, instantly drew his sword, and put himself in an attitude to plunge it into me. I called out *friend, friend*, and he as speedily, to my great joy, responded, "Ah, Monsieur, *friend*," and returning his sword to its place he departed. I think he was a French soldier, and it is doubtful whether he or myself was the most frightened.   (p. 283)

Thacher's personalization of history is also an important factor in his account of the final surrender. Of course, he included the general exultation at the events of this "most glorious day" (p. 288) and a recitation of the terms and official actions connected with the British capitulation, but he also provided descriptions of minor incidents and humorous anecdotes which gave the military achievement a human form. For example, in the entry for October 19, the day of the formal surrender Thacher contrasted the attitude and appearance of the three armies:

The French troops, in complete uniform, displayed a martial and noble appearance, their band of music, of which the timbrel formed a part, is a delightful novelty, and produced while marching to the ground a most enchanting effect. The Americans, though not all in uniform, nor their dress so neat, yet exhibited an erect, soldierly air, and every countenance beamed with satisfaction and joy. . . . The royal troops, while marching through the line formed by the allied army, exhibited a decent and neat appearance, as respects arms and clothing. . . . But in their line of march we remarked a disorderly and unsoldierly conduct, their step was irregular, and their ranks frequently broken. But it was in the field, when they came to the last act of the drama, that the spirit and pride of the British soldier was put to the severest test: here their mortification could not be concealed. Some of the platoon officers appeared to be exceedingly chagrined when giving the word *"ground arms,"* and I am a witness that they performed this duty in a very unofficer-like manner; and that many of the soldiers manifested a *sullen temper*, throwing their arms on the pile with violence, as if determined to render them useless. (pp. 289-90)

Such a passage is significant not only for the subtlety with which Thacher elevated the Americans over the petulance of the defeated British and the elegance of the French, but also because of his admission that he conceived of the war as a drama. This view of life as art has been shared by many diarists, allowing them to structure or perceive a structure in the events they record. It is with such literary license that Thacher included material that occurred far from his position at that time, describing it with a skill that tempts the reader to believe Thacher actually saw them. In this way Thacher's diary is able to be a record of the conflict without totally losing the individual flavor one expects from a diary.

VI *Josiah Atkins (?-1781)*

When in January 1781 Josiah Atkins enlisted in the Continental Army, he was not only ignorant of the skills of "military art," but also unprepared for the spiritual demands of his new role. It was easy enough for him to learn the former, but almost impossible for him to accept the latter. Atkins joined the army out of an extreme patriotism which enabled him to endure the danger and fatigue of a military campaign, but even his patrio-

tism was barely able to reconcile him to bearing arms or ne-
glecting Sunday worship. In an early entry he wrote of being
"obliged to *pass by*" a church "while others are worshiping in
the courts of my God!" and complained: "—O Lord my God,
how lamentable my circumstances! Once I liv'd in peace at
home, rejoicing in the divine favor & smiles: but now I'm on
the field of war surrounded with circumstances of affliction &
heart felt disappointment! . . . Once I enjoy'd the pleasant
company of many friends; but now I am among *strangers* in a
strange land."[10] In using the expression "stranger in a strange
land" Atkins was identifying his situation with Moses's exile
in Sinai before the exodus from Egypt.[11] In doing so he
suggested that his suffering, like that of Moses, might be a
precursor to a divinely ordained deliverance of his people
from oppression.

Soon after this attempt to find a spiritual justification for the
Revolution and his participation in it, Atkins's faith in the
American cause underwent its most severe test. Marching
across George Washington's plantation, Atkins found the very
symbol of the war he had portrayed as a liberation from slavery
was, himself, the owner of slaves:

Alas! That persons who pretend to stand for the *rights of mankind* for
the *liberties of society*, can delight in oppression, & that even of the
worst kind! These poor creatures are enslav'd: not only so, but
likewise deprived of that which nature affords even to beasts. Many
are almost without provision, having little for support of nature; &
many are as naked as they came into this world. What pray is this but
the strikingly inconsistent character pointed out by the apostle,
*While they promise them liberty, they themselves are the servants of
corruption*! But when I speak of *oppression* it readily suggests to my
mind my own troubles & afflictions. Am I not oppressed, as being
oblig'd to leave my own state of peace & happiness, friends & relation, wife and Child[ren], shop & tools, & customers, against my mind
and expectation, & come these hundreds of miles distance in the
capacity of a soldier carrying the cruel & unwelcome instruments of
war.   (pp. 24-25)

Atkins's awareness of the hypocrisy of the slaveholding "patriots" was made more painful by reminding him of the conflict
between his own belief in peace and love among men and his
present position. In attempting to reconcile this dilemma Atkins found the diary to be an important asset.

In Virginia, Atkins's unit joined with the force led by the Marquis de Lafayette as it played cat and mouse with the British army under Cornwallis. Atkins was engaged in only one major encounter, the Battle of Green Spring on July 6, 1781. A month later Atkins became ill and was sent to a hospital to recover. When he had sufficiently recuperated to join his regiment Atkins was offered alternative choices:

This day I have been sent for two ways: A man sent, & desir'd to hire me in order to instruct him how to make files, gimblets, knives and forks, &c. & the doctor sent for me, to come & live with him, in order to assist him in his hurry of business, dealing out medicines, dressing wounds &c. — I am at no loss which will be the most profitable invitation to me. It must be the former, I being best acquainted with that work. But (doctor is so importunate, that tho' I am sure I shall make a poor doctors mate, yet I promised him to come tomorrow, if I shou'd be no worse. (p. 50)

Atkins offered his "thirst for medical knowledge" as an explanation for this choice, but one cannot avoid recognizing that by entering the hospital service, Atkins was able to aid the American cause while avoiding the moral disquiet of his combat role. Despite a fatiguing schedule which required him to travel from hospital to hospital administering over a thousand doses of medicine a day, and which exposed him to diseases as threatening as British bullets, Atkins considered himself enjoying particular advantages:

Providence has call'd me from home, from friends & acquaintance, into this distant land, & among entire strangers, where is no man, I ever knew, or ever saw before (save one) yet he hath given me friends. I am us'd with friendly notice, while other recruits as good (perhaps much better) are treated as strangers. How comes this about! From whom comes preferment? & whence the favors I now enjoy? Truly, these things are from the Lord. Did I ask it? No! Did I expect it? No! Did it even enter my heart? By no means. How surprisingly sweet are favors which come from and unexpected quarter! . . . What great reason then have I to devote all my spare moments to him who grants me so many unexpected unask't untho't of favors! (p. 53)

Atkins had found such friends and such satisfaction in his "strange land" that he noted, "I have almost forgot my native home," but he did not forget the source from which he believed these benefits came. He prayed to be made able not only to constantly thank God for his physical situation, but to pray "for greater mercies, even *spiritual* ones, which relate to my superior part, my immortal soul!" and to remember "I have no *continuing city here*, that I am a *pilgrim & stranger on earth*" (p. 54). Atkins was still a "stranger," but the word had a different meaning than when he first applied it to himself.

His exile did not last long. Less than six weeks after accepting employment in the hospital, Atkins became so ill that he found he had to return north to recuperate. To do so he would first have to return to his regiment and secure a pass. Suffering from fever and ague Atkins traveled sixty miles through bad weather before he found his regiment preparing for the siege of Yorktown, the last important engagement of the war. Atkins probably did not live to celebrate the victory; he returned only as far as the hospital in which he served and died. His death is a fitting conclusion to the diary, providing in Atkins's own terms the only satisfactory conclusion to the temporary isolation of the soul in the physical world.

VII   *Civilian Diaries*

Certainly the weapons of war developed in the last century have made civilians increasingly vulnerable to the direct effects of battle, but civilians have never really been isolated from the effects of war. The American Revolution was no exception, especially since the internal division of the loyalty of the populace extended the conflict beyond the battlefield. Lacking participation in the events that were affecting them, many civilians turned to the writing of diaries to record and consider the anxieties of their situations.

It may be more than coincidence that the works I have chosen as the best civilian diaries of the war period were written by individuals who were not clearly committed to one side or another and through their semineutrality became subject to victimization by one or both of the sides. James Allen was the son of William Allen, Chief Justice of Pennsylvania (1750-1774), who had helped finance Independence Hall and had fought against the Sugar Duties and the Stamp Act. James's grandfather was Andrew Hamilton, the lawyer who defended John Peter Zenger in the famous case supporting the freedom of the press. However, while the Allen family were active in support of American rights, they opposed separation from England and ultimately became targets for the Revolutionary party. Margaret Morris, a Quaker widow living in New Jersey, was uninvolved in the politics of the conflict, but the location of her home placed her and her family between the warring armies. Samuel Rowland Fisher was one of many Quakers whose pacifistic refusal to support the Revolution led to their persecution and imprisonment.

Among other diaries related to events of the period are several worth attention, especially those of: Nicholas Cresswell, and Englishman who came to America in 1774 with the intention of settling but chose to return because of his attitude toward the Revolution;[12] John Boyle, whose "Journal of Occurrences"[13] is spotty but contains many interesting entries including one describing the Boston Massacre; and Samuel Curwen, an American Loyalist who offered in his diary an account of exile in England.[14]

VIII   *Margaret Morris (1737-1816)*

"Observe, oh man, how swift thy moments fly away, and how soon death may overtake thee, and send Faith as a spy into the Holy Land; try to taste some of the fruits of it, and it will quicken thy desires after it, and strip Death of its terrors."[15] Written on November 21, 1751, Margaret Morris's[16] fourteenth birthday, these are the first lines of the Quaker spiritual journal which she kept sporadically for twenty-five years. The entries offer interesting testimonies to God's mercy whether it be in saving her from serious illness or allowing her to be resigned to the death of her child. This journal shows the willingness to submit to divine will and the resourcefulness which allowed her to face the difficulties of her life.

At the end of 1776, with the British about to take Philadelphia not far from her home in Burlington, New Jersey, Mrs. Morris's record underwent a significant change. Religion ceased to be the dominant subject of the work, which then became a diary of incident, focusing on the problems Mrs. Morris and her neighbors faced as the result of the nearby armies. This diary is actually a compilation of diary "scraps" which Mrs. Morris collected to send to her sister and her family. It is properly prefaced by a letter to her sister explaining

Mrs. Morris's attitude in writing it and reservations about having it read critically. "It is," she wrote, "by no means fit for mixed companies or general communication. Part of it was written in a serious, others in a waggish mood, and most of it after the family were abed, and I sat up to keep guard over my fences &c. while the soldiers were next door, for fear they should pull them down to burn. . . . I shall have no objection to your reading it out to our own family, provided you turn the critic out of doors and let only the partial friends hear the thoughts of my heart at the time I wrote them."[17] In the document that followed, Margaret Morris continued the strength of character and confidence in God evident in the earlier spiritual journal and added a newly evident capacity for humor in the face of real and perpetual dangers—it is a combination which makes partisans of her readers, for an honest critic is likely to be favorably disposed to thoughts candidly expressed.

When this diary began Mrs. Morris's home was between Hessian troops stationed near by and American war galleys on the river. The galleys proved the greatest threat because the Americans suspected that British troops might be hidden in the town:

A number of men landed on our bank this morning, and told us it was their settled purpose to set fire to the town. I begged them not to set my house on fire; they asked which was my house, and they said they knew not what hindered them from firing on it last night, for seeing a light in the chambers they thought there were Hessians in it, and they pointed their guns at it several times. I told them my children were sick, which obliged me to burn a light all night. Though they did not know what hindered them from firing on us, I did; it was the guardian of the widow and the orphan, who took us into his safe-keeping, and preserved us from danger; oh, that I may keep humble, and be thankful for this, as well as other favours vouchsafed to my little flock.   (p. 216)

Again, as in the spiritual journal, it was Mrs. Morris's faith which gave her confidence. With this confidence she was able to find humor in her situation as she demonstrated in the following excerpt:

A snow-storm last night has almost stopped the navigation, and sent our guarda-costas out of our sight down the river; surely this will be a quiet day—me-thinks I will call for my work-basket, and set myself down to sewing—but hark! a rap at the door—that face (J.V.) [James Verree] is full of intelligence. "Well, what news, neighbour?" "Oh, bless me! great news, indeed! why, haint you heard it?" "No, we have seen nobody from town today; do tell us." "Why, the Hessians are actually just here; Master P., W.D., &c. &c., are all gone out to see what they can do." "Well! and will they bring them all into town? I'm sure we are but poorly provided just now for a great deal of company." J.V. still goes on—"Oh! Ah! you will have enough of them; I expect to have my house full! I saw a man from Holly, yesterday, who says he saw fifty of the light-horse, all very fine English horses—oh, it was a terrible sight to see how they all foamed at the mouth and pranced —and fifty Hessians all quartered at Holly; but Putnam is surely coming with 1500 men." "Well, but neighbour, I should suppose it was a very fine sight to see so many fine horses together, and prancing." "Oh no, bless my spirits! it is a terrible sight to see how they foamed at the mouth!" "Well, we shall hear by and by what the ambassadors have done—I hope they won't come in to-night with the Hessians, for I am quite unprovided to entertain company." (Observe, Patty, it was I that was in such a fidget and not provided for company.) "Whip the fellows, I got supper enough for twenty of them the first night of the alarm, and I'm resolved I'll trouble myself no more about them till I see some of them in earnest."   (pp. 219-20)

Here, in one of her "waggish" moods, Mrs. Morris demonstrated an ear for dialogue, capturing Varree's comic panic and her own satiric replies.

Threatened by both sides, Mrs. Morris strove to maintain her neutrality, but this neutrality was far from passive. Compassionately willing to aid those suffering on either side, she placed herself in danger. In one incident she narrowly avoided disaster after her young son used a spyglass to look at the American galleys:

They manned a boat, and set her on shore; a loud knocking at my door brought me to it; I was a little fluttered, and kept locking and unlocking that I might get my ruffled face a little composed; at last I opened it, and half a dozen men all armed, demanded the key of the empty house. I asked them what they wanted there; they said to search for a d – –d tory who had been spying at them from the mill. The name of a tory, so near my own door, seriously alarmed me, for a poor refugee, dignified by that name, had claimed the shelter of my roof, and was at that very time concealed like a thief in an auger-hole; I rung the bell violently, the signal agreed on if they came to search, and when I thought he had crept into the hole, I put on a very simple look, and cried out, "Bless me, I hope you are not Hessians," "Do we look like Hessians?" asked one of them rudely, "Indeed, I don't know." "Did you ever see a Hessian?" "No, never in my life: but they are men, and you are men, and may be Hessians, for anything I know; but I'll go with you into Col. Cox's house, though indeed it was my son at the mill; he is but a boy, and meant no harm; he wanted to see the troops."

So I marched at the head of them, opened the door, and searched every place, but we could find no tory; strange where he could be. We returned—they greatly disappointed—I, pleased to think my house was not suspected.   (pp. 217-18)

Despite this and other threats from the gondola men Mrs. Morris willingly nursed them and their families from the fever until they had recovered. In such actions she sought no further reward except the satisfaction of doing good, yet in almost every case she was rewarded beyond her expectations. The Tory refugee she protected appears to have been responsible for saving her house from cannonading by the British fleet and her nursing of the Americans in the gondolas resulted in an unasked-for reward:

I thought I had received all my pay, when they thankfully acknowledged my kindness, but lo! in a short time afterwards, a very rough, ill-looking man came to the door and asked for me. When I went to him, he drew me aside and asked if I had any friends in Philadelphia. The question alarmed me, supposing there was some mischief meditated against that poor city; however, I calmly said: "I have an ancient father-in-law, some sisters, and other near friends there." "Well," said the man, "do you wish to hear from them, or send anything by way of refreshment to them? If you do, I will take charge of it, and bring you back anything you may send for."   (p. 232)

Morris's reward was the opportunity to do further good to others by sending fresh provisions to her friends in Philadelphia, and this charity in turn spawned a succession of rewards and charities. The first occurred two days later as the gondola man returned "with a letter, a bushel of salt, a jug of molasses, a bag of rice, some tea, coffee and sugar, and some cloth for a coat for . . . [her] poor boys." This bounty sent her by her sisters was recognized as a blessing and an opportunity from God—she wrote:

How did our hearts and eyes overflow with love to them, and thanks to our Heavenly Father, for such seasonable supplies. May we never forget it. Being so rich, we thought it our duty to hand out a little to the poor around us who were mourning for want of salt; so we divided the bushel, and gave a pint to every poor person that came for it, and had a great plenty for our own use. Indeed, it seemed as if our little store increased by distributing it, like the bread broken by our Savior to the multitude, which, when he had blessed it was so marvelously multiplied.   (p. 233)

Through such entries, Margaret Morris's diary of the Revolution became a more effective testament to a divinely ordained pattern in the world than was her earlier, more overtly spiritual record. Acting upon the world in accordance with a set of moral principles, Mrs. Morris found the world answering in kind, and her diary took on this same order. Thanked and blessed by soldiers to whom she had given food she received it "not as my due, but as belonging to my *Master* who had reached a morsel to them by my hand" (p. 225). Just as such an attitude rebounded to her praise, so her diary as it turned outward toward the war, which to her Quaker faith was the antithesis of God's will, turned inward toward her and her faith in God.

IX *James Allen (1742-1778)*

Allen's diary began long before the outbreak of the Revolution as a diary of personal events; and, while the war and its effects became the primary subject of the diary, the personal quality of the diary was maintained. Allen announced this personal nature in his very first entry on November 6, 1770:

I have often thought that committing to writing little occurrences in private matters might in some future period of life afford amusement in the perusal, & have frequently regretted, my inability of recalling to mind many past scenes of my earlier days. To run over the employments of times past with the catalogue of former acquaintance, thro' all their changes, must be an high gratification. These reflections have led me into the design of keeping a Diary, in which I do not propose to admit any occurrences of a publick nature; I shall leave those to Gazettes & Magazines, and only preserve the remembrance of such private interesting scenes & conversations as will be entertaining in a review. And I will take special care, not to make my

Diary a register of such things as ought to be forgotten, or can possibly do an injury to any one; & on this principle neither the follies or vices of any one shall find admission, here.[18]

Despite the motivation Allen expressed, he managed few entries in the first nine months, the last of which was ended with the admission that he had found "the fatigue and trouble of keeping it regularly too great" and was considering abandoning it. He formally ended the diary eight months later with the statement that his "business will not admit of so much leisure as a journalist should have" (p. 179). Allen tried to resume the diary, but was ineffective until July 26, 1775, when he entered his first statement regarding the Revolution:

The Congress is now sitting here & have just published their Declaration & address to the inhabitants of Great Britain. Hitherto our arms have been successful; but God knows what will be the event of this war, as there seems to be a thorough determination on both sides to prosecute it. Many thinking people believe America has seen its best days, & should it even be victorious, peace & order will with difficulty be restored. The inconveniences are already sensibly felt; Debts as yet are paid & suits commenced, but it cannot last long; as people already plead inability. My profession is visibly on the decline, & when it is no longer useful, I shall suffer considerably. . . . I cant conceive what will become of all those who have no estates, but live genteely on their annual profits of business, when that business ceases. . . . We have no hopes but that the struggle will be soon over: if it continues, America is ruined whoever gets the better. These reflections are in the mouth of all thinking people. We however keep up our spirits & gloomy as things appear, prefer our situation to a mean acquiescence. It is a great & glorious cause. The Eyes of Europe are upon us; if we fall, Liberty no longer continues an inhabitant of this Globe: for England is running fast to slavery. The King is as despotic as any prince in Europe; the only difference is the mode; & a venal parliament are as bad as a standing army.   (pp. 184-85)

This entry is not only longer and more unified than those which precede it, but it also allows the expression of feeling that justifies the effort it requires.

There was a significant conflict between Allen's announcement in this entry that the American struggle was a "great and glorious cause" and his statement later in the diary that as a member of the Pennsylvania Assembly he had "been very active in opposing independance & change of Government" (p. 187). Such seeming contradictions are the kind of material that differentiates a diary from history and furnishes for its reader a task and an opportunity rarely offered readers of histories. With a little effort the reader can discover that for many Americans like Allen support for the principles and positions which led to the Revolution was not the same as support for independence. Allen's work not only demonstrates the difficulty in differentiating Whig from Tory, but forces a recognition that in the past as in the present human beings are not always content with simplistic answers to complex problems. Allen, himself, marched in the Pennsylvania militia not only to avoid suspicion of being a British sympathizer but also because he believed that "discrete people mixing with them, may keep them in Order." In a single sentence he expressed "zeal for the great cause we are engaged in," yet admitted, "I frequently cry out—Dreadful Times!" (p. 186).

Of course, many Americans did choose either an extreme allegiance to one party or another or withdrew from positions of visibility and action. Certainly Allen would have believed that Yeats's lines "the best lack all conviction while the worst are full of passionate intensity" applied to his society. In March 1776 he wrote:

The plot thickens; peace is scarcely thought of—Independancy predominant. Thinking people uneasy, irresolute & inactive. The Mobility triumphant. Every article of life doubled. 26,000 troops coming over; The Congress in Aquilibrus: on the question, Independence or no? Wrapt in the contemplation of these things I cry out—"O! Rus quando ego te aspiciam &c. I love the Cause of liberty; but cannot heartily join in the prosecution of measures totally foreign to the original plan of Resistance. The madness of the multitude is but one degree better than submission to the Tea-Act.   (p. 186)

Such entries convincingly show that Allen's failure to embrace the war effort was not the result of a lack of concern.

Allen's refusal to support fully the position of either side in the conflict put him in great difficulty. Elected as a Representative to the Pennsylvania Assembly, Allen had the opportunity for security and advancement by embracing independence, but he did not. Neither did he join his brothers in fleeing to the protection and cause of the British.[19] Unable to benefit by the successes of either side and victimized by both,

James Allen watched the war with growing despair. Finally his family, "linked together by the purest and most disinterested affection," was "totally unhinged," and he himself was ordered "to surrender . . . & stand a trial for high Treason" (p. 440). Becoming ill, a situation which he blamed on "the uneasiness of my mind at the state of public affairs & ye distress of my family" (p. 440), Allen terminated the diary on July 15, 1778. He died two months later.

Historians may question the accuracy of Allen's information and patriots may question Allen's political stance, but the impartial reader will be caught up in his dilemma and, accepting the statements of the narrative, see Allen as a tragic hero. The nature of Allen's tragic flaw, if indeed one can be determined from the diary, is not obvious. Some readers may see it as an inability to choose the better of two imperfect alternatives; others may see it as an unwillingness to accept the consequences that arose from the assertion of radical independence. For this study, however, it is more important to recognize the possibility of applying such critical judgments to diary material than to reach a conclusion about the particular question.

X   Samuel Rowland Fisher (1745-1834)

Samuel Fisher was sent to prison after a trial that made a mockery of justice; his crimes: an unwavering adherence to his religious principles and an untactfully candid expression of the beliefs that resulted from them. His tormentors were not a hardened military establishment or a foreign tyranny, but American officials, supporters of a revolution being fought for the principles of freedom. Such a subject alone might well attract our attention, but what holds it is the skill with which Fisher presented it and his own role in it.

One of the most striking things about Fisher's role is his passivity. Warned three weeks prior to his arrest that a potentially incriminating letter of his was in the possession of Thomas McKean, the chief justice, and Jonathan Seargent, the states attorney, Fisher did nothing. Informed that a warrant was coming for his arrest, he sat calmly down to dinner. When asked for bail to assure his appearance at his trial, he not only refused to provide it, but also refused to let any of his friends provide it for him. One explanation Fisher gave for such actions was: "I was firmly persuaded I had done nothing worthy of any Punishment."[20] Another reason was that he chose to do nothing which might have indicated his acceptance of the American government or its officials, whom he referred to as "the present rulers." He even refused the offer of a lawyer as the only lawyers allowed in the court were those who had taken an oath of loyalty to the United States Government. By his blanket assertion of innocence and his refusal to recognize the authority of the court, Fisher attempted to show that the moral responsibility rested with those who had imprisoned him. When he told the judge, "I have nothing to do with the Tryal & if you will try me it must be your Act" (p. 159), he was attempting to emulate the strategy and moral position of Christ before Pilate.

The charge against Fisher that he "Falsly, traitorously and maliciously" wrote letters in an "attempt to convey intelligence to the Enemies of . . . the United States of America" (p. 155) is, in light of the text which he copied verbatim into the diary, clearly absurd. The item on which the prosecution focused its case consisted of the lines: "We have nothing here that I know of very material or interesting lately—The prospect of there not being sufficient of Grain for bread till harvest seems well founded. Flour now sells from 30 / to 35 / p.ct." (p. 157). The states attorney claimed that by this statement Fisher "was giving the Enemy very material intelligence in respect to the Scarcity of provisions" (pp. 160-61). Fisher answered that had he wished to convey secret intelligence, he was not such a "Blockhead" as to do so "in an open letter with my name signed to it" or by a means by which it would be "subject to inspection before it could enter the Brittish Lines" (p. 162).

On the basis of the evidence the jury twice acquitted Fisher, but the states attorney refused to allow the court to accept its judgment. One juror even commented, "You may as well keep us here, for if we are kept six days & nights more I can never agree to any thing else without wronging my Conscience" (p. 165). Nevertheless the jury was sent out a third time, at which time, Fisher suggested, they were threatened until they agreed to return with a verdict of guilty. Fisher was then sentenced to forfeit half of his possessions and to be jailed for the duration of the war. This section dealing with the arrest and trial comprises less than 10 percent of the document, but it is highly significant because in establishing the injustice of Fisher's imprisonment it prepares the reader to look favorably on Fisher's subsequent actions and attitudes.

Following his "conviction" Fisher learned that he might be released if he would post bail for his future good behavior, but for Fisher any act, no matter how small, that compromised his principles was too great. He even refused to pledge "good behavior," since this he believed would be an admission of guilt, and he insisted that he was "not conscious of having misbehaved" (p. 188). Neither would he send a "representation" of his case to the council, because such an act would be an admission of its official existence. Numerous friends worked to obtain Fisher's release, but they were stymied not only by those who had imprisoned him, but by Fisher himself. When his brother suggested Fisher might be exchanged for a prisoner held by the British, he answered that, "I could not be easy to be discharged on condition of binding myself to that or any other acknowledgm't, which would give occasion for any to say I had swerved from my principles, by evading suffering" (p. 306).

To some, Fisher's adamancy may seem like stubbornness, and it is to Fisher's credit that he did not ignore the possibility. His diary recorded this self-examination in which he questioned not only if he was wrong in not acknowledging "the present rulers," but also whether his actions were the result of a prideful desire to appear righteous. It was not easy for him to write: "To become as I now am noticed on account of my imprisonment, is a thing the farthest both from my intention and expectation, & tho I have no doubt of the sufficiency at this day of the Almighty Power being as great as ever to release the innocent, yet I am ready to doubt there being any rectitude in my conduct, or that I am suffering innocently" (p. 409). Like Thomas à Becket in Eliot's *Murder in the Cathedral*," Fisher recognized that to seek martyrdom would be as much a betrayal of his principles as to avoid it by abandoning them, and he learned to avoid finding self-righteous comfort in his predicament.

Fisher believed that his trials rightly borne would give him spiritual rewards denied to his persecutors. He wrote, "I have a firm hope that if I am preserved steady & watchful I may experience a calmness and serenity which these unjust Rulers may not readily arrive at." But as he wrote this passage Fisher caught himself on the verge of self- righteousness and so tempered his statement by continuing, "Yet such is the State of my Mind that if it be consistent with divine Wisdom & Justice, I have desired the worst of them might yet come to see their conduct in its true Light; & thereby escape that measure of distress & calamity being returned upon their own heads, which they have seemingly long sought to bring on those who could not join with them" (p. 400).

Believing "that tis much safer to have our tryals & rightly to bear up under them than to be exempt from a share" (p. 449), Fisher continued in prison not only until a pardon came, but until he was sure that in leaving prison he need not perform any act which might have compromised his principles. Even then he expressed concern that some people might suspect his release was a result of some slackening of his principles.

The diary ended without note of any widespread recognition by his fellows of Fisher's sacrifice; instead it concluded with Fisher's attendance at the yearly meeting of the Society of Friends at which "a secret satisfactory sensation passed thro' my mind" (p. 457). As the goals of Fisher's diary and his sacrifice were directed more toward inner peace than public vindication, such a conclusion was entirely satisfactory. If the work were fiction, we might well praise the author for avoiding the extremes of heroic victory and tragic defeat to find the ending in keeping with the soul of the created character.

CHAPTER 6

Life Diaries

MOST of the diaries discussed thus far are diaries of situation.[1] They were created to record a special activity or to perform a limited role. Once that situation ended they usually stopped. True, some have run on for weeks or even years like an abandoned windmill turning in the breeze of habit, but their vitality ended with their concluded purpose. Life diaries transcend limitations of function and incident. Diaries of life may originate as diaries of incident, but once animated they rarely revert to a limited function; rather, they decay and die like the men who keep them. In the life diary, events like travel or courtship and the concerns about religion and politics may form important episodes in the work, but they do not dominate it.

It is almost as impossible to define the essence of such a diary as it is to define the essence of its author. Unless a man is so limited in his activities, attitudes, and insights that he never changes he will be many different characters in the course of his life; the child searching for knowledge, the adolescent finding an identity, the young adult creating his life's goals, the mature individual working to achieve and perfect them, and the old man ordering his memories. Focusing on one of these selves would slight the others. Thus with a life diary we must be especially willing to consider the concept of change and to describe its unifying elements in ways that preserve a sense of its dynamic character.

Many a life diary is like the child of its author; dependent on the parent for sustenance yet possessing a life of its own. The regularity and identity of such a diary is rarely shaken by events in the life of the diarist. The diaries of Winthrop, Sewall, and Byrd tend toward this type. Other life diaries were more integral parts of the lives of their authors, changing and growing as their diarists did. John Adams's diary and, to a considerable extent, Cotton Mather's diary responded actively to enable their authors to deal with life changes. This process is clearly distinct from that which appears in nonperiodic autobiographies. There can be little sense of prior direction in a work that is free to respond in this manner.[2] Over the long periods of a life diary the importance of the temporal dimension as a factor in the literary analysis of a work of diary literature becomes most obvious.

I *John Winthrop (1587-1649)*

While by its length and varied subject matter Winthrop's work may be clearly categorized as a life diary, it is not clear whose life the diary chronicles. In title, focus, and content Winthrop seems distant from his own diary. Only by careful examination can a reader discover his pervasive presence behind the impersonal façade, but only by such a discovery can we be fully satisfied by the work. In titling his work *The History of New England* Winthrop engendered expectations which he was not able to meet. Not only were most of his materials restricted to a portion of New England, the Massachusetts Bay Colony, but his revelations were limited to those which he received unsought. There are no indications that he either engaged in any major attempt to research material not open to his view or that he attempted any major revision of earlier material as new information became available. The prime concession Winthrop made to his title was his third-person style; with few but significant exceptions Winthrop referred to himself in the third person, assuming the pose of an external objective observer.

It is the desire to appear objective that offers the most obvious explanation for Winthrop's attempt to present his work as a history. Referring to himself as "he" (or occasionally a communal "we") rather than "I," Winthrop could endorse his own actions and deprecate those who opposed him without seeming to be self-interested. This motive appears to have been operating when he wrote passages such as the following (one of many involving controversies between Winthrop and Thomas Dudley). At the time of this entry Winthrop, the gov-

ernor, had just answered charges leveled against him by Dudley, his assistant governor:

Though the governor might justly have refused to answer these
seven articles, wherewith the deputy had charged him, both for that
he had no knowledge of them before, (the meeting being only for the
deputy his personal grievances,) and also for that the governor was
not to give account of his actions to any but to the court; yet, out of his
desire of the public peace, and to clear his reputation with those to
whom the deputy had accused him, he was willing to give him satisfaction, to the end, that he might free him of such jealousy as he had
conceived, that the governor intended to make himself popular, that
he might gain absolute power, and bring all the assistants under his
subjection; which was very improbable, seeing the governor had
propounded in court to have an order established for limiting the
governor's authority, and had himself drawn articles for that end,
which had been approved and established by the whole court;
neither could he justly be charged to have transgressed any of them.[3]

The absence of the first person in Winthrop's defense helps
the reader to forget Winthrop's partisan position.

However, the advantages of pretended objectivity do not
seem to have been the whole reason for this unusual approach
to diary keeping. Another, and at least as compelling an argument, can be made that the Puritan view of the workings of the
world was the principal basis for this practice. The Puritans
believed that an overview of time and space would show all
acts to be preordained as part of a divine plan, while from a
closer perspective the involvement of God in the present
could be seen in the way individual natural and human events
seemed directed toward divine goals. Accordingly, the Puritans held that the historian's role was to reveal God's plan by
showing the purposeful integration of events; the role of most
individuals was to learn God's plan from histories, sermons
and, of course, the Bible and to act in accordance with it. Puritan diaries could serve as histories by showing an overall pattern of events such as that which confirmed the author's election or by directing the author's actions toward conformity
with God's will.

Winthrop's diary provides numerous examples of events
which reveal God's constant intervention in the world. A sea-
man in a boat loaded with gunpowder declares he will smoke
his pipe even "if the devil should carry him away quick" (I, p.

82), an event which follows as the gunpowder ignites, tearing him to pieces. In a similar entry a servant who, "reproved for his lewdness, and put in mind of hell, answered, that if hell were ten times hotter, he had rather be there than he would serve his master" (I, pp. 103-104), and is drowned. But God could warn as well as condemn, and every calamity avoided was credited to divine providence, as was the case when two of Winthrop's own daughters "were sitting under a great heap of logs, plucking birds." The wind blew some of the feathers into the house, prompting their mother to demand that they move. Almost immediately the logs fell down, revealing the wind as God's instrument (I, p. 99).

In other entries Winthrop demonstrated that God used contemporary events to reinforce established principles or teach new spiritual lessons. For example, in one entry Winthrop claimed that, by sudden shifts in the value of commodities, "God taught us the vanity of all outward things" (II, p. 19). A similar lesson appears in the following passage:

A godly woman of the church of Boston, dwelling sometimes in London, brought with her a parcel of very fine linen of great value, which she set her heart too much upon, and had been at charge to have it all newly washed, and curiously folded and pressed, and so left it in press in her parlor over night. She had a negro maid went into the room very late, and let fall some snuff of the candle upon the linen, so as by the morning all the linen was burned to tinder, and the boards underneath, and some stools and a part of the wainscot burned, and never perceived by any in the house, though some lodged in the chamber over head, and no ceiling between. But it pleased God that the loss of this linen did her much good, both in taking off her heart from worldly comforts, and in preparing her for a far greater affliction by the untimely death of her husband, who was slain not long after at Isle of Providence. (II, pp. 30-31)

Such adversity was frequently exalted as a sign of God's concern for the individual's soul, a far more important object than possessions or even family. A famine was provided so New Englanders might recognize that they were to eat their food "in the sweat of their brows" (II, p. 92).

Taken together these divine interventions were seen by Winthrop as showing the special relationship between God and New England. Winthrop had articulated such a belief in a sermon delivered before he had ever set foot in America.[4]

Winthrop declared that the Puritans about to settle in New England had entered into a covenant with God to set up a community to serve Him and advance His principles. Such a covenant was a communal analogue of the covenant of grace by which the individual Puritan might hope to be worthy of salvation and without which he would perish. The covenant Winthrop proposed in his sermon required that each individual identify with the whole Puritan community in New England: "We must," he wrote, "delight in each other, make others' Conditions our own, rejoice together, mourn together, labor and suffer together, always having before our eyes our Commission and Community in, our Community as members of the same body."

As the author of these words and first governor of the Massachusetts Bay Colony, Winthrop strongly felt this identification with his community, and his diary was a product of that consciousness. In addition to entries revealing the providential manipulation of individual destinies, Winthrop showed those directed at the community. To demonstrate this function let us examine two entries—the first from a section of one of the early pages of the diary, the second from one of the last.

At Watertown there was (in the view of divers witnesses) a great combat between a mouse and a snake; and, after a long fight, the mouse prevailed and killed the snake. The pastor of Boston, Mr. Wilson, a very sincere, holy man, hearing of it, gave this interpretation: That the snake was the devil; the mouse was a poor contemptible people, which God had brought hither, which should overcome Satan here, and dispossess him of his kingdom   (I, pp. 83-84)
. . . .

The synod met at Cambridge. . . . Mr. Allen of Dedham preached. . . .

It fell out, about the midst of his sermon, there came a snake into the seat, where many of the elders sate behind the preacher. It came in at the door where people stood thick upon the stairs. Divers of the elders shifted from it, but Mr. Thomson, one of the elders of Braintree, (a man of much faith,) trode upon the head of it, and so held it with his foot and staff with a small pair of grains, until it was killed. This being so remarkable, and nothing falling out but by divine providence, it is out of doubt, the Lord discovered somewhat of his mind in it. The serpent is the devil; the synod, the representative of the churches of Christ in New England. The devil had formerly and lately attempted their disturbance and dissolution; but their faith in the seed of the woman overcame him and crushed his head.(II, pp. 347-48)

Through these interpretations of events in nature, Winthrop showed first a prophecy of the success of the colony in fulfilling its covenant; second, of its return to its guiding principles after a dangerous desertion from them. These passages were part of a thematic pattern running throughout the diary.

Like their counterparts in nature, human events figured in the working out of God's design: politics, commerce, diplomacy, and warfare all played important parts. The diary includes entries detailing religious controversies such as that surrounding Ann Hutchinson and her Aninomian "heresies," and battles such as those with the Pequot Indians. The subjects are diverse, but clearly different from the personal concerns to be found in most diaries. However, the individual is not really absent, just hidden by identification with or submission to the identity of the group. Its existence is pointedly seen in an exception such as the following passage: "My son, Henry Winthrop, was drowned at Salem" (I, p. 51). Here Winthrop was able to restrict to a single line an entry which was not pertinent to a diary of the colony, but he betrayed his feelings by momentarily dropping his pose of a third-person narrator. This is a sign of the underlying tension between Winthrop's personal and public impulses in his diary record.

Winthrop could not be totally successful in eliminating or disguising his personal perspective and attitudes in his diary, and as a result a careful reader can see the first-person diary beneath the impersonal "history." There is, of course, the danger that a reader knowledgeable about Winthrop's actions and attitudes may read too much into the diary, but, kept in appropriate perspective, recognition of a tension between Winthrop's private and public roles as they appear in the diary provides its unifying and directing forces.

II *Samuel Sewall (1652-1730)*

In discussing diary literature, especially American diary literature, it is frequently necessary to assert that the form and its individual works have been neglected. However, in the case of Sewall's diary we encounter a rare exception, a diary that has acquired a widespread reputation for excellence. Several respected critics have declared it to be one of the best diaries written in English, and no less a diary scholar than William Matthews has called it "probably the best American diary."[5] It would be a great comfort to accept the support of critical opinion; but, unfortunately, while I find much of value in Sewall's diary, I cannot endorse the widely accepted claim of its preeminent position.

The reason for this judgment is not so much a disagreement about the nature of the diary as it is a problem of criteria. In this volume I have asserted the primacy of intrinsic literary merit, and I have attempted to place the quality and unity of style, subject, and structure as the crucial determinants of that merit. Sewall's diary truly excels in the quality of its subject, but it is weaker in the other areas than its reputation would lead one to expect.

In the introduction to his excellent edition of Sewall's diary, Mr. Halsey Thomas wrote:

Sewall's diary meets the test of a good diary or book of memoirs of any period: he knew and had continuing and far from casual contacts with all the notable people of his place and time. For several decades Sewall was an important figure in Massachusetts Bay, a man entrusted with numerous public offices, a man of wealth, and a member of the *in*-group. Though he lived in a small town and was conversant with all of its goings-on, lawful and otherwise, both as a recipient of gossip and officially in his capacity as magistrate, Sewall was by no means a small-town person. Throughout the diary there are constant references to the happenings of the great world. Every time a ship came into port Sewall eagerly received the corantos and gazettes with the news of the home and foreign countries, and lost no opportunities to question the captains and passengers. When a newspaper was finally established in Boston in 1704, he preserved his copies, annotated them, made rough indexes, and had them bound.[6]

This interest in and access to vital events can, and in the case of Sewall's work did, make a valuable diary; however, such content cannot by itself make a literarily valuable diary. Sewall's diary does not sufficiently impose or reveal a unity of event or character to supply a highly coherent pattern, and its style, though readable, has no special merit. Therefore, while Sewall's diary excels in several respects, an assessment of its merit as a work of literature must be more moderate.

One of the obstacles to such merit is the length of the period covered as compared to the amount of material written. In comparison with Pepys's diary, with which it is sometimes compared, Sewall's work attempted to cover fifty-six years in a fraction of the space that Pepys's covered ten. If Sewall's diary had been limited in focus, this situation might not have posed so great a problem. However, the very breadth of Sewall's interest, which produced so many items of value, fragmented the work as a whole. As a result, an appreciation of the diary depends on a sensitivity to the vitality of the society which Sewall revealed, rather than to any artistic control. Even some of the more coherent sets of entries depend for their full meaning on the reader's ability to link them to the general context of events in the diary.

Most anthologists have done an adequate job of portraying the strong points of Sewall's work, but because they cannot devote enough space to the context, they often give a distorted picture of the work as a whole. As an example, let us consider Sewall's recantation of his part in the Salem witchcraft trials included in the following entry:

Copy of the Bill I put up on the Fast day; giving it to Mr. Willard as he pass'd by, and standing up at the reading of it, and bowing when finished; in the Afternoon.

Samuel Sewall, sensible of the reiterated strokes of God upon himself and family; and being sensible, that as to the Guilt contracted, upon the opening of the late Commission of Oyer and Terminer at Salem (to which the order for this Day relates) he is, upon many accounts, more concerned than any that he knows of, Desires to take the Blame and Shame of it, Asking pardon of Men, And especially desiring prayers that God, who has an Unlimited Authority, would pardon that Sin and all other his Sins; personal and Relative: And according to his infinite Benignity, and Soveraignty, Not Visit the Sin of him, or of any other, upon himself or any of his, nor upon the Land: But that He would powerfully defend him against all Temptations to Sin, for the future; and vouchsafe him the Efficacious, Saving Conduct of his Word and Spirit.   (pp. 366-67)

As readers of a diary we will be more concerned with the "reiterated strokes of God" than with the historically more significant witch trials. Sewall spent little time in the diary on the witch trials or on his decision to repent of them, but the diary is full of comments on the sufferings of his family and himself which he interpreted as divine warning or punishment. In the section just preceding the above entry Sewall wrote:

Mr. Willard had the Meeting at his house to day, but We had no Invitation to be there as is usual.

On the 22th of May I buried my abortive son; so neither of us were then admitted of God to be there, and now the Owners of the family admit us not: It may be I must never more hear a Sermon there. The Lord pardon all my Sins of Omission and Commission: and by his Almighty power make me meet to be partaker of the Inheritance with the S^{ts} in Light. *Secund-day Jany 11, 1696 81/7* God helped me to pray more than ordinarily, that He would make up our Loss in the burial of our little daughter and other children, and that would give us a Child to Serve Him, pleading with Him as the Institutor of Marriage, and the Author of every good work.   (p. 366)

To ignore either Sewall's concern about his ostracism from the Reverend Willard's meetings on earth or from God's "spiritual" church (symbolized by the misfortunes of his family) is to miss not only the full meaning of his bill of guilt, but also the dual nature of the diarist himself. Although Sewall's professions of lawyer and judge are today clearly secular, such was not the case in the late seventeenth century. Those accused of witchcraft in Salem were tried by laymen, not clergymen; those accused of civil offenses might be condemned from the pulpit.

    For Sewall, spiritual forces acted in this world and had to be considered seriously. In one entry he noted having heard Increase Mather preaching "from Rev. 22. 16—bright and morning Star" and mentioning a "Sign in the Heaven," and that the following evening he "saw a large Cometical Blaze, someting fine and dim, pointing from the Westward, a little below Orion" (p. 462). The imputation was that these events were linked by more than coincidence. Even Sewall's dreams were treated as divine messages which should be recorded in the diary so that their message might be better understood. Like Winthrop, Sewall could see a theological lesson in a news item such as the following:

Crabtree, a middle-aged woman, through some displeasure at her Son whom she beat, sat not down to Supper with her Husband and a Stranger at Table: when they had done, she took away, and in the

Room where she set it, took a piece of grisly meat of a Shoulder of Mutton into her mouth which got into the top of the Larynx and stopt it fast, so she was presently choak'd. Tho. Pemberton and others found it so when they opened her Throat. She gave a stamp with her foot and put her finger in her mouth . . . and [she] di'd immediately. What need have all to Acknowledge God in whose Hand their breath is, &c.   (p. 287)

One of the most unified sections of the diary is that covering Sewall's courtship period after the sudden death of his second wife. The common topic and cast of characters hold the group of entries together, but even here a full understanding of the group depends on an appreciation of diverse and often distant entries in the diary. For example, in their material on Sewall many anthologists include and literary historians cite entries in which Sewall carefully recorded giving a prospective bride "about ½ pounds of Sugar Almonds cost 3^s per £" (p. 965), or dickering about whether it would cost £40 or £100 a year to maintain a coach for her. Such passages make Sewall seem mercenary and devoid of romantic sentiment; however, there are other entries in which he wrote of his "flood of tears" at the death of his first wife (p. 864) or the way his "bowels yern towards" a woman who had rejected his suit (p. 911). Moreover, the reader of the whole diary will be aware that even eleven years and two marriages later Sewall could write of being "much affected" when he realized that it was "the same day of the week and Moneth that the Wife of my youth expired" (p. 1063). Such an understated assertion helps to put the courtship entries in a different light. Sewall the character is no longer seen as a comic fool, and Sewall the diarist can be given credit for recognizing the elements of humanity.

Another complex self-portrait emerges from a set of entries dealing with his conflict with Ebenezer Pemberton, then minister of the South Church. Sewall and Pemberton had argued before, but probably never with such emotion as was recorded in the diary for November 28, 1710. Pemberton began an attack in Sewall's own house, first with mocking sarcasm and then with open accusations of judicial favoritism:

Mr. Pemberton quickly begun to say, What you have been holding a Court to day! Had it over again; I was a little amus'd at the word Court; however, I began to relate what had been done. Mr. Pember-

ton with extraordinary Vehemency said, (capering with his feet) If the
Mathers order'd it, I would shoot him thorow. I told him he was in a
passion. He said he was not in a Passion. I said, it was so much the
worse. He said the Fire from the Altar was equal impartial. Upbraid-
ing me, very plainly, as I understood, it with Partiality. The President
said, The Governour was barbarously Treated (meaning Dr. Cotton
Mather's Letter to his Excellency). I answered; That was put to the
Council. Mr. Mayhew told me afterward, that I said his Carriage was
neither becoming a Scholar nor Minister. The Truth is I was surpris'd
to see my self insulted with such extraordinary Fierceness, by my
Pastor, just when I had been vindicating two worthy Embassadors of
Christ (his own usual Phrase) from most villanous Libels. (p. 646)

Ther, walking to dinner, Pemberton resumed his attack, revealing he imagined injustice that prompted it:

In the Way Mr. Pemberton charg'd me again, I was griev'd and said,
What in the Way! He answer'd, No body hears. But Mr. Sergeant
heard so much, that he turn'd back to still us. Mr. Pemberton told me
that Capt. Martin, the Commadore, had abus'd him, yet I took no
notice of it: I answer'd, you never laid it before me. He said, You
knew it. I said, I knew it not. (For every Rumor is not ground sufficient for a Justice of Peace to proceed upon; and Mr. Pemberton
never spake word of it to me before). He said Capt. Martin call'd him
Rascal in the Street, and said had it not been for his coat, he would
have can'd him. Mr. Pemberton said I excluded him, or he was
excluded from Dining with the Superiour Court by the Invitation of
Capt. Martin.   (p. 646)

Sewall's crime in defending the Mathers against slander is
here shown to be his failure to similarly defend Pemberton.
Sewall's logical and judicial explanations were ignored, and
Pemberton compounded his assault by having part of the Fif-
ty-eighth Psalm sung in church the next Sunday, including the
following verses:

> Speak, O ye Judges of the Earth
>   if just your Sentence be:
> Or must not Innocence appeal
>   to Heav'n from your Decree?
> Your wicked Hearts and Judgments are
>   alike by Malice sway'd;
> Your griping Hands, by weighty Bribes,
>   to Violence betrayed.

> To Virtue, strangers from the Womb
> their Infant Steps went wrong:
> They prattled Slander, and in Lyes
> employ'd their lisping Tongue.   (p. 648n)

To this Sewall replied in the diary, "Tis certain, one may make Libels of David's Psalms; and if a person be abused, there is no Remedy: I desire to leave it to GOD who can and will Judge Righteously" (p. 649).

This was not the only incident in which Pemberton showed his hostility toward Sewall; yet, when finally Pemberton was on his deathbed it was Sewall he called for to be with him, speak to him, and to clasp his hand (p. 845). Such episodes are important to any assessment of Sewall's character.

As the product of such complex and far-reaching chains of entries, Sewall's is not an easy diary to grasp, but it will eventually yield its value to a persistent reader. It is clearly worth the effort, for even if the work is not the almost unequalled masterpiece it has often been considered to be, it is still a very fine diary.

III *William Byrd (1674-1744)*

In writing about American diary literature one cannot avoid mentioning the work of William Byrd, because Byrd's diary and its author have been the subject of much critical attention. Byrd's skill as a writer has been long apparent from those of his works written for the public including a book of verse, *Tunbridgalia*, and three travel accounts: *A History of the Dividing Line*, *A Progress to the Mines*, and *Journey to the Land of Eden*. These histories are essentially revised diaries and their excellence shows Byrd's potential as a diarist. However, this potential was not fully realized and the suggestion that Byrd was a "Virginian Pepys" is an exaggeration of his performance.

Byrd kept a diary for most of his life, but only four sections are known to exist. These were secret diaries, three of which were written in a shorthand that was not deciphered and made public until the second quarter of the twentieth century. The fourth document is the secret counterpart of Byrd's *History of the Dividing Line*. The first of these shorthand diaries covers the period from 1709 to 1712 and treats Byrd's life as a young country gentleman in Virginia. Byrd's social and political position during this period gave him an excellent vantage point from which to observe and describe the life of genteel society and the events of government. However, these subjects were not the primary focus of the work. At this point in his life Byrd was married to Lucy Park, whose will and temper equalled Byrd's own. The result was a series of conflicts on home management and personal deportment that formed the major thematic elements of this diary section. Byrd and his wife argued about all sorts of minor details, from which piece of meat should be served first to whether or not Mrs. Byrd might pluck her eyebrows. While positive factors in making the diary interesting, as indications of immature behavior, the actions of both Byrd and his wife left much to be desired. Lucy defied her husband by having servants whipped and branded against his will, while he purposely angered her by cheating her at cards and kissing another woman in front of her:

In the evening I went to Dr. [Barret's] where my wife came this afternoon. Here I found Mrs. Chiswell, my sister Custis, and other ladies. We sat and talked till about 11 o'clock and then retired to our chambers. I played at [r-m] with Mrs. Chiswell and kissed her on the bed till she was angry and my wife also was uneasy about it, and cried as soon as the company was gone. I neglected to say my prayers, which I should not have done, because I ought to beg pardon for the lust I had for another man's wife. However I had good health, good thoughts, and good humor, thanks be to God Almighty.[7]

All sorts of events were confided to the diary in complete frankness; Byrd did not even omit mention of lovemaking on a billiard table.

The diary of the period of 1717-1721 is equally frank. It covers a period in which Byrd was a widower living in England and courting and proposing marriage to several women, while buying the sexual favors of numerous others. The contrasts which assume a thematic force in this book include the differing qualities of the two types of relationships. When Byrd was courting a Miss Smith, he would alternate entries describing his writing of submissive letters and dreaming romantic dreams, with other entries telling of casual sexual encounters with female servants. More detailed contrasts are also informative. For example, consider the following excerpt:

About 5 o'clock I wrote a letter to my milliner. Then I went to Mrs. B-r-t and drank tea till seven and then walked in the park with Mrs. D-n-s and Mrs. [Noel]. Then I picked up a woman and went home with her and ate some mutton steak and committed uncleanness. About one o'clock I went home and neglected my prayers.[8]

The union by proximity of fornication and menu items was unintentionally given a further ironic twist by Byrd's concern for his missed prayers.

A third shorthand diary covers the period from 1739 to 1741.[9] Written late in Byrd's life, this diary has entries considerably shorter and of comparatively lesser interest than the earlier diaries. Unfortunately none of the shorthand diaries really lives up to its potential. Regularity in a diarist is usually a virtue because this trait promises fullness and consistency. In the periods covered by extant diary material Byrd rarely let a day go by without an entry. This consistency by itself would be commendable, but Byrd went further, regularizing length and form. The first two shorthand diaries have entries averaging about 150 words each. The third volume has entries of half that length.

Even the very short entries of the third diary might have provided an adequate record, but Byrd further reduced the entry by including a pattern of common details. A typical entry from one of the shorthand diaries begins with a note on the hour Byrd awoke, his morning reading, his morning prayers, and his breakfast menu. To this material he frequently added a standardized note that he "danced his dance" (probably a reference to daily exercises) and a comment on the weather. Entries usually end with a statement about his evening prayers or his failure to pray. In between the reader may also expect some note about Byrd's dinner. Subtraction of these standard materials leaves a relatively brief entry with little space for the development of descriptive details, characterization, and the like; inclusion of them leaves a work with persistent interruptions of the flow of ideas. Even Byrd's honesty and skill with language could not fully overcome these obstacles.

The other extant diary, *The Secret History of the Dividing Line*, describes two expeditions to survey the boundary between Virginia and North Carolina. This diary differs from the shorthand diaries not only in matters of form such as the absence of standard items, but also in the unifying effect of its subject matter. As a travel diary, this work has a coherence imposed by situation which is more effective than that in the other works. Of course, one cannot be sure whether it was the isolation from the input of other interests or the positive attraction of the events of the expedition that most contributed to this success. Another factor which should also be considered is that a sense of the public trust placed in those undertaking this survey may have conveyed a special sense of purpose and audience.

Byrd's sense of purpose was modified by his intention of revising the secret version before presenting his account to the public. With this intention he was as free to express his opinions as he was in the shorthand diaries. Byrd's literary talent applied to the open expression of his views produced a satire marked by such techniques as the use of character titles instead of names. Thus, his fellow commissioners became: Firebrand, Meanwell, Humdrum, Shoebrush, and so on, while Byrd himself was renamed Steady.

With a sharp wit and the license of secrecy Byrd proceeded to declare that if one of the North Carolina commissioners "had not formerly been a Pyrate himself, he seem'd intimately acquainted with many of them."[10] A Virginia commissioner, who begged to be excused because his wife was ill, was simultaneously pardoned and condemned when he paid to have a doctor visit his wife. This commissioner, Byrd wrote, "treated his Company handsomely, and by the help of a Bowl of Rack Punch his Grief disappear'd so entirely, that if he had not sent for Arsmart [the physician], it might have been suspected his Lady's Sickness was all a Farce. However to do him Justice, the Man wou'd never be concern'd in a Plot that was like to cost him 5 Pistoles" (p. 33).

Byrd's views of the people among whom the expedition passes were rarely complimentary, but his most effective satire was directed against his fellow commissioners. On the surface, however, Byrd attempted to treat them more kindly, believing: "When People are join'd together in a troublesom Commission, they shou'd endeavor to sweeten by Complacency & good Humour all the Hazards & Hardships they are bound to encounter, & not like marry'd People make their condition worse by everlasting discord" (p. 89). Unfortunately, the expedition was plagued by constant dissension. Much of the hostility was between the North Carolina and Virginia groups, but Byrd paid more attention in the diary to the more serious and more personal dissension among members of his own Virginia Commission. In one entry he described the conflicts between two Virginia surveyors, "Astrolabe" and "Orion": "At Night Young Astrolabe came to Us, & gave great Jealousy to Orion. His Wigg was in such Stiff Buckle, that if he had seen the Devil the Hair wou'd not have stood on end" (p. 45). In another entry Byrd averted a more serious dispute: "At last I join'd their Hands, & made them kiss One another. Had not this Pacification happen'd thus luckily, it would have been impossible for Meanwell to put up the Indignity of holding up a Clubb at him, because in a court of honour, the Shaking of a Cudgel at a Gentleman, is adjudged the same affront as striking him with it. Firebrand was very sensible of this, & had great Reason to believe that in due time he must have been call'd to an Account for it by a Man of Meanwells Spirit" (p. 175).

Byrd himself was not exempt from attack from either Orion, who slandered Byrd along with Astrolabe, or Firebrand, who endorsed Orion's slander and for a time refused to sign Byrd's official journal. Byrd noted that when asked why he refused to sign, Firebrand's "Invention cou'd find no other Reason, but, because it was too Poetical, However, he thought proper to Sign this Poetical Journal at last, when he found it was to be sent to England without" his signature (p. 129).

Another persistent subject of the diary was the sexual escapades of the commissioners and their servants. Byrd himself appears to have been chaste during this period, a situation which the content of Byrd's other diaries would suggest was not likely to be a falsification for pretended modesty. He did confess to a dream about a romantic intrigue with one of the three Graces, but this imaginary intrigue was no competition for the real debaucheries of his fellows as they were depicted in this tavern scene:

My Landlord had unluckily sold our Men some Brandy, which produced much disorder, making some too Cholerick, and other too loving. (So that a Damsel who came to assist in the Kitchen wou'd certainly have been ravish't, if her timely consent had not prevented the Violence. Nor did my Landlady think herself safe in the hands of such furious Lovers, and therefore fortify'd her Bed chamber & de-

fended it with a Chamber-Pot charg'd to the Brim with Female Am-
munition. I never cou'd learn who the Ravisher was; because the Girl
had walk't off in the Morning early, but Firebrand & his Servant were
the most suspected, having been engag'd in those kind of Assaults
once before.   (pp. 147, 149)

Through such entries many of the well-bred Christian
commissioners were portrayed as far less moral than the "heathen" Indians they encountered who, within the limits of their
own situation and code of behavior, acted decently. Byrd recognized the virtues of the Indians in the public version of the
journal in which he even advocated their intermarriage with
whites as a step toward their conversion to Christianity, assert-
ing, "Had the English done this at the first Settlement of the
Colony, the Infidelity of the Indians had been worn out at this
Day, with their Dark Complexions, and the Country had
swarm'd with People more than it does with Insects" (p. 120).
Byrd asserted the superiority of Christianity to the Indians'
native beliefs, but his lengthy retelling of one Indian's portrait
of the afterlife was presented in positive terms:

In the Evening I examin'd our Indian Ned Bearskin concerning his
Religion, & he very frankly gave me the following Account of it. That
he believ'd there was a Supream Being, that made the World & every
thing in it. That the same Power that made it still preserves & governs
it. That it protects and prospers good People in this World, &
punishes the bad with Sickness & Poverty. That after Death all Mankind are conducted into one great Road, in which both the good &
bad travel in Company to a certain Distance when this great Road
branches into 2 Paths the One extremely Levil, & the other
Mountainous. Here the good are parted from the bad, by a flash of
Lightening, the first fileing to the Right, the other to the Left. The
Right hand Road leads to a fine warm country, where the Spring is
perpetual, & every Month is May, And as the Year is always in its
Youth, so are the People, and the Women beautiful as Stars, & never
scold. . . . The left hand Path is very rough & uneven, leading to a
barren Country, where 'tis always Winter, the Ground was cover'd
with Snow, & nothing on the Trees but Iciles. All the People are old,
have no teeth, & yet are very hungry. Only those who labour very
hard make the Ground Produce a Sort of Potato pleasant to the Tast,
but gives them the dry Gripes, & fills them full of Sores, which stinks
and are very painfull. The Women are old & ugly arm'd with sharp
Claws like a Panther, & with those they gore the Men that slight their
passion.   (pp. 199, 201)

This entry first mirrors Benjamin Franklin's deistic statement of personal faith expressed in his letter to Ezra Stiles and repeated in his *Autobiography*: "I never doubted, for instance the existence of the Deity; that he governed it by his providence; that the most acceptable service to God was doing good to man; that our souls are immortal; and that all crime will be punished, and virtue rewarded, either here or hereafter." The entry later echoes "the choice of Hercules" in John Adams's diary.

Returning to the "civilized" world after months on the primitive frontier, Byrd's thankfulness at being home emphasized the distance between these two worlds in terms of physical comforts. Yet the diary revealed that Byrd was acutely aware that there might be a greater distance between the inner qualities of the men of the Virginia aristocracy than between these so-called aristocrats and the common people. It was this discrepancy between the expectation and reality of what Byrd expected from the frontier that elevated this work above the shorthand diaries, but it was the skill apparent in all the works that made Byrd's achievement possible.

IV *Multi-generation Diaries*

Given the frequency with which individuals kept diaries in early America, and the public discussion about and advocacy of the practice, it is not surprising that we should encounter instances in which several members of the same family kept diaries. The final two diaries to be discussed at length in this volume, those of Cotton Mather and John Adams, are both part of a family tradition of diary keeping which extended for at least three generations.

Cotton Mather's father, Increase, and his grandfather Richard both kept diaries.[11] These earlier works, however, are relatively brief and of significantly lower quality than those of Cotton Mather. John Adams's descendants and their families produced numerous diaries, some of which are more extensive and of comparable quality to John's. Both John and his wife, Abigail, kept diaries, and their children were advised to continue the practice. In this second generation the most significant work is that of John Quincy Adams. Spanning approximately seventy years and three million words, it presents special problems for the serious reader of diary literature. John Quincy Adams's wife and children also produced diaries, of which the most notable is that of Charles Francis Adams.

The diaries of these three generations of Adamses skillfully cover one and a quarter centuries, and provide a detailed portrait of the lives of their authors and the nation they helped to shape. Such monumental materials require special consideration before useful generalizations can be made. However, one general trend seems sufficiently clear to be suggested. As subsequent analysis will indicate, John Adams's diary was directed toward the future, preparing the attitudes and actions of its author. Most of the diaries of John Quincy Adams and Charles Francis Adams were rooted more closely in the present. It may be that in the fourth generation Henry Adams's decision to write an autobiography, *The Education of Henry Adams*, completed a cycle as the work turned in form and perspective toward the past. The consideration of such hypotheses regarding multi-generation diaries can help to clarify the relationship between form and content in individual diaries.

V   *Cotton Mather (1663-1728)*

Before beginning a consideration of Cotton Mather's diary, it is worthwhile to consider those diaries his father, Increase Mather, and his grandfather Richard Mather kept. The latter's diary consists of a literate description of his migration to America in 1635 marked by comments on storms at sea and signs of God's providence in natural events. Increase Mather kept at least two overlapping diaries: one for the years 1675-1676, which, though kept regularly, rapidly deteriorated into a series of brief notes about religious duties and another running from 1674 to 1687, of which only extracts now exist. Although there is no direct statement in any of the works establishing any father-to-son influence related to the practice of diary keeping, the importance of spiritual insight, historical records, and parental guidance was valued by each. A reading of the public and private statements of the three men leads to but does not prove the hypothesis that the practice of the sons was affected by the models of the fathers. However, the record also provides evidence of the individuality of each of the three. Certainly there is no lack of original and dynamic thought in the works of Cotton Mather.

To most of those who have any association at all with the name Cotton Mather, those associations are of dogmatic Puritanism, antiscientific fundamentalism, religious persecution, and sexless, passionless life. The events most frequently associated with him are the Salem witch trials. The diary shows us a very different man; one who could speak of being "assaulted" with doubts, "tempted . . . to look upon the whole *Christian Religion*, as–(I dare not mention what!)" because he perceived so much evil in a world he believed was controlled by God: "As for the *dark Things* that occur, in His *Providence*; and the *unaccountable Proceedings* of that glorious One, in His Government of His Church, and His Permission of *ill Things* to be *suffered*; yea, and which is worse, to be *done*, by His own most faithful Servants; and his permission of *Evil Spirits*, to do astonishing Things for a considerable While, in the Countenancing and Encouraging of Christianity. I did re-solve humbly to rely upon his unsearchable Wisdome."[12] Even though Mather pulled back from the *"unpardonable sin"* of denouncing God, his need to question shows him to have been a more complex individual than one might have expected.

The charge of an antiscientific bias can be refuted by noting such things as Mather's great pride that his scientific writings had been rewarded by a nomination as a fellow of the Royal Society, and his willingness to risk his reputation in the community and actual attempts on his life to support the still novel technique of smallpox inoculation (11, pp. 246, 144). Similarly, while Mather could not be considered a tolerationist by modern standards, he did challenge the extreme forms of religious persecution by his own society. In the margin of the diary he wrote:

Among other things, I ran the Hazard of much Reproch by testifying in that Sermon, against the *Persecution* of erroneous and conscientious Dissenters, by the *civil Magistrate*. I feared, that the *Zeal* of my Countrey had formerly had in it more *Fire* than should have been; especially, when the mad *Quakers* were sent unto the *Gallowes*, that should have been kept rather in a *Bedlam*. I did therefore on this great Occasion bear my Testimony; hoping, that if the General Assembly now thank'd mee for it, *their* doing so, would bee accepted both by God and Man. I think, I am the only *Minister* Living in the Land, that have testifyed against the *Suppression* of *Haeresy*, by *Persecution*. And I hope, the Lord will own mee with a more singular Success, in the Suppression of Haeresy by Endeavours more *spiritual* and *evangelical*.   (I, p. 149)

The diary's portrait of Mather at the witch trials plays down the belief in the existence of witches and devils that fill his public work *The Wonders of the Invisible World* and shows that while he defended the honesty of the judges and the proceedings, he cautioned against the use of "spectral evidence" and campaigned for the treatment of the symptoms of the "afflicted" accusers as an alternative to the execution of the convicted "witches":

The *Divels*, after a most praeternatural Manner, by the dreadful Judgment of Heaven took a *bodily Possession*, of many people, in *Salem*, and the adjacent places; and the Houses of the poor People, began to bee filled with the horrid Cries of Persons tormented by *evil Spirits*. There seem'd an execrable *Witchcraft*, in the Foundation of this wonderful Affliction, and many Persons, of diverse Characters, were accused, apprehended, prosecuted, upon the *Visions* of the Afflicted.

For my own part, I was alwayes afraid of proceeding to convict and condemn any Person, as a *Confaederate* with afflicting Daemons, upon so feeble an Evidence, as a *spectral Representation*. Accordingly, I ever testified against it, both publickly and *privately*; and in my *Letters* to the *Judges*, I particularly, besought them, that they would by no means admitt it; . . .

Nevertheless, on the other side, I saw in most of the *Judges*, a most charming Instance of *Prudence* and *Patience*, and I knew their exemplary *Pietie*, and the *Agony* of Soul with which they sought the Direction of Heaven. . . . For this Cause tho' I could not allow the *Principles*, that some of the Judges had espoused, yett I could not but speak honourably of their *Persons*, on all Occasions; and my *Compassion*, upon the Sight of their *Difficulties*, raised by my Journeys to *Salem*, the chief Seat of these diabolical Vexations, caused mee yett more to do so. And meerly, as far as I can learn, for the Reason, the mad people thro' the Countrey, under a fascination on their *Spirits*, aequal to what our *Energumens* had of their *Bodies*, reviled mee, as if I had been the Doer of all the hard Things, that were done, in the Prosecution of the *Witchcraft*.

In this *Evil-Time*, I offered, at the beginning, that if the *possessed* People, might bee scattered far asunder, I would singly provide for six of them; and wee would see whether without more bitter methods, *Prayer* with *Fasting* would not putt an End unto these heavy Trials: But my offer (which none of my Revilers, would have been so courageous or so charitable, as to have made) was not accepted.   (I, pp. 150-52)

Mather himself practiced such "excorcism," recording his procedure in the diary:

About this Time, I had many wonderful Entertainments, from the *Invisible World*, in the Circumstances of a Young Woman, horribly *possessed* with *Divels*. The Damsel was cast into *my* cares, by the singular Providence of God; and accordingly besides my Cares to releeve her, to *advise* her, to *observe* the prodigious things that befel her . . . *I* did alone in my Study, *fast* and *pray* for her Deliverance. And, unto my Amazement, when I had kept my *third* Day for her, shee was finally and forever delivered from the hands of *evil Angels*; and I had afterwards the Satisfaction of seeing not only *her* so brought home unto the Lord, that shee was admitted unto our *Church*, but also many other, even some scores, of young People, awakened by the Picture of *Hell*, exhibited, in *her* Sufferings, to *flee from the Wrath to come*.   (I, pp. 160-61)

The diary sheds some light on the motives which led Mather to aid rather than condemn. One of the most important was Mather's sense of his own wickedness; Mather denounced "the incredible vilenesses" of his own life, called himself "the most loathsome Wretch in the world," and repented with the aid of a constant "pouring out" of prayers, secret fasts, and periods of lying prostrate on the floor. He was able to write that after such humiliations "I received from Heaven, in a manner, *which I may not utter*, a wonderful *Assurance*, that my Sins are all pardoned, by the infinite Grace of God" (I, p. 233). Of course, such professions of guilt and periods of repentence were not as frequent or extreme as those expressed by Wigglesworth in his journal; and, significantly, Mather's outpourings of emotion were consistently and speedily rewarded by convictions of divine forgiveness. Moreover, statements about special messages conveyed in ways he dared not make public suggest that he shared an enthusiasm relatable to that of many sects persecuted by his own society and by those who claimed to be afflicted by "spirits."

In viewing his own sins Mather occasionally showed a

willingness to take responsibility for the actions of others. When Mather found that "Horrible Crimes, are by strange Dispensations of Heaven, discovered in some Communicants of my Church," he, considering that these warnings might be signs that God is "offended at *mee* for the Iniquities of those that are under *my Charge*," spent a day *"Fasting* in my Study, that I may obtain the Pardon of all my own vile Sinfulness" (I, p. 242). And again Mather obtained the assurance of God's forgiveness.

Such acceptance of the guilt of others carried with it more than a hint of pride. When in his absence his daughter fell into the fire in his study, Mather concluded, "Alas, for *my Sin*, the just God throwes *my Child* into the *Fire"* (I, p. 283). And when he expected "some Affliction" as the penalty for *"Slothfulness* of Spirit," the same daughter's illness several days later was taken as the punishment (I, p. 303). In such statements Mather seems to have been describing a world which revolved around him.

This turning of the external subjects of the diary to focus on Mather himself is evident in three distinct roles Mather played: the spiritual role of a soul seeking salvation, the public role of minister and author seeking the welfare of his congregation and of society in general, and his private role as a son, husband, and father. These roles identify the three major themes of the diary. The early pages of the preserved portion of the diary (and probably most of any lost or omitted earlier material) are almost entirely about Mather's relationship to God, his prayers, his resolutions, and his inner struggles. This aspect of the diary never completely ended even after the diary had expanded beyond the limits of a spiritual journal developing its own identity. Prayers, fasts, and other religious duties were the basic fabric upon which the design of Mather's life and society was woven. Mather's religious duties as recorded in the diary were so consistent that the reader may almost lose sight of them, but if at any point they had ceased, their absence would have been the most noticeable event in the diary.

Over half of the diary was imposed upon a pattern which Mather called *Devices of Good*, a series of questions, one for each day of the week. Sunday's question was, *"What Service to be done for my Saviour in the FLOCK whereof I am the*

Pastor?" Monday's, "What to be done in *MY FAMILY*?" Tuesday's on alternate weeks were, *What Service to be done for Christ, and my RELATIVES ABROAD,*" and "*my Personal enemies . . . what good may I do unto them?*" and so on (II, pp. 23-26). The responses to these questions generally appear in the diary headed by the number of the day of the week and the words "Good Devised, (usually abbreviated as G.D.)." Such themes interplayed week upon week draw attention beyond their original spiritual purpose, yet it was the spiritual role that gave form to the diary.

Mather's entries showing the good he devised for his enemies reveal just one aspect of the diary's extension into his public role. One example of this situation is observable in the following pair of entries. In the first Mather wrote:

3. G.D. There is a Merchant in this Town, who has been wickedly, absurdly, sordidly abusive to me. It lies in my Power many Wayes to hurt him. I will totally abstain from doing the least Hurt unto him. I will earnestly pray unto God, for all Sorts of Blessings upon him; and particularly, that the Danger of his Breaking, and coming to nothing, may be prevented. And I will sett myself to invent wayes to do him good Offices.   (II, p. 44)

Such attacks and public opposition Mather took as signs of Satan's assaults and thus further proof of his own merit and so continued in his behavior. But approximately six months later he noted:

This Day I was *buffeted* with a libellous Letter from a Merchant in this Town, fill'd with Scurrilities that I suppose were hardly ever aequalled in the World. The Divel stared in every Line of it. A Legion together could scarce have out-done it. It is a little odd; tho' the Libeller, were one of the last, whom I find mention'd among the Enemies for whom I projected Kindnesses, yett one Article of his Foam is, that I am a Stranger to the Practice of a forgiving Spirit which I preach unto others.   (II, p. 99)

Of course the merchant could not have known about Mather's prayers for him, but Mather expected that God would order the world by His, not human, knowledge.

In other actions recorded in the diary, Mather publicly labored for what he considered the good of others: the writing of numerous books and tracts, the distribution of Bibles, the de-

livery of speeches, and so on. Together these give the reader a
picture of constant activity. Such actions gained Mather a substantial reputation, but each success also attracted enmity. External records show that Mather's reception by his contemporaries was generally positive, but the diary shows that
Mather felt it was otherwise. In a section toward the end of the
diary Mather reviewed the good he had devised under the
heading "Dark Dispensations but Light Arrising in Dark-
ness." The following are only three examples from twenty-
seven Mather listed:

I. *What has a gracious Lord given me to do*, for the Welfare of the
seafaring Tribe? In *Prayers* for them; in *Sermons* to them; in *Books*
bestow'd on them; and in various Projections and Endeavours, to
render the *Sailors*, an happy Generation!
    AND YETT, there is not a Man in the world, so Reviled, so slan-
dered, so cursed, among the *Sailors*.
. . . .
    IX. *What has a Gracious Lord given me to do*, that the *Colledge*
may be own'd for the bringing forth such as are somewhat known in
the World, and have read and wrote as much as many have done in
some other Places?
    AND YETT, the *Colledge* forever putts all possible Marks of Dises-
teem upon me. If I were the greatest *Blockhead* that ever came from
it, or the greatest *Blemish* that ever came to it, they could not easily
show me more Contempt than they do.
. . . .
    XIV. *What has a gracious Lord given me to do*, in a Variety of *Serv-
ices*? For many *Lustres* of years, not a Day has passed me, without
some *Devices*, even *written Devices*, to be *serviceable*.
    AND YETT, my *Sufferings*, they seem to be (as tis Reason they
should be,) more than my *Services*. Every Body points at me, and
speaks of me, as by far the most afflicted Minister in all *New England*.
And many look on me as the *greatest Sinner* because the *greatest
Sufferer*: and are pretty Arbitrary in their Conjectures on my
punished Miscarriages.   (II, pp. 705-708)

This conflict between Mather's estimation of his own worth
and the treatment he received dominates the diary's record of
Mather's public life.
    Mather's private life is also an important part of the diary.
His joys and sufferings in marriage, his anxiety with each
death or deliverance from death of his many children—all of
these are vital to the diary. As these relationships threaded

through the work are traced by the reader, the tragedy of Mather's private life emerges. Surely Mather would have denied the tragedy, for throughout the diary he took pains to search out proof that all events, whether pleasant or painful, seemed directed by God or by Satan with God's permission and thus must lead to the best possible result. A drought was God "chastising this poor land" (I, p. 361); the death of a disliked relative was an act of God. Mather even tried to systematize such interpretations, resolving, "As whatever Trouble befalls me in general, I would presently fetch and form out of it, a poenitent Confession of some Sin, which the Trouble may lead me to take notice of; so if I particularly suffer any troublesom Circumstance in my Health, I would be led thereby, presently to think on some analogous Distemper in my Soul or Miscarriage in my Life, which I should make an Article of Repentance before the Lord" (II, p. 201). Thus when Mather fell out of a canoe into a fishpond, he tried to find God's Message: "sollicitous to make all the Reflections of Piety, on my Disaster, and on my Deliverance. But not yett able to penetrate into the whole Meaning of the Occurence. Am I quickly to go under the Earth, as I have been under the Water!" (II, p. 367). In this way Mather was quick to seize on good fortune as an instance of providential aid. For example, when Mather wished he had the money to purchase a library of books recently placed on sale, the money was equally pressed on him by a man whose ill treatment Mather had forgiven (II, p. 2).

Mather was not always given a favorable response to his prayers. In a moving series of entries Mather treated his wife's illness:

21 d. 5 m. Tuesday. My *Faith* and my poor Consort's *Patience,* is mightily tried, by her continuing in a dubious, dangerous, deplorable Condition of Illness.

The Physicians, this Evening, seem to have laid aside all Expectation of her ever being restored, from the wasting scorbutic Feaver, and still continuing Salivation, that followes her.

. . . .

I retired into my Bed-Chamber, and spent good Part of the Night, prostrate on the Floor, (with so little of Garment on as to render my lying there painful to my tender Bones), crying to God for the Life of my poor Consort, but humbly committing her Case, and submitting

my Will, to His glorious Providence. I think, before I went unto my
Rest, I obtained some further Satisfaction, that my God has heard me!
I shall have a blessed Answer, tho' I do not as yett foresee all the
Circumstances.   (I, pp. 436-37)

With alternate despair and hope, he faced the loss of his own
faith. At first his prayers and fasts seemed answered by a
miraculous recovery, but the hoped-for cure did not occur:

My poor Consort falls into new Returns of Languishment; yea, her
Feebleness growes again to that Extremity, as to render her Condition, as dubious perhaps as ever. I am kept up all Night, that I may see
her dy, and therewith see the terrible Death of my Prayer and Faith.
But in this Extremity, when I renew my Visits unto Heaven, and go to
resign my dear Consort unto the Lord, and consent that she shall be
taken from me, a strange Irradiation comes from Heaven upon my
Spirit, that her Life shall not as yett come unto an End.   (I, p. 437)

Mather was so moved by his grief that he seemed almost to
abandon his Puritan principles and wholly give way to enthusiasm. In one entry he wrote, "I found a strange Impression on my Mind, intimating to me that Heaven was willing to
converse with me, after a familiar Manner, if I would now look
and wait in a suitable Posture for it, It was q. said to me, *Go
into your great Chamber and I will speak with you!*" Casting
himself onto the floor and confessing his own "Loathsome-
ness" before God, Mather felt strangely "caused to speak"
promises not only of God's favor but special attention.
Through Mather's own voice he was promised that God would
love him, make him a *"chosen Vessel* to do good in the World,"
dispatch angels to preserve Mather's "treatise of, THE
TRIUMPHS OF CHRISTIANITY," and "be a *Father* to
Mather's children" (I, pp. 437-38).
     When Mather began to accept his wife's approaching death,
he found that this acceptance supported his position as the
recipient of special attention from God. He termed his wife's
temporary remissions "admirable Demonstrations, of His
being loath to deny me any thing that I importunately ask of
Him," but cautioned that death must eventually come and that
he might be shortsighted in not considering that God might
have more marvelous blessings than the recovery from illness
(I, pp. 441-42). Even after the entry recording his wife's death

after an illness of over four months, Mather recorded that upon asking her to tell him what faults in his conversation she would suggest he correct, "she replied (which I wondered at) that she knew of none" (I, p. 448). Nevertheless we should not accuse Mather of too much self-love in such diary entries as we might if the same statements had appeared in another form, because the goal of the diary was not objectivity but the self-improvement which can only come from a candid admission of feelings.

Another personal tragedy in the later portion of the diary was the fall of Mather's son Increase. Mather's high hopes for this child are evident in the entry recording his birth. In his study, praying to God to relieve his wife from the pains of childbirth, Mather, on hearing of the birth, continued praising God and reported having "received a wonderful Advice from Heaven, that this my Son shall bee a Servant of my Lord Jesus Christ throughout eternal Ages" (I, p. 307). In naming the boy after his own father, a man famous for his piety and wisdom, Mather set a high standard for the child. Repeated statements in the diary that Mather perceived indications of further divine favor toward young Increase are further proof of his expectations. Thus when Increase was "taken with Convulsion fits," Mather recorded in the diary:

The Lord now not only called mee, but also helped mee, to resign my Son unto Him. Nevertheless, that I might more effectually conform to the Dispensations of Heaven, when I saw an *Angel of Death*, with a *drawn Sword* thus over my Family, I thought it my Duty to betake myself unto more than ordinary Supplications. Wherefore, altho' I have already kept *one Day* of *Prayer* with *Fasting* this week, yett on *Satureday* I kept *another*. I then heartily and cheerfully gave away my Son, unto the Lord Jesus Christ, professing, that if the Child may not be a *Servant* of His, I was far from desiring the Life of it; but, if the Child might serve Him exceedingly, I cry'd unto him, to speak for it, the Word, by which it might live. . . . Towards the Evening, the Convulsions left the Child. (I, pp. 336-37)

With these expectations and divine promises in mind, Mather determined to spare no effort in the child's improvement and the diary shows Mather expressing greater concern for "Cresy" than for his other children. When the accidental death of a child in the neighborhood moved Mather to preach a sermon designed to move children to prepare for death and divine judgment, he added: "And I will make that sad Accident, an occasion of more than ordinarily importunate Admonitions unto my own Children, especially unto my son *Increase*, to become serious and prayerful and afraid of Sin, and concern'd to gett a part in their only Saviour" (II, p. 64).

Whether despite or because of such special attention, Increase early gave Mather cause for concern. When the child was not yet twelve years old, Mather wrote of his concern that "vicious and wicked Lads" might "corrupt and ensnare him" (II, p. 76). But Mather's "daily Admonitions" to his "poor Son Increase" (II, p. 212), and the son's promises to "no longer persist in a prayerless Life" did not keep the boy from misbehavior (II, p. 203). Then in 1717 Mather wrote in the diary:

> The Evil that I greatly feared, is come upon me. I am within these few hours, astonished with an Information, that an Harlot big with a Bastard, accuses my poor Son *Cresy*, and layes her Belly to him. Oh! Dreadful Case! Oh, Sorrow beyond any that I have mett withal! what shall I do now for the foolish Youth! what for my afflicted and abased Family? My God, look mercifully upon me.
>
> The most sensible Judges upon the strictest Enquiry, beleeve the youth to be Innocent. But yett, oh! ye Humiliations!   (II, p. 484)

Mather could not openly accept that this, the most prayed-for child on earth, was lost to God, and his prime concern seems his own reputation (II, p. 323).

VI *The Diary of John Adams (1735-1826)*

In his diary, John Adams noted several uses and advantages which he hoped to gain from such a work. It would, he hoped, provide moral lessons, reveal truths about human nature, improve his writing style, aid his memory, and provide future entertainment for himself and his family. But its central use, he concluded, would be "to give me a true Compunction for the Waste of Time and urge me of Course to a better improvement of it. Besides," he added, "Writing is one of the greatest Pleasures and it sooner rouses my ambition, warms my imagination, and fixes me in a train of thinking, than any other Thing I can do—."[13] It was as this instrument for ambition that the diary became a living entity acting on and, at times, directing the actions of its creator.

Adams used his diary to impose order on his life and so foster productivity. One way he did so was through the formulation of resolutions:

I am now entering on another Year, and I am resolved not to neglect my Time as I did last Year. I am resolved to rise with the Sun and to study the Scriptures, on Thursday, Fryday, Saturday, and Sunday mornings, and to study some Latin author the other 3 mornings. Noons and Nights I intend to read English Authors. This is my fixt Determination, and I will set down every neglect and every compliance with this Resolution. May I blush whenever I suffer one hour to pass unimproved. I will rouse up my mind, and fix my Attention. I will stand collected within my self and think upon what I read and what I see. I will strive with all my soul to be something more than Persons who have had less Advantages than myself.   (I, p. 35)

Such standards, though useful in directing a life, are essentially static. A more dynamic use of the diary was as a place for analyzing experience and planning future activities by trial action. Like fantasy, in which an individual may imagine a possible course of action and mentally experience the risks and rewards of various alternatives, diary writing can be used for active planning. As in the following situation, Adams would begin many entries by proposing possibilities:

Shall I, by making Remarks, and proposing Questions [to] the Lawyers att the Bar, endeavour to get a great Character for Understanding and Learning with them. But this is slow and tedious, and will be ineffectual, for Envy, Jealousy, and self interest, will not suffer them to give a young fellow a free generous Character, especially me. Neither of these Projects will bear Examination, will avail.(I, p. 78)

Finally, after a series of such paragraphs, he was able to present the problem in such a way that the decision he sought to make seemed evident:

Shall I look out for a Cause to Speak to, and exert all the Soul and all the Body I own, to cut a flash, strike amazement, to catch the Vulgar? In short shall I walk a lingering, heavy Pace or shall I take one bold determined Leap into the Midst of some Cash and Business? That is the Question. A bold Push, a resolute attempt, a determined

Enterprize, or a slow, silent, imperceptible creeping. Shall I creep or
fly.   (I, p. 78)

The result of this consideration proved consistent with what
we know of Adams. He chose to be bold in stressing his worth
and his own beliefs. It was this fierce determination to support
uncompromisingly his own convictions that eventually pre-
cipitated his political destruction.

This struggle to achieve shaped both Adams' life and the
diary he kept for almost fifty years. Strongly motivated to
achieve, Adams used the diary to express an unrealistically
high level of aspiration, confessions of his failure to meet his
goals, and the downgrading of those with whom he was in
competition:

> What am I doing? Shall I sleep away my whole 70 Years. No by
> every Thing I swear I will renounce the Contemplative, and betake
> myself to an active roving Life by Sea or Land, or else I will attempt
> some uncommon unexpected Enterprize in Law. Let me lay the Plan
> and arouse Spirit enough to push boldly. I swear I will push myself
> into Business. I will watch my Opportunity, to speak in Court, and
> will strike with surprize-surprize Bench, Bar, Jury, Auditors and all.
> Activity, Boldness, Forwardness, will draw attention. Ile not lean,
> with my Elbows on the Table, forever like Read, Swift, Fitch, Skin-
> ner, Story, &c.   (I, p. 73)

Endorsing the Protestant ethic of work, Adams attacked
failure as a probably indication of vice. In the following entry,
Adams supported an attack by recording his subject's lame ex-
cuses:

To temper such a stiff and egotistical self-portrait we may
consider Mather's assertion that he accepted his son's sins as
his own (II, p. 485), and the fact that he refused to "utterly cast
off the wretched child" (II, p. 489). Finally, after "the Wretch"
had "brought himself under public Trouble and Infamy by
bearing a Part in a Night-Riot, with some detestable Rakes in
the Town," Mather cast him out (II, p. 611). Yet even here he
tempered the action by entreating his son's grandfather and
namesake to "take Pains" for the youth's "recovery" (II, p.
612). Eventually he took the son back despite worsened behavior, but this action did not lead to a happy conclusion. Ultimately Increase went to sea and died, leaving his father with
unresolved hopes for the young man's salvation:

For, I am now advised, that my Son *Increase*, is lost, is dead, is gone. The Ship wherein he was bound from Barbados to St. Peters had been out five Months, and was not arrived; and some singular Circumstances of the Vessel also concur to confirm the Apprehension that it is perished in the Sea. Ah! My Son *Increase*! My Son! My Son!

My Head is Waters, and my Eyes are a Fountain of Tears! I am overwhelmed! And this at a Time when the domestic Inhumanities, and Diabolisms which I am treated withal, are so insupportable! O my God, I am oppressed; undertake for me.

But, the Soul of the Child! If the Papers which he left in my Hands, were sincere and His Heart wrote with his pen, all is well! Would not my GOD have me to hope so? (II, p. 753)

In the above passage the interplay among the spiritual, personal, and private provides a capsule of the whole diary. Here Mather's relationships with his God, his family, and the external world are inseparable. The passage is also significant in that it and the event it chronicled signaled the end of the diary. Mather lived a few years beyond this point, but the true diary (discounting lists and letters) lasted only the few months until all rumors of Increase's survival from shipwreck had ceased. Perhaps the diary ended because Mather, who acknowledged that he saw his own image in his children, found that image in the diary as well and could no longer face it without painful memories. Certainly the incident must have dampened Mather's enthusiasm for thoughts of an earthly future. Diary and son represented the preparation for living; thus, the life diary ended as it no longer looked toward life.

Green told me, to day, that he had lived in Woodstock 13 Years and had nothing but bad luck, all the Time. Now he was about to try whether Change of Place, would alter his fortune. I asked what bad Luck? He said he had fail'd in Trade like a fool—and after Dinner he [said] that the richest Men were such as had fail'd in Trade. His Uncle John Chandler broke once, and very nigh breaking another Time. His Uncle Tommy Green broke once. John Spooner broke once. So I dont entirely despair.—This News I was not att all surprized to hear, for I thought fifteen Year ago, that Jno. Green would turn out so. He was a boaster of his Vices—a great affecter of licentiousness—and at last got in Love, like a fool, with a Girl, much too good for him. (II, pp. 22-23)

This association of achievement with deserving effort is a common one among those with a strong need to achieve. One probable reason for this association is that, if one holds the contrary belief that unscrupulous action will result in reward, his own effort seems futile. Consequently, Adams consistently showed himself unwilling to accept the fact that those who achieved their positions by unscrupulous means might triumph; he predicted their defeats, and he rejoiced whenever his prediction became a reality.

But of all the people Adams condemned for their vices and failures, none was so frequently a target as Adams himself. The diary is full of confessions that instead of being devoted to productive effort, his time had been wasted in excessive sleep or, "spent in a softening, enervating dissipating, series of hustling, pratling, Poetry, Love, Courtship, Marriage," all of which he described as, "unmanly Pleasures" (I, p. 73). We see from this list that Adams disapproved of many things which are seen as worthy in contemporary society. In the case of marriage, Adams, at this point in his life, viewed the choice of a husband or a wife as a rational decision which should be isolated from emotional considerations; however, his failure to wed Hannah Quincy (and her subsequent marriage to another), which Adams described as, "a great sacrifice to Reason," were very much the product of chance:

Accidents, as we call them, govern a great Part of the World, especially Marriages. Sewal and Esther broke in upon H. and me and interrupted a Conversation that would have terminated in a Courtship, which would in spight of the Dr. have terminated in a Marriage, which Marriage might have depressed me to absolute Poverty and obscurity, to the End of my Life. But the Accident seperated us, and gave room for Lincolns addresses, which have delivered me from very dangerous shackles, and left me at Liberty, if I will but mind my studies, of making a Character and a fortune.   (I, p. 87)

Here Adams clearly chose wealth and reputation over romance, and despite his assertion that acquisitions made through personal achievement are to be preferred to those attained by birth or marriage, he finally chose to marry much above his station rather than below it. This is not to say that his affection for Abigail was pretended; however, we cannot be sure what the result might have been if her economic and social position had been different. It is worth noting there is no reference in the diary to Adams's courtship and marriage, and there are few references of any kind to his wife. On the other hand, the diary contains much in praise of Hannah Quincy, such as the following piece of gushing prose:

If I look upon a Law Book and labour to exert all my Attention, my Eyes tis true are on the Book, but Imagination is at the Tea Table with Orlinda [a code name for Hannah Quincy], seeing That Face, those Eyes, that Shape, that familiar friendly look, and [hear]ing Sense divine come mended from her Tongue ⟨*When I should be at my Devotions*⟩ When the rest of the family are at their devotions I am paying ⟨*mine*⟩ my Devoirs across a Tea Table to Orlinda ⟨*When I attempt to Sle*⟩ I go to bed and lie ruminating on the same, till morning Wakes me, and robs me of my Bliss. . . .

Oh Tea, how shall I curse thy once delightful but new detested stream. May I never taste thy Waters more, for thy Waters will forever bring the Remembrance of Orlindas Cruelty, my eager Wishes and fatal Disappointment. Or if I must taste, for my cup from thy stream may I drink whole Buckettsfull from Lethe to forget my Woe, ⟨*which that would otherwise without such an Antidote always renew*⟩.

In the battle between practicality and passion, it was practicality which finally won out.

For Adams, anything that was not useful was to be shunned. The only art to be valued was that with a moral lesson.[15] He was an avid reader, but read for what he might learn. He was interested in literary style, but this interest was primarily because stylistic eloquence was useful in all of the professions in which he engaged. Adams did not totally condemn the study of such unproductive activities as dancing, fencing, and music (possibly because he was motivated to view any mastery as desirable); but, as he explained in the diary, he would rather that his children "should be ignorant of em all than fond of any one of em" (II, p. 47). Beyond the importance of mastery, such activities were regarded as a mark of vanity.

Early in the diary Adams acknowledged that vanity was his "cardinal Vice and cardinal Folly," requiring "the strictest caution and watchfulness" (I, p. 25); and, as the diary progressed, his concern grew, until he could even welcome personal attacks because they reminded him to avoid vain behavior. "Good treatment," he concluded, "makes me think I am admired, beloved, and [my] own Vanity will be indulged in me. So I dismiss my Gard and grow weak, silly, vain, conceited, ostentatious. But a Check, a frown, a sneer, a Sarcasm rouses my Spirits, makes me more careful and considerate" (I, p. 69).

Although Adams became progressively concerned about the danger of vanity, his growing confidence and increasing success shifted his attention away from himself and toward others, particularly those whom he perceived as being directly or indirectly in competition with him. The reason for a remark that a friend "pretends to more genius than he has" came later in the same entry when Adams disclosed that the friend had publicly teased Adams about his knowledge thus casting doubt on Adams's level of achievement (I, p. 59).

Similarly, when a local squire boasted about his knowledge of the law (Adams's profession), Adams not only labeled him "a finished Example of self Conceit, and Vanity," but also concluded that "the instances of this Mans Vanity are innumerable—his Soul is as much Swollen as his Carcass" (II, p. 46). It is doubtful that Adams would have attacked the squire so bitterly had the man pretended to knowledge about medicine or business instead of law. Even Benjamin Franklin stands accused by Adams in the diary:

He [Franklin] has a Passion for Reputation and Fame, as strong as you can imagine, and his Time and Thoughts are chiefly employed to obtain it, and to set Tongues and Pens male and female, to celebrating him. Painters, Statuaries, Sculptors, China Potters, and all are set to work for this End. He has the most affectionate and insinuating Way of charming the Woman or the Man that he fixes on, it is the most silly and ridiculous Way imaginable, in the Sight of an American, but it succeeds, to admiration, fullsome and sickish as it is, in Europe. (II, p. 367)

Adams's accusation here stemmed not only from simple jealousy, which he readily admitted, but also from a conviction that the European regard for Franklin and deference to him over Adams were the result of his reputation and not any real superiority.

Adams found such a situation intolerable, because although he considered fame desirable and reputation a thing to be prized, he felt they were only valuable when they signified real achievement. Strongly motivated to achieve, Adams believed that significant achievement deserved notice. Anything less would be the meanest form of ingratitude and stand in opposition to natural order. Similarly, Adams considered nothing more despicable than undeserved fame, and whenever he saw someone enjoying or attempting to acquire an undeserved reputation, Adams felt it his duty to oppose this injustice.

Among his own achievements, Adams placed great value on his writing style, and his written works contributed greatly to his reputation. In this achievement the diary served not only as an example of his talent but as a place for its development. Adams consciously planned to make the improvements of style one of the principal uses of his diary (I, p. 127). One indication of this attempt can be seen in the early drafts of works included in the diary that were later published. In the manuscript of such entries there are many examples of changes made for the purpose of improving their style.

Adams's belief that art should serve a useful purpose strengthened rather than weakened his desire to master the elements of effective style. He recognized that it was through a mastery of style that one could communicate knowledge and influence emotions, and consequently, at different times in his life, he either assumed or considered assuming the roles of: student, minister, lawyer, politician, legislator, and diplomat. In each case, the value of an effective style is obvious.

Since style was an important tool for the achievement he so values, Adams could not be satisfied with a haphazard method for its attainment and concluded that he would "learn the Art soonest, and most perfectly" by reading and observing with a design to learn. Mere imitation and trust in the accidental acquisition of skill could not be trusted. Adams concluded:

To form a style, therefore, read constantly the best Authors. Get a Habit of clear Thinking and strength and Propriety and Harmony of Expression. This one Principle of Imitation would lead me thro the whole human System. A Faculty acquired accidentally, without any Endeavours or forsight of the Effect. . . . Let me recollect, and con over, all the Phenomena of Imitation that I may take advantage of this Principle in my own make, that I may learn easier and sooner.(I, pp. 84-85)

Adams followed this resolution not only in his further study of effective style but also in his own productions. Consequently, even though Adams rarely corrected his diary entries, he appears to have been reasonably careful in his style.

As this last quotation suggests, Adams was an attentive reader. He strove at all times to make those works that he most admired not merely a part of his experience, but an active part of his being. His diary shows his development of a balanced style, a forceful turn of phrase, a satiric wit, and an ear for dialogue. However, the most significant of all Adams's writing skills was characterization, which put his ability to understand human motives to good use. In attempting to understand the diary this skill can hardly be overestimated.

One particular feature of Adams's treatment of characters in the diary was his tendency to treat them as types or as representative of the human race as a whole. This tendency was enhanced by the influence on Adams of a literary genre called the prose *character*. This genre, based on principles observed in the writings of Theophrastus in the fourth century, was imitated in both British and French literature during the seventeenth and eighteenth centuries, and ultimately influenced other forms such as the essay and novel.

The Theophrastan *character* was a description or story of a fictional individual who was the embodiment of a group or class and who, though portrayed as a real person, was shown in such a way as to reveal the dominant features of that class or group. In the *character* the features which distinguish the individual from the type he is intended to represent are played down, but their existence is not denied. The heightening of certain dominant traits of persons described in the diary in the manner of the prose *character* does not necessarily detract from the realism of their portraits. Instead, by making dominant traits stand out, Adams made the person so described more vivid and real in the mind of the reader than if a more balanced portrait had been attempted.

Adams's natural tendency to form sharply defined opinions of the people he encountered was suited to the prose character, as the following entry from Adams's period as a schoolteacher shows:

I sometimes, in my sprightly moments, consider my self, in my great Chair at School, as some Dictator at the head of a commonwealth. In this little State I can discover all the great Genius's, all the surprizing actions and revolutions of the great World in miniature. I have severall renowned Generalls but 3 feet high, and several deep-projecting Politicians in peticoats. I have others catching and dissecting Flies, accumulating remarkable pebbles, cockle shells &c., with as ardent Curiosity as any Virtuoso in the royal society. Some rattle and Thunder out A, B, C, with as much Fire and impetuosity, as Alexander fought, and very often sit down and cry as heartily, upon being out spelt, as Cesar did, when at Alexanders sepulchre he recollected that the Macedonian Hero had conquered the World before his Age. At one Table sits Mr. Insipid foppling and Fluttering, spinning his whirligig, or playing with his fingers as gaily and wittily as any frenchified coxcomb brandishes his Cane or rattles his snuff box. At another sitts the polemical Divine, plodding and wrangling in his mind about Adam's fall in which we sinned all as his primmer has it. In short my little school like the great World, is made up of Kings, Politicians, Divines, L.D. [LL.D.'s?], Fops, Buffoons, Fidlers, Sychophants, Fools, Coxcombs, Chimney sweepers, and every other Character drawn in History or seen in the World. (I, pp. 13-14)

Here in Adams's fantasy are capsule portraits of the schoolchildren, not just as future adults, but also as types observable in the adults of Adams's generation. For the reader, these types become meaningful because they are applicable to his generation as well. He can recognize that "Mr. Insipid" and the would-be "Alexander" might be spiritual counterparts of some of his own associates.

Adams's adaptation of technique in the *character* contributed to the creation in the diary of portraits such as the following:

What Passion is most active and prevalent in Dr. Savel's mind? The Desire of Money. He retails Sugar by the Pound, [. . .] by the bunch, Pins, Pen knifes, to save these Articles in his family, and neat a few Shillings Profit. He makes poor People who are in his Debt pay him in Labour. He bargains with his Debtors in the 2 other Parishes for Wood, which he sends to the Landing Place, and to Dr. Marshes. Thus by practice of Physick, by trading and bargaining and scheming he picks up a Subsistance for his family and gathers very gradually, Additions to his Stock. But this is low. The same Application, and scheming in his Profession, would raise and spread him a Character, procure him profitable Business and make his fortune. But by this contemptible Dissipation of mind, among Pins, Needles, Tea, Snuff Boxes, Vendues, Loads of Wood, day labour &c. he is negligent of the Theory of his Profession, and will live and die unknown.—These driveling souls. oh! He aims not at fame, only at a Living and a fortune! (I, pp. 52-53)

This portrait might well be a *character* of the avaricious man. It is developed in the manner of the prose *character* by the inclusion of "many concrete but independent actions."[16] There is no necessary order to the instances of behavior listed. It is the accumulated effect of a number of actions that creates the portrait of the person described in a *character*. Adams concluded the entry by commenting on the person described, and thus highlighted his relationship to the character trait discussed. Adams's own value system was the opposite of that of Dr. Savel; his goal was fame, and his fear, to die unknown. Through such insights into Adams's own personality, portraits of others advance the principal focus of the diary.

In examining the *characters* which Adams incorporated in the diary, the reader sees a portrait emerge which is of greater consequence to the diary than any of the character studies exhibited thus far. It is a portrait of Adams himself, and, as with others, Adams resorted to a type. The figure Adams used for this purpose was Hercules as portrayed in a classical fable:

.—Two Ladies are before him: The one, presenting to his View, not the Ascent of Virtue only, tho that is steep and rugged, but a Mountain quite inaccessible, a Path beset with Serpents, and Beasts of Prey, as well as Thorns and Briars, Precipices of Rocks over him, a Gulph yawning beneath, and the Sword of Damocles [over] his Head.—The other displaying to his View, Pleasures, of every Kind, Honours, such as the World calls by that Name, and showers of Gold and Silver.

If we recollect what a Mass of Corruption human Nature has been, in general, since the Fall of Adam, we may easily judge what the Consequences will be.   (II, p. 75)

Adams viewed himself and all the members of his society as facing this choice between vice and virtue. He was not hopeful about the chances for others to surmount this temptation. While not himself a Calvinist, he shared the Calvinist's view of the depravity of the average human being. However, despite the reference to the "Fall of Adam" in the last sentence, Adams did not base his opinion about human depravity on a belief in original sin. His conclusion was drawn not from a consideration of scripture, but rather from an examination of historical evidence. It was in this evidence that Adams found corruption.

The first mention in the diary of the choice of Hercules came at a point in Adams's life at which he had found his own behavior deserving of criticism. He himself was guilty of pretending to be more virtuous than he was:

Pretensions to Wisdom and Virtue, superiour to all the World, will not be supported by Words only. If I tell a man I am wiser and better than he or any other man, he will either despize, or hate, or pity me, or perhaps all 3.—I have not conversed enough with the World, to behave rightly. I talk to Paine about Greek, that makes him laugh. I talk to Sam Quincy about Resolution, and being a great Man, and study and improving Time, which makes him laugh. I talk to Ned, about the Folly of affecting to be a Heretick, which makes him mad. I talk to Hannah and Easther about the folly of Love, about despizing it, about being above it, pretend to be insensible of tender Passions, which makes them laugh. I talk to Mr. Wibirt about the Decline of Learning, tell him, I know no young fellow who promises to make a figure, cast Sneers on Dr. Marsh for not knowing the Value of old Greek and Roman Authors, ask "when will a Genius rise, that will shave his Beard, or let it grow rather and sink himself in a Cell, in order to make a figure." I talk to Parson Smith about despizing gay Dress, grand Buildings, great Estates, fame, &c. and being contented with what will satisfy the real Wants of Nature.
All This is Affectation and Ostentation. 'Tis Affectation of Learning, and Virtue and Wisdom, which I have not, and it is a weak fondness to shew all that I have, and to be thot to have more than I have. (I, pp. 67-68)

It was during this period of self-criticism that Adams adapted the fable to suit his own situation:

The other night, the Choice of Hercules came into my mind, and left impressions there which I hope will never be effaced nor long unheeded. I thought of writing a Fable, on the same Plan, but accommodated, by omitting some Circumstances and inserting others, to my own Case.
Let Virtue address me—"Which, dear Youth, will you prefer? a Life of Effeminancy, Indolence and obscurity, or a Life of Industry, Temperance, and Honour? Take my Advice, rise and mount your Horse, by the Mornings dawn, and shake away amidst the great and beautiful scenes of Nature, that appear at that Time of the day, all the Crudities that are left in your stomach, and all the obstructions that are left in your Brains. Then return to your Study, and bend your whole soul to the Institutes of the Law, and the Reports of Cases, that have been adjudged by the Rules, in the Institutes. Let no trifling

Diversion or amuzement or Company decoy you from your Books, i.e. let no Girl, no Gun, no Cards, no flutes, no Violins, no Dress, no Tobacco, no Laziness, decoy you from your Books. (By the Way, Laziness, Languor, Inattention, are my Bane, am too lazy to rise early and make a fire, and when my fire is made, at 10 o'clock my Passion for knowledge, fame, fortune or any good, is too languid, to make me apply with Spirit to my Books. And by Reason of my Inattention my mind is liable to be called off from Law, by a Girl, a Pipe, a Poem, a Love Letter, a Spectator, a Play, &c.) But, keep your Law Book or some Point of Law in your mind at least 6 Hours in a day.   (I, p. 72)

As Adams became habituated to the examination of his world in terms of this choice, the standards which he set were absolute. Only the two paths were offered. It was only after a long period of self-examination that Adams finally began to consider himself one of the select few who had chosen the virtuous path. He was, therefore, especially proud whenever he chose to sacrifice his own good in the furtherance of his principles. His decision to defend the soldiers involved in the Boston massacre was one such choice.

By viewing life according to the pattern of the fable, he could consider the difficulties and opposition which he faced as the necessary result of his choice. Therefore, adversity only served to further convince Adams of his own virtue.

Adams saw himself reaping the final rewards of Hercules—not any present luxury or rest, but rather a final vindication after death. Any achievement, even his election to the presidency, was not as great a source of pride as the struggle and danger of the path of virtue. The diary is a record of his struggle. It was Adams's guide to the path that should be followed and his warning against the path taken by most men. A comparison between Adams's use of the diary to serve as evidence of his virtue and the Puritan's as search for proof of election is an important one. Even today the diary is proof of Adams's worth. If not another one of his works was extant, the diary would be sufficient evidence that John Adams was a man worthy to be remembered.

CHAPTER 7

Afterword

THE American diary tradition did not end with the coming
of the nineteenth century; it continued to develop and to
in new directions. Changes in the diary form can be related to
almost all of the major political, social, and artistic
movements; however, if one factor ought to be singled out as
contributing most significantly to the shift between the diaries
treated in this volume and those of the period that followed, it
should be the shift in the people's sense of national identity as
America moved from colony to new nation.

The "revolution in the system of religion" which Paine in
his *Age of Reason* had predicted would follow political revolution did not come to pass. As religion was not directly affected
by the American Revolution, so spiritual journals like those
written during the colonial sentiment grew more diverse, so
the range of spiritual journals widened. Some of these
spiritual journals are so different that they can be considered
to constitute new types.

One important new form which evolved from the spiritual
journal is the Transcendentalist journal. Emerson and those
who shared his views moved from a vision of an external God
to one that was part of each individual, and they accepted the
journal as a means of relating to this divine spirit of the universe. Indeed, this process is evident in Emerson's journal. As
the work progressed the word "God" was mentioned less frequently, but the concerns earlier writers associated with God
remained central.

The Transcendentalists' journals display two other characteristics more common and pronounced in later American
diaries than those of the colonial period: extreme length and
self-conscious literary intent. The journals of Emerson and

Thoreau each run thousands of printed pages long, several times longer than any of those studied in this work. Several colonial diaries did furnish materials for public works such as autobiographies and sermons, but in such cases artistic concerns were minor. An artistic goal was at the root of many of the Transcendentalists' diary entries.

Thoreau's *Walden* is only one example of the works of art that were derived from the pages of American diaries. In writing *Walden*, Thoreau not only imposed the artistic structure of a year's cycle of the seasons on the events of a twenty-six-month residence at Walden Pond; he also imposed this structure on entries taken from a decade of journal keeping. While this process of revision made *Walden* a more advanced artistic work than the journals, its greatness was made possible by them. It was in his journals that the moment of inspiration was captured for later revision.

After the Revolution Americans not only increasingly accepted the creative arts but they looked forward to a distinctly American literature that would have international recognition. Many of the growing number of professional writers and artists kept artistic notebooks which preserved moments of inspiration. The ideas and images recorded were important to many of the greatest writers of the period including Irving, Hawthorne, and James. In some cases a brief comment in a notebook became the impetus for a work of fiction; however, in others long entries were reworked as an important part of a fictional work. For example, Hawthorne in writing his *Blithedale Romance* borrowed significantly from the pages of his *American Notebooks*.

Independence allowed America to turn its attention westward. No longer restricted by British regulations, Americans could explore and develop western lands; no longer seeing the future determined by a European model, Americans could look to the frontier for clues to their special identity. Americans, especially the diplomats of the new nation, continued to keep diaries of travel eastward, but more significant in the development of the American diary tradition were the diaries of exploration and travel west. American explorers such as Lewis and Clark, Pike, Schoolcraft, and Fremont captured the attention of thousands of readers with their diaries of the American

West. Many of these works began as dry, official records but quickly developed into diaries of considerable merit.

War continued to inspire diary records. Just as the Revolution had spurred the production of diaries so the battles of the young republic, especially those of the Civil War, prompted many such records. In the best of these works human tragedy rather than significant encounters forms the core. Examples are works such as Mary Boykin Chesnut's *Diary from Dixie* and Kate Stone's *Brokenburn*, which picture the Civil War from the Southern Celebrations at its beginning to the Southern suffering at its end. These diaries are able to personalize the terrible effects of the conflict.

Life diaries were far more common in the nineteenth century than in the colonial period. Moreover, their entries tended to be more regular and more extensive than those of the earlier works, making them more voluminous. For example, John Quincy Adams's life diary is several times as extensive as that of his father, John. Along with this tendency toward extreme length, these works reveal an enhanced awareness of the artistic potential of the form. Reflecting the increasing diversity and complexity of American life, these diaries offer important opportunities for study.

The development of the American diary in the nineteenth century reflected the development of America itself. In shaping a nation from the wilderness, Americans of the seventeenth and eighteenth centuries had to find their national identity. Early settlers had tried to impose principles they had brought from Europe. Soon, however, they altered these intentions, because they found that as they changed the land, the land changed them. Diaries provide important clues to their writers' searches for their individual and national identities. Since 1800, American diarists have been trying to refine their vision of both self and nation, but they seem more secure about their present situation. Colonial diaries provide evidence of the existence of distinctly American situations and attitudes; later diaries assert their importance. *American* territorial expansion, *American* literature, *American* society are the concerns of the diarists of the new nation.

Notes and References

Chapter One

1. William Matthews, *American Diaries* (Berkeley, 1945), p. ix.
2. Anne Robeson Burr, *The Autobiography* (London, 1909), pp. 56-65.
3. John Adams, *Diary and Autobiography of John Adams*, ed. L. H. Butterfield, (Cambridge, 1966), II, p. 64.
4. Daniel B. Shea, Jr., *Spiritual Autobiography in Early America* (Princeton, 1968), p. x.
5. Gordon Williard Allport, *Personal Documents in Psychological Sciences*, Bulletin of the Social Science Research Council No. 49 (New York, 1942), p. 96.
6. Typical of the derogation of the diary form is the opinion of a French critic, E. Schoser, who regretted that Amiel, the great diarist, "lacked the qualities necessary for the production of real works." The error of such an assessment is pointed out in Tolstoy's accurate prophecy that the works of the critic would barely outlive their author "while the accidental unreal work of Amiel, his *Journal*, will always remain a living book, needed by men and fruitfully affecting them." Leo Tolstoy, "Introduction to Amiel's *Journal*," in *What Is Art?* Trans. Aylmer Maude (London, 1929), p. 13.
7. Ralph Waldo Emerson, *The Journals of Ralph Waldo Emerson*, ed. William H. Gilman, Alfred R. Ferguson, George P. Clark, and Merrell R. Davis (Cambridge, 1960), I, pp. 3-4.
8. Franz Kafka, *The Diaries of Franz Kafka 1910-1913* (New York, 1948), p. 36.
9. Leon Edel, *Literary Biography* (London, 1957), p. 13.
10. Andre Gide, *The Journals of Andre Gide*, trans. Justin O'Brien (New York, 1947), I, pp. 18-19.
11. George Gordon Byron, *Byron, A Self Portrait*, ed. Peter Quennell (London, 1967), I, p. 234.
12. Walt Whitman, *Complete Poetry and Selected Prose*, ed. James E. Miller, Jr. (Boston, 1959), p. 395.
13. J. Lyndon Shanley, *The Making of Walden* (Chicago, 1957), pp. 22-23.
14. Henry David Thoreau, *Thoreau's Journals* (Boston, 1949), VIII, p. 134.

15. Bronson Alcott, *The Journals of Bronson Alcott*, ed. Odell Shepard (Boston, 1938), p. 398.

16. Ms. Diary of Bronson Alcott, entry for October 3, 1835, p. 387, in Harvard University Library, Cambridge, Massachusetts.

17. Nathaniel Hawthorne, Letter to Horatio Bridge May 3, 1843, quoted in *The American Notebooks*, ed. Randall Stewart (New Haven, 1932), p. xxii.

18. Alcott, *Journals*, p. 136.

19. Emerson, *Journals*, V, p. 167.

20. Ralph Waldo Emerson, *Journals of Ralph Waldo Emerson*, ed. Edward Waldo Emerson and Waldo Emerson Forbes (Boston, 1913), IX, p. 522. Entry for June 24, 1863.

21. See Whitman's "Out of the Cradle Endlessly Rocking" and Poe's "Alone."

Chapter Two

1. Michael Wigglesworth, *Diary of Michael Wigglesworth*, ed. Edmund Morgan (Gloucester, 1970), p. 5. Hereafter all references to this work are from this edition and appear in parentheses in the text. Readers may find it useful to compare Wigglesworth's journal to that of Thomas Shepard whose sense of unworthiness before God seems less extreme. See *God's Plot* (Amherst, 1972).

2. This date marks the beginning of the extant portion of the diary. It is possible that an earlier one existed.

3. Joseph Campbell, *Hero with a Thousand Faces* (Cleveland, 1949).

4. It may be more than coincidence that the most significant decline in Wigglesworth's diary production coincided with the point at which his wife could have recognized her pregnancy.

5. An interesting diary to consider along with Brainerd's is that of David McClure (New York, 1899). Most of this work covers a religious mission to the Indians on the frontier in 1772-1773.

6. David Brainerd, *Memoirs of the Reverend David Brainerd, Missionary to the Indians*, ed. Jonathan Edwards and revised by Sereno Edwards Dwight (New Haven, 1822), p. 30. Reprinted 1970 by Scholarly Press. Hereafter all references to this work are from this edition and appear in parentheses in the text.

7. The proper term for this religious group is the Society of Friends, but the popular term Quaker is accepted.

8. See George Fox, *Journal*, ed. John L. Nickalls (Cambridge, Eng., 1952).

9. John Woolman, *The Journal and Main Essays of John Woolman* (New York, 1971), p. 23. Hereafter all references to this work are from this edition and appear in parentheses in the text.

10. John Wesley, 1703-1791, founder of Methodism. His diary includes a mission to America. See Rev. John Wesley, *The Journals of John Wesley A.M.*, ed Nehemiah Curnock (London, 1909-16).

11. George Whitefield, 1714-1770, Methodist evangelist preacher. His first of several missions to America occurred in 1739. See George Whitefield, *Journals* (London, 1960).

12. Francis Asbury, *Journals and Letters of Francis Asbury*, I (Nashville, 1938), p. 722. Hereafter all references to this work are from this edition and appear in parentheses in the text.

13. Lorenzo Dow, *The Life, Travels, Labors and Writings of Lorenzo Dow; Including His Singular and Erratic Wanderings in Europe and America* (New York, 1881), pp. 13-14.

Chapter Three

1. George Winship Parker's Introduction to Sarah Kemble Knight, *The Journal of Sarah Kemble Knight*, originally edited by Theodore Dwight (New York, 1935), p. iii. Hereafter all references to this work are from this edition and appear in parentheses in the text. Two critics provide commentary and are rare exceptions to the general tendency to ignore the place of diaries as literature. Robert O. Stephens in "The Odyssey of Sarah Kemble Knight," *CLA* 7 (March 1964), 247-55, shows how Knight's description of her adventures follows a "mock heroic" style born of a familiarity with Homer. Peter Thorpe in "Sarah Kemble Knight and the Picaresque Tradition" provides an alternate explanation, attributing Madam Knight's style to her adaptation of techniques from picaresque literature.

2. David McClure, *Diary of David McClure*, ed. F. B. Dexter (New York, 1899), pp. 117-18.

3. Carl Bridenbaugh's Introduction to Dr. Alexander Hamilton, *A Gentleman's Progress: The Itinerarium of Dr. Alexander Hamilton*, ed. Carl Bridenbaugh (Chapel Hill, 1948), p. xxv. Hereafter all references to this work are from this edition and appear in parentheses in the text.

4. Philip Vickers Fithian, *Journal and Letters of Philip Vickers Fithian 1773-1774: A Plantation Tutor of the Old Dominion*, ed. Hunter Dickinson Farish (Charlottesville, 1968), p. 162. Hereafter all references to this work are from this edition and appear in parentheses in the text.

5. Fithian's other diaries for 1774-1776 appear with the plantation diary in the three volumes of Philip Vickers Fithian, *Journals and Letters*, ed. J. R. Williams (Princeton, 1904).

6. For a biography of John Morgan see Whitfield J. Bell, Jr., *John Morgan Continental Doctor* (Philadelphia, 1965).

7. Most of his work has not yet been published. The manuscript

for the travel journal of 1764 and a later portion describing his work as a physician (1781-1784) are in the collection of the Pennsylvania Historical Society.

8. This and the following quotation come from the manuscript diary for August 1764.

9. One of the people Morgan met during his travels was the famous diarist and biographer James Boswell. Unfortunately Morgan left no extant record of this portion of his trip.

10. John Morgan, "A Visit to Voltaire," *Pennsylvania Magazine of History and Biography*, X (1866), 45. Hereafter all references to this work are from this edition and appear in parentheses in the text.

11. Henry St. John, 1st Viscount Bolingbroke, 1678-1751, English politician and philosopher.

12. The diary of John Adams, discussed later in this work, includes a considerable number of entries covering his diplomatic missions.

13. Gouverneur Morris, *A Diary of the French Revolution,* ed. Beatrix Cary Davenport (Boston, 1939), I, p. 246. Hereafter all references to this work are from this edition and appear in parentheses in the text.

14. Beginning in August 1792 Morris's diary underwent two significant alterations. Entries became briefer and less personal until they finally deteriorated to notes on the day's weather. The diary resumed in October of 1794 as Morris left France; but, although it continued until the year of Morris's death (1816) it never regained the vibrancy of the earlier portion. Certainly the unity of situation was missing. This diary is available in Volume II of *The Diary and Letters of Gouverneur Morris,* ed. Ann Cary Morris (New York, 1888).

Chapter Four

1. John Smith, *Hannah Logan's Courtship,* ed. Albert C. Myers (Philadelphia, 1904), p. 96. Hereafter all references to this work are from this edition and appear in parentheses in the text.

2. William Black, "Journal of William Black," ed. R. Alonzo Brock, *Pennsylvania Magazine of History and Biography* I (1877), 242. Hereafter all references to this work are from this edition and appear in parentheses in the text. (References to pages 40-49 are to Volume II.)

3. Sarah Wister, *Sally Wister's Journal,* ed. Albert Cook Meyer (New York, 1969), pp. 91-94. Hereafter all references to this work are from this edition and appear in parentheses in the text.

4. Frances (Burney) D'Arbley, *Evelina* (New York, 1958), pp. 24-25.

5. Sarah (Sally) Jones, Sally Wister's aunt, "was only one year older than the niece," Sally Wister, *Journal*, p. 65n.

6. Anne Home Livingston, *Nancy Shippen, Her Journal Book*, ed. Ethel Armes (Philadelphia, 1935), p. 139. Reprinted by Arno Press 1968. Hereafter all references to this work are from this edition and appear in parentheses in the text.

7. Françoise Maintenon, Marquise de Aubigne, morganatic second wife of Louis XIV.

8. As in many published versions of diaries, the editor inserted letters in chronological sequence. Such letters can alter the effect of the diary even as they add valuable information. A reader should recognize the difference between such editorial insertions and those letters which the diarist copies into a work.

Chapter Five

1. Rogers kept several diaries during the French and Indian War, including scouting journals and an account of the siege of Detroit. A later work covers his service as an officer at Fort Michillimackinec.

2. George Washington kept a diary which (with substantial gaps) runs from 1748 to 1799, but most of this work, including material covering the Revolution, is limited to brief notes and to terse lists of facts. The standard edition of the complete diary is *The Diary of George Washington, 1748-1799*, ed. John C. Fitzpatrick (Boston, 1925). The early frontier portion has been published separately in *The Journal of Major George Washington* (Williamsburg, 1959).

3. Among the better diaries of soldiers during the Revolution are those of Amos Farnsworth, a private at the Battle of Bunker Hill, whose erratic spelling need not spoil an effective narrative, and General William Heath, most of whose diary was written in a period in which he was no longer entrusted with combat operations. Among the most interesting of the diaries kept by British soldiers during the Revolution is that of Frederick Mackenzie, a British adjutant whose work includes accounts of the battles of Lexington and Concord.

4. Arnold was not present when the agreement Beebe objects to was made; he only accepted it later to prevent a massacre by the Indians. See Frederick R. Kirkland, ed., "Journal of a Physician in the Expedition against Canada," *Pennsylvania Magazine of History and Biography*, 59 (October 1935), 33ln.

5. Dr. Lewis Beebe, "Journal of a Physician in the Expedition against Canada," ed. Frederick R. Kirkland, *Pennsylvania Magazine of History and Biography*, 59 (October 1935), 331. Reprinted in book form by New York Times and Arno Press, 1970. Hereafter all references to this work are from this edition and appear in parentheses in the text.

6. Dr. Albigence Waldo, "Valley Forge, 1777-1778. Diary of Sur-

geon Albigence Waldo, of the Connecticut Line," *Pennsylvania Magazine of History and Biography*, 21 (1897), 299-323. Hereafter all references to this work are from this edition and appear in parentheses in the text.

7. Charles Herbert, *A Relic of the Revolution*, ed. Rev. R. Livesey (Boston, 1847), p. 50. Hereafter all references to this work are from this edition and appear in parentheses in the text. This edition was reprinted by the New York Times and Arno Press, 1968.

8. Dr. James Thacher, *Military Journal during the American Revolution*, ed. Peter Decker (New York, 1969), p. 100. Hereafter all references to this work are from this edition and appear in parentheses in the text.

9. Baron DeKalb's remarks are quoted from Don Higgenbotham, *The War of American Independence* (New York, 1971), p. 399.

10. Josiah Atkins, *The Diary of Josiah Atkins*, ed. Steven E. Kagle (New York, 1975). Hereafter all references to this work are from this edition and appear in parentheses in the text.

11. *Exodus* 2.22.

12. Nicholas Cresswell, *The Journal of Nicholas Cresswell, 1774-1777* (New York, 1924).

13. John Boyle, "Journal of Public Occurrences in Boston," *New England Historical and Genealogical Register*, LXXXIV (1930), 142ff.

14. Samuel Curwen, *Journal of Samuel Curwen Loyalist*, ed. Andrew Oliver (Cambridge, 1972).

15. Margaret Morris, "Private Diary of Margaret Morris," in *Letters of Doctor Richard Hill and His Children*, ed. John Jay Smith (Philadelphia, 1854), p. 339. Hereafter all references to this work are from this edition and appear in parentheses in the text.

16. Born Margaret Hill.

17. Margaret Morris, "Private Journal Kept during a Portion of the Revolutionary War," in *Letters of Doctor Richard Hill and His Children*, ed. John Jay Smith (Philadelphia, 1854), p. 210. This volume, containing both Morris diaries, has modernized spelling and punctuation. The Revolutionary War journal with an unaltered form is available in the limited edition of *Margaret Morris, Her Journal*, ed. John W. Jackson (Philadelphia, 1949).

18. James Allen, "The Diary of James Allen, Esquire, of Philadelphia," *Pennsylvania Magazine of History and Biography*, IX (1885), 197.

19. James Allen's three brothers shared his views opposing both the British mistreatment of the colonies and American separation from the mother country. Andrew Allen had been a member of Congress but left it when Congress concluded to declare independence; William Allen, a lieutenant General in the American forces during

the Canadian Campaign, resigned his commission and formed the Pennsylvania Loyalists to fight on the side of the British. They and the eldest brother, John Allen, sought the protection of the British General Howe in December 1776. See the notes to Allen's diary pp. 176-7, 191-3.

20. Samuel Rowland Fisher, "The Journal of Samuel Roland Fisher," *Pennsylvania Magazine of History and Biography*, 41 (1917), 149.

Chapter Six

1. One possible exception may be that of John Woolman. The fact that what survives has been edited makes it difficult to decide the extent to which the original work was focused as a spiritual journal.

2. As these comments should indicate, I define a life diary in terms that make it distinct from what Fothergill calls "serial autobiography." Both terms refer to diaries kept over a long period; however, the crucial distinction of a life diary is that it transcends limits of focus and situation, while a "serial autobiography" is distinguished by the author's "autobiographical consciousness ... the sense that one is living a *Life*, that an organic story links one's days together." Robert A. Fothergill, *Private Chronicles* (London, 1974), p. 153.

3. John Winthrop, *Winthrop's Journal*, ed. J. Franklin Jameson (New York, 1908), I, p. 88. Hereafter all references to this work are from this edition and appear in parentheses in the text.

4. Entitled "The Model of Christian Charity," this sermon was delivered aboard the *Arbella*, flagship of the fleet that brought Winthrop and his party to New England in 1630.

5. William Mathews, *American Diaries, An Annotated Bibliography of American Diaries Written Prior to the Year 1861* (Berkeley, 1945), p. 7.

6. Samuel Sewall, *The Diary of Samuel Sewall*, ed. Halsey Thomas (New York, 1973), pp. v-vi. Hereafter all references to this work are from this edition and appear in parentheses in the text.

7. William Byrd, *The Secret Diary of William Byrd of Westover 1709-1712*, ed. Louis B. Wright and Marion Tinling (Richmond, 1941), p. 101.

8. William Byrd, *The London Diary (1717-21) and Other Writings*, ed. Louis B. Wright and Marion Tinling (New York, 1958), p. 161.

9. William Byrd, *Another Secret Diary of William Byrd of Westover 1739-1741*, ed. Maude H. Woodfin (Richmond, 1942).

10. William Byrd, *The Secret History of the Dividing Line*, ed.

William K. Boyd (New York, 1967), p. 43. Hereafter all references to this work are from this edition and appear in parentheses in the text.

11. See Richard Mather, *Journal of Richard Mather* (Boston, 1850); and Increase Mather, *Diary* (Cambridge, 1900).

12. Cotton Mather, *Diary of Cotton Mather,* ed. Worthington Chauncey Ford (New York, 1957), I, p. 3. Hereafter all references to this work are from this edition and appear in parentheses in the text.

13. John Adams, *Diary and Autobiography of John Adams,* ed. L. H. Butterfield (Boston, 1961), I, pp. 127-28. Hereafter all references to this work are from this edition and appear in parentheses in the text.

14. John Adams, *Earliest Diary of John Adams,* ed. L. H. Butterfield (Boston, 1966), p. 70.

15. Edmund Morgan, "John Adams and the Puritan Tradition," *New England Quarterly,* XXXIV (December 1961), 521.

16. Benjamin Boyce, *The Theophrastan Character* (Cambridge, 1947), p. 273.

Selected Bibliography

PRIMARY SOURCES

1. American Diaries (seventeenth and eighteenth century)

ADAMS, JOHN. *The Adams Papers: Diary and Autobiography of John Adams*. Ed. L. H. Butterfield. Four Vols. Cambridge: Belknap Press, 1961.

———. *The Earliest Diary of John Adams*. The Adams Papers. Ed. L. H. Butterfield. Cambridge: Belknap Press, 1966.

ALLEN, JAMES. "The Diary of James Allen, Esquire, of Philadelphia." *Pennsylvania Magazine of History and Biography*, 9 (1885), 176-96, 278-96, 424-41.

ASBURY, FRANCIS. *Journals and Letters of Francis Asbury*. Two Vols. Nashville: Abingdon Press, 1958.

ATKINS, JOSIAH. *The Diary of Josiah Atkins*. Ed. Steven E. Kagle. New York: New York Times and Arno Press, 1975.

BEEBE, DR. LEWIS. "Journal of a Physician in the Expedition against Canada." Ed. Frederick R. Kirkland. *Pennsylvania Magazine of History and Biography*, 59 (October 1935), 321-61. Rept. Arno, 1970.

BLACK, WILLIAM. "Journal of William Black." *Pennsylvania Magazine of History and Biography*. 1 (1877), 117-32, 233-49, 404-19, and 2 (1878), 40-49.

BOYLE, JOHN. "Public Journal, January 1759-April 1778." *New England Historical and Genealogical Register*, 84 (1930), 142-71, 248-72, 357-82, and 85 (1931), 5-28, 117-33.

BRAINERD, DAVID. *Memoirs of the Rev. David Brainerd; Missionary to the Indians on the Border of New York, New Jersey, and Pennsylvania*. Ed. Sereno Edwards Dwight. New Haven: S. Converse, 1822. Rept. Michigan: Scholarly Press, 1970.

BYRD, WILLIAM. *The Secret Diary of William Byrd of Westover 1709-1712*. Eds. Louis B. Wright and Marion Tinling. Richmond: The Dietz Press, 1941.

———. *William Byrd of Virginia, The London Diary (1717-1721) and Other Writings*. Eds. Louis B. Wright and Marion Tinling. New York: Oxford University Press, 1958.

———. *Another Secret Diary of William Byrd of Westover 1739-1741: With Letters & Literary Exercises 1696-1726*. Ed. Maude H. Woodfin. Richmond: The Dietz Press, 1942.

————. *William Byrd's Histories of the Dividing Line Betwixt Virginia and North Carolina* (with introduction and notes by William K. Boyd and a new introduction by Percy G. Adams). New York: Dover Publications, 1967.

CRESSWELL, NICHOLAS. *The Journal of Nicholas Cresswell, 1774-1777.* London: J. Cape, 1925.

DICKINSON, JONATHAN. *Jonathan Dickinson's Journal or God's Protecting Providence.* Eds. Evangeline Walker Andrews and Charles Mclean Andrews. New Haven: Yale University Press, 1945.

DOW, LORENZO. *The Life and Travels, Labors and Writings of Lorenzo Dow; Including His Singular and Erratic Wanderings in Europe and America.* New York: R. Worthington, 1881.

FARNSWORTH, AMOS. *Diary Kept by Lieut. Amos Farnsworth of Groton, Mass., during a part of the revolutionary war. Apr. 1775-May 1779.* Ed. Samuel A. Green. Cambridge: J. Wilson and Son, 1898.

FISHER, SAMUEL ROLAND. "Journal of Samuel Roland Fisher, of Philadelphia, 1779-1781." Ed. Anna Wharton Morris. *Pennsylvania Magazine of History and Biography.* 41 , (1917), 145-97, 274-333, 399-457.

FITHIAN, PHILIP VICKERS. *Journal and Letters of Philip Vickers Fithian 1773-1774: A Plantation Tutor of the Old Dominion.* Ed. Hunter Dickinson Farish. Charlottesville: University Press of Virginia, 1968.

————. *Journal, 1775-1776: Written on the Virginia-Pennsylvania Frontier and in the Army around New York.* Eds. Robert Greenhalgh Albion and Leonidas Dodson. Princeton: Princeton University Press, 1934.

HAMILTON, DR. ALEXANDER. *A Gentleman's Progress: The Itinerarium of Dr. Alexander Hamilton.* Ed. Carl Bridenbaugh. Chapel Hill: University of North Carolina Press, 1948.

HERBERT, CHARLES. *A Relic of the Revolution.* Ed. Rev. R. Livesey. Boston: C. H. Pierce, 1844. Rept. Arno, 1968.

KNIGHT, SARAH KEMBLE. *The Journal of Madam Knight.* New York: Peter Smith, 1935.

LIVINGSTON, ANNE HOME (SHIPPEN). *Nancy Shippen, Her Journal Book: The International Romance of a Young Lady of Fashion of Colonial Philadelphia with Letters to Her and about Her.* Ed. Ethel Armes. Philadelphia: J. B. Lippincott, 1935. Rept. Arno, 1968.

MATHER, COTTON. *Diary of Cotton Mather.* Ed. Worthington Chauncey Ford. New York: Frederick Ungar Publishing Co., 1957. Two Vols.

————. *The Diary of Cotton Mather for the Year 1712.* Ed. William

Manniere II. Charlottesville: University of Virginia Press, 1964.

MATHER, INCREASE. *Diary by Increase Mather*. Ed. Samuel A. Green. Cambridge: J. Wilson, 1900.

MATHER, RICHARD. *Journal of Richard Mather 1635. His Life and Death 1670*. Boston: David Clapp, 1850. Rept. 1874.

McCLURE, DAVID. *The Diary of David McClure*. Ed. F. B. Dexter. New York: Knickerbocker Press, 1899.

MORGAN, DR. JOHN. "A Visit to Voltaire." *Pennsylvania Magazine of History and Biography*, 10 (1886), 43-50.

MORRIS, GOVERNEUR. *A Diary of the French Revolution*. Ed. Beatrix Cary Davenport. Boston: Houghton Mifflin Co., 1939.

———. *Diary and Letters of Governeur Morris*. Ed. Anne C. Morris. Two. Vols. New York: Scribner's, 1888. Rept. DaCapo, 1969.

MORRIS, MARGARET. *Margaret Morris: Her Journal with Biographical Sketch and Notes*. Ed. John W. Jackson. Philadelphia: George S. MacManus Co., 1949.

———. "The Private Diary of Margaret Morris, Daughter of Dr. Richard Hill," and "Private Journal Kept During the Revolutionary War for the Amusement of a Sister." In *Letters of Doctor Richard Hill and His Children*. Ed. John Jay Smith. Philadelphia: Privately Printed, 1854. Rept. Arno, 1969.

SEWALL, SAMUEL. *The Diary of Samuel Sewall 1674-1729*. Ed. M. Halsey Thomas. Newly edited from the manuscript at the Massachusetts Historical Society. New York: Farrar, Straus & Giroux, 1973.

SHEPARD, THOMAS. *God's Plot: The Paradoxes of Puritan Piety, Being the Autobiography & Journal of Thomas Shepard*. Ed. Michael McGiffert. Amherst: University of Massachusetts Press, 1972.

SMITH, JOHN. *Hannah Logan's Courtship*. Philadelphia: Ferris and Leach, 1904.

STILES, EZRA. *The Literary Diary of Ezra Stiles*. Ed. F. B. Dexter. Three Vols. New York: Charles Scribner's Sons, 1901.

THACHER, DR. JAMES, *Military Journal of the American Revolution*. Hartford: Hurlbut, Williams, and Co., 1862. Rept. Arno, 1969.

WALDO, DR. ALBIGENCE. "Valley Forge, 1777-1778. Diary of Surgeon Albigence Waldo, of the Connecticut Line." *Pennsylvania Magazine of History and Biography*, 21 (1897), 299-323.

WIGGLESWORTH, MICHAEL. *Diary of Michael Wigglesworth*. Ed. Edmund Morgan. Gloucester: Peter Smith, 1970.

WINTHROP, JOHN. *Winthrop's Journal: The History of New England 1630-1641*. Ed. James Kendall Hosmer, L.L.D. New York: Charles Scribner's Sons and Co., 1908. Rept. Barnes and Noble, 1959.

WISTER, SALLY. *Sally Wister's Journal*. Ed. Albert Cook Meyers. New York: The New York Times and Arno Press, 1969.

WOOLMAN, JOHN. *The Journal and Major Essays of John Woolman.* Ed. Phillips P. Moulton. New York: Oxford University Press, 1971.

2. Other Materials

ALCOTT, BRONSON. *The Journals of Bronson Alcott.* Ed. Odell Shepard. Two Vols. Boston: Little, Brown and Co., 1938.

BRADFORD, WILLIAM, and WINSLOW, EDWARD. *Mourt's Relation.* New York: S. Wiley, 1848.

BYRON, GEORGE GORDON. *Byron, A Self Portrait.* Ed. Peter Quennell. London: John Murray, 1967.

CURWEN, SAMUEL. *Journal of Samuel Curwen Loyalist.* Ed. Andrew Oliver. Two Vols. Cambridge: Harvard University Press, 1972.

EMERSON, RALPH WALDO. *Journals of Ralph Waldo Emerson.* Eds. Edward Waldo Emerson and Waldo Emerson Forbes. Ten Vols. Boston: Houghton Mifflin and Co., 1909-1914.

————. *The Journals and Miscellaneous Notebooks of Ralph Waldo Emerson.* Eds. William H. Gilman, Alfred R. Ferguson, George P. Clark and Merrell R. Davis. Fourteen Vols. Cambridge: Belknap Press, 1960-1978.

GIDE, ANDRÉ. *The Journals of André Gide.* Trans. Justin O'Brien. New York: Alfred A. Knopf, 1947.

HAWTHORNE, NATHANIEL. Letter to Horatio Bridge May 3, 1843, quoted in *The American Notebooks.* Ed. Randall Stewart. New Haven: Yale University Press, 1932.

KAFKA, FRANZ. *The Diaries of Franz Kafka 1910-1913.* New York: Schocken Books, 1948.

MACKENZIE, FREDERICK. *Diary of Frederick Mackenzie.* Two Vols. Eyewitness Accounts of the American Revolution Ser. no. 1, 1968; rept. of 1930 ed.

THOREAU, HENRY DAVID. *Journal of Henry D. Thoreau.* Eds. Bradford Torrey and Francis H. Allen. Fourteen Vols. Boston: Houghton Mifflin Co., 1949.

WASHINGTON, GEORGE. *The Diaries of George Washington, 1748-1799.* Ed. John C. Fitzpatrick. Four Vols. Boston and New York: Houghton Mifflin Co., 1925.

————. *The Journal of Major George Washington.* Charlottesville: University Press of Virginia, 1959. Rept. 1972.

WESLEY, REV. JOHN. *The Journals of Rev. John Wesley, A. M.* Ed. Nehemiah Curnock. London: Epworth Press, 1909-16.

WHITEFIELD, GEORGE. *Journals.* London: Banner of Truth Trust, 1960.

WHITMAN, WALT. *Complete Poetry and Selected Prose.* Ed. James E. Miller, Jr. Boston: Houghton Mifflin Co., 1959.

SECONDARY SOURCES

1. Bibliography
FORBES, HARRIETTE MERRIFIELD. *New England Diaries 1602-1800: A*

2. Other Materials
ALLPORT, GORDON WILLARD. *Personal Documents in Psychological Science*. Bulletin of the Social Science Research Council no. 49. New York: Social Science Research Council, 1942. Discusses psychology of diary-keeping process.
BACON, WALLACE A., and BREEN, ROBERT S. *Literature as Experience*. New York: McGraw Hill, 1959. Discusses the relationship between art and life.
BELL, WHITFIELD J., JR. *John Morgan, Continental Doctor*. Philadelphia: University of Pennsylvania Press, 1965. Biography covers period of diary.
BOYCE, BENJAMIN. *The Theophrastan Character*. Cambridge: Harvard University Press, 1947.
BURR, ANNE ROBESON. *The Autobiography*. London: Constable and Co. Limited, 1909.
CAMPBELL, JOSEPH. *Hero with a Thousand Faces*. Cleveland: World, 1949.
CROWDER, RICHARD. *No Featherbed to Heaven: A Biography of Michael Wigglesworth 1631-1705*. Michigan: Michigan State University Press, 1969. Covers material relevant to Wigglesworth's diary.
DETOCQUEVILLE, ALEXIS. *Democracy in America*. Ed. J. P. Mayer. Garden City: Doubleday, 1969.
EDEL, LEON. *Literary Biography*. London: Rupert Hart-Davis, 1957.
FOTHERGILL, ROBERT A. *Private Chronicles*. London: Oxford University Press, 1974. This excellent analysis of the British diary tradition provides valuable commentary on the diary form.
GUMMERE, RICHARD MOTT. "Byrd and Sewall, Two Colonial Classicists." *Publications of the Colonial Society of Massachusetts*, 42 (1964), 156-73. Illustrates some classical elements in the works of these two diarists.
HIGGENBOTHAM, DON. *The War of American Independence*. New York: The Macmillan Co., 1971.
MARGOLIES, ALAN. "The Editing and Publication of 'The Journal of Madam Knight.'" *Papers of the Bibliographical Society of America*, 58 (1964), 25-32. Traces the process of authenticating *Descriptive Catalogue of Diaries, Orderly Books, and Sea Journals*. New York: Russell and Russell, 1923.
MATTHEWS, WILLIAM. *American Diaries: An Annotated Bibliog-*

raphy of American Diaries Written Prior to the Year 1861. Berkeley and Los Angeles: University of California Press, 1945.

———. *American Diaries in Manuscript 1580-1954. A Descriptive Bibliography*. Athens: University of Georgia Press, 1974. and preparing an accurate edition of a diary. This work shows the difficulties and pitfalls encountered by editors and commentators.

McCLELLAND, DAVID *The Achieving Society*. Princeton: D. Van Nostrand Co., Inc., 1961.

MILLER, PERCY, and JOHNSON, THOMAS H., eds. *The Puritans*. 2 Vols. New York: Harper and Row, 1963. Anthology of Puritan writing including diaries with prefatory sections that offer an excellent introduction to the period.

———. *The New England Mind*. Vol I. *The Seventeenth Century*. Cambridge: Harvard University Press, 1939. Vol. II. *From Colony to Province*. Cambridge: Harvard University Press, 1953. Excellent analysis of New England culture.

MORGAN, EDMUND. "John Adams and the Puritan Tradition." *New England Quarterly*, 34 (December 1961)518-21.

MURDOCK, KENNETH B. *Literature and Theology in Colonial New England*. New York: Harper and Row, 1963. Considers diaries of colonial New England and their relation to the religious concerns and practices of the period.

PASCAL, ROY. *Design and Truth in Autobiography*. London: Routledge and Kegan Paul Ltd., 1923. Discusses distinction between diary and other autobiography, pp. 3-5.

PEARCE, ROY HARVEY. "Sterne and Sensibility in American Diaries." *Modern Language Notes*, 59 (June 1944), 403-407. Discusses use of literary expressions of sensibility in American diaries as an indication that this attitude from Sterne's writings had an influence in America prior to its appearance in American novels. Pearce mentions Waldo among other diarists.

PIERCY, JOSEPHINE. *Studies in Literary Types in Seventeenth Century America, 1607-1710*. Hamden, Connecticut: Archon Books, 1969. Part of chapter on "Personal Records," pp. 78-82, includes commentary on the diaries of Sewall, Cotton Mather, Anne Bradstreet, Michael Wigglesworth, John Winthrop.

PONSONBY, ARTHUR, ed. *English Diaries*. 2nd ed. London: Methuen and Co., Ltd., 1923. Introduction provides discussion of some principles related to the writing of diaries.

SHANLEY, J. LYNDON. *The Making of Walden*. Chicago: University of Chicago Press, 1957. Shows process of converting diary material into autobiographical essay.

SHAW, PETER. *The Character of John Adams*. Chapel Hill: University of North Carolina Press, 1976. Excellent analysis of personality relevant for study of the diaries.

SHEA, DANIEL B., JR. *Spiritual Autobiography in Early America*. Princeton: Princeton University Press, 1968. An effective analysis of American spiritual autobiography, it includes valuable analyses of the autobiographical writings of John Woolman and of Richard, Increase, and Cotton Mather.

SPENGEMANN, WILLIAM, and LUNDQUIST, L. R. "Autobiography and the American Myth." *American Quarterly*, 17 (Fall 1965), 501-19. Discusses autobiographical writing in America as a "cultural act" in which the author became a created character.

STEPHENS, ROBERT O. "The Odyssey of Sarah Kemble Knight." *CLA*, 7 (March 1964), 247-55. Emphasizes Knight's use of classical models to support the consideration of her diary as a literary work.

THORPE, PETER. "Sarah Kemble Knight and the Picaresque Tradition." *CLA*, 10 (December 1966), 114-21. Analysis of Knight's diary as in keeping with the tradition of picaresque fiction.

Index

Adams, Abigail, diary of, 159
Adams, Charles Francis, diary of, 160
Adams, Henry, 160
Adams, John, 120; diary of, 19, 25, 62, 143, 159-60, 170-82, 185
Adams, John Quincy, diary of, 159-60, 185
Age of Reason, The (Paine), 183
Alcott, Bronson, journals of, 25, 26
Allen, James, diary of, 130, 135-38
Allen, William, 130
Allport, Gordon, 19
American Notebooks (Hawthorne), 184
André, John, 124
Antony and Cleopatra (Shakespeare), 76
Arnold, Benedict, 102-103, 123-24
Asbury, Francis, diary of, 51, 52-54
Atkins, Josiah, diary of, 101, 127-28

Barlow, Joel, 58
Becket, Thomas à, 140
Beebe, Lewis, diary of, 101-108, 109, 123
Black, William, diary of, 85-86
Blithedale Romance, The (Hawthorne), 184
Bolingbroke, Henry St. John, 73-74
Boston Massacre, 131, 182
Boswell, James, biography of Johnson, 22, 24, 26
Boyle, John, diary of, 131
Bradford, William, diary of, 23, 27
Brainerd, David, diary of, 30, 38-46
Bridenbaugh, Carl, 63
Brokenburn (Stone), 185

Bryant, William C., diary of, 25
Burgoyne, John, 119, 122
Burney, Fanny, 88
Byrd, Lucy Park, 154
Byrd, William, diaries of, 142, 153-59
Byron, George Gordon, diary of, 23

Campbell, Joseph, 36
Cato, 75
Chandler, John, 173
Chesnut, Mary Boykin, 185
Cicero, 75
Civil War, 98, 185
Clark, George Rogers, journal of, 184
"Columbiad" (Barlow), 58-59
Conway, Thomas, 109
Cooper, James F., 25
Cresswell, Nicholas, diary of, 131
Curwen, Samuel, diary of, 131

Dana, Richard Henry, diary of, 25
DeKalb, Baron, 123
"Democratic Vistas" (Whitman), 26
Diary, definition, 15-20; as art, 20-24; tradition in America, 24-28, 185; spiritual journals, 29-57; Puritan diaries, general, 29-30, 99; Quaker diaries, general, 46-47; Methodist diaries, general, 51; travel diaries, 58-81; romantic diaries, 82-97; war diaries, general, 98-99; military diaries, general, 100-101; civilian diaries, general, 130-31; life diaries, general, 142-43; multi-generation diaries, general, 159-60; changes in diary form, 183-85
Diary from Dixie (Chesnut), 185

Dickinson, Emily, 27
Dow, Lorenzo, diary of, 51, 54-57
Dudley, Thomas, 143-44

Edel, Leon, 22
Education of Henry Adams, The, 160
Edwards, Jonathan, 27, 39, 41, 52
Eliot, T. S., 140
Emerson Ralph Waldo, journal of, 21, 25, 26, 183-84
Evelina (Burney), 88

Fisher, Samuel Rowland, diary of, 131, 138-41
Fithian, Philip Vickers, diaries of, 58, 67-71, 82
Flahaut, Comtesse de, 77-78
Fox, George, diary of, 46-47
Franklin, Benjamin, 120, 176; *Autobiography* of, 25, 159
Fremont, John Charles, journal of, 184
French and Indian Wars, 27, 98
French Revolution, 76-81

Gates, Horatio, 104, 119, 122
Gide, André, journal of, 22, 26
Goethe, Johann, diaries of, 21
Green, Thomas, 173

Hamilton, Dr. Alexander, diary of, 58, 63-67
Hamilton Andrew, 130
Hancock, John, 118
Hannah Logan's Courtship. See Smith, John, diary of
Hawthorne, Nathaniel, 184; diary of, 25
Harvard College, 34
Heath, William, 121
Herbert, Charles, diary of, 101, 114-21
History of New England, The. See Winthrop, John, diary of
History of the Dividing Line, A (Byrd), 153
Howe, William, 119
Hutchinson, Ann, 147

Iliad (Homer), 76

Irving, Washington, diary of, 25, 184

James, Henry, 184
Jefferson, Thomas, 76
Johnson, Samuel, 26
Jones, Sally, 88
"Journal of Occurrences." *See* Boyle, John, journal of
Journey to the Land of Eden (Byrd), 153

Kafka, Franz, 21
Kemble, Fanny, diary of, 21
Knight, Sarah Kemble, diary of, 58, 59-63

Lafayette, Marquis de, 76, 109
Law, Jonathan, 63
Lee, "Lighthorse Harry," 103
Lewis, Meriwether, journal of, 184
Livingston, Anne Home, diary of, 82, 83, 92-97
Livingston, Henry B., 93
Locke, John, 74
Logan, Hannah, 82, 83-85, 92
Logan, William, 83
Longfellow, Henry Wadsworth, diary of, 25
Louis XVI, 76
Louisiana Purchase, 27

Maintenon, Marquise de, 94
Marlowe, Christopher, 93
Matthews, William, 148
Mather, Cotton, 152; diary of, 25, 30, 143, 159, 160-70, 172-73
Mather, Increase, 150, 152; diary of, 159, 160
Mather, Increase (son of Cotton), 169-70, 172
Mather, Richard, diary of, 159, 160
McClure, David, journal of, 63
McKean, Thomas, 138
Melville, Herman, diary of, 25
Memoirs of Brainerd (Edwards), 38-39
Mirabeau, Comte de, 76
Moby Dick (Melville), 112
Morgan, John, diary of, 71, 75
Morris, Governeur, diary of, 75-81

Morris, Margaret, journal of, 131-35
Murder in the Cathedral (Eliot), 140

Necker, Jacques, 76
Newton, Isaac, 74
Norris, Deborah, 87-88

Otto, Louis G., 93-97

Paine, Thomas, 183
Pemberton, Ebenezer, 151-53
Pemberton, Thomas, 151
Pepys, Samuel, diary of, 149
"Personal Narrative" (Edwards), 41
Pike, Zebulon, journal of, 184
Poe, Edgar A., 27
Progress to the Mines, A (Byrd), 153
Putnam, Israel, 133

Quebec Act, 27
Quincy, Hannah, 174-75, 181
Quincy, Samuel, 181

Revolutionary War, 27, 58, 71, 72, 88, 92, 98-141, 184-85
Rogers, Robert, 98
Romantic Movement, 59

Salem witchcraft trials, 149-50, 161-63
Sally Wister's Journal. See Wister, Sally, journal of
Savel, Dr., 179-80
Scipio, 75
Seargent, Jonathan, 138
Secret History of the Dividing Line, The; see Byrd, William, diaries of
Sewall, Samuel, diary of, 30, 82, 142, 147-53
Shippen, Nancy; see Livingston, Anne Home
Shippen, William, 93
Singleton, John, 64
Smallwood, General, 86-87, 90
Smith, John, 92; diary of, 82, 83-85
"Song of Myself" (Whitman), 49
Spooner, John, 173
Stamper, Mary (Molly), 85-86

Stendhal, journal of, 26
Stiles, Ezra, 159
Stirling, Lord, 109
Stodard, Major, 86-87, 90-92
Stone, Kate, 185
Sullivan, General, 101, 104

Thacher, James, journal of, 101, 121-27
Theophrastan *character*, 178-80
Thomas, Halsey, 148
Thoreau, Henry David, 23, 24, 25, 26, 184
Tocqueville, Alexis de, 67
Transcendentalism, 26, 27, 28, 183-84
Tunbridgalia (Byrd), 153

Verree, James, 133
Voltaire, François M. A., 73-75

Walden (Thoreau), 23, 24, 25, 26, 184
Waldo, Albigence, diary of, 101, 108-14
Washington, George, 98, 103, 123, 125-26
Wesley, John, diary of, 51, 53
Whitefield, George, diary of, 51
Whitman, Walt, 26, 27, 49-50, diary of, 25
"Wide World, The" (Emerson), 21
Wigglesworth, Edward, 35
Wigglesworth, Mary Reyner, 37
Wigglesworth, Michael, 52; diary of, 25, 30, 31-38, 82
Winthrop, Henry, 147
Winthrop, John, diary of, 21, 27, 30, 59, 142, 143-47, 150
Wister, Sally, journal of, 83, 86-92
Wonders of the Invisible World, The (Mather), 162
Woolman, John, journal of, 23-24, 47-51, 54, 55, 56

Yeats, William Butler, 137

Zenger, John Peter, 130

818.03
K 11

108 877